# NEVER BIRD
# IN THE ROAD

**Memories & Lessons From A Lifetime of Birding**

## TOM STRIKER

LIBRARY OF CONGRESS
CATALOGING-IN-PUBLICATION DATA
Names: Striker, Tom, author
Title: Never Bird in the Road / Tom Striker


ISBN 978-1-7357425-0-2 (Paperback)
ISBN 978-1-7357425-1-9 (eBook)
1. Striker, Tom - Nonfiction    2.  Birding – Nonfiction
3. Binoculars – Nonfiction    4.  Field Guides – Nonfiction
5. Memoir – Nonfiction    6.  Attracting Birds - Nonfiction


Printed in the United States of America


Book and Cover Design by Joan Kellogg
Cover Photograph by Kathy Tickner

# SPECIAL THANKS

Books are not written alone. Joan Howard brought this book to life and I will be forever grateful.

Joan Kellogg designed the book and its cover, and guided me through the maze of publishing.

Jaime Davis, owner of Blue Ridge Bird Seed Company and Dr. Chuck Anderson, retired physician and long-time friend, kindled my fire to start writing with a clever combination of praise and guilt.

Carol Crawford's gentle but thorough editing reminded me of the guy with the shovel that follows the elephants in the parade.

Special thanks to early readers Dave and Kathy Tickner, to Joe Siegrist (President, Purple Martin Conservation Association) for his thorough review of the Purple Martin chapter, and to Adrian Lesak, Kate Fitzmier and Shamus Terry of Vortex Optics for their critical review of the Binoculars chapter.

Suggestions from Allen Jackson, Bernie Daniel and Mike DeBruhl at the North American Bluebird Society added immeasurably to the completeness and accuracy of the Bluebirds chapter.

Outstanding birders Giff Beaton and Patty McLean reviewed the book for ornithological accuracy. Any remaining errors are mine.

Thanks to Suzanne Zuckerman, Brian Lupa, Robert Kimsey, Kathy Tickner, Barb Hauer, Joyce Twing, Charlie Hesse, Bill Schmid, David Fann and Stan Tekiela for sharing their wonderful photographs.

There's no way to say an adequate "Thank You!" to Sonja, my wife and partner in life for more than 50 years. She was my very first reader and remains my number one fan.

## ALSO BY TOM STRIKER

*Becoming A (Better) Birder*

### WITH ROBERT KIMSEY
*Birding Blue Ridge*

## PRAISE FOR NEVER BIRD IN THE ROAD

*A very good introduction to binoculars for birding presented in an approachable and welcoming style. Striker's experience shows, with real world examples.*

Kate Fitzmier & Adrian Lesak, Vortex Optics

*My birding class was fantastic because of Tom. He is "a teacher's teacher!" Extremely knowledgeable and passionate about his subject and he transmits both to every student in class!*

Cindy Wooten – Folk School Student

*The Bluebird chapter is thorough and comprehensive and summarizes my proactive approach to proper management of bluebirds.*

Allen Jackson, President, NJ Bluebird Society & NABS Board of Directors

*The Purple Martin chapter is very good. You did your homework well!*

Joe Siegrist, President – Purple Martin Conservation Association

*The advice on becoming a better birder has a logical start and progresses through the basics of getting started in birding. It's well done and gets right to the point.*

Stan Tekiela, Author / Naturalist

*Lots of good stories and great info about bins, birds and birding! Interesting, accurate and fun!*

Giff Beaton, Author of Birding Georgia and Dragonflies & Damselflies of Georgia

# TABLE OF CONTENTS:

**"Success is when you look back at your life
and the memories make you smile."**
*Unknown, but reported to be someone's grandmother*

## FOREWORD (Lynda Striker Robinson)

Learning to bird is a lot like learning a language. I grew up in a household where my mother spoke fluent German and my father spoke *bird*. Mom came to the US at age five but her brother insisted they continue to speak German at home, so she is incredibly at ease with her native tongue. Hearing conversations within my mother's side of the family in fluent German gave me an ear for the language. With no formal training, I am still able to understand quite a bit, although most of the words I remember are the fun ones, like *Kartoffelpuffer* (potato pancake) and *geschlafen* (slept) and of course all the bad words!

Learning the language of birds might be a little easier for me since I grew up hearing the proper names of birds. One of my sister's first words was *Gunshinch*, her two-year old attempt at goldfinch. Our friends would recognize a *red bird* on one of our many bird feeders, and we would subconsciously correct that it was a Cardinal. As with German, I also concentrated on the fun bird words, like Great Blue Heron, Sandhill Crane and Blue-footed Booby. The chapters in bird books that best held my interest were on the big birds, hawks and water birds. However, there is great satisfaction in correct language as well, the nitty-gritty detail of the bird world that comes from knowing the difference between a Pine Siskin and a Pine Warbler.

Exploring the language of birding is just like traveling to another country. One must travel properly equipped, with a bird book, *binocs* (hint: binoculars is the novice term; to sound like a pro, it is binocs,) a hat, and some way to keep a list. There must be some sort of proof that you saw all those species.

My father recognizes things in nature that most would overlook. I don't remember the destinations of our family trips as clearly as I remember my father randomly chirping "Brown Thrasher," "Black Vulture," "Sharp-shinned Hawk, a young male." For the longest time, I wasn't sure if he wasn't simply making things up. He'd identify some flying object and I'd look up just in time to see more road signs or cows in the fields. Through the years, as I learned more birds, I began to see them, too, by knowing where to look, up high or in the shrubs. Camping trips turned into birding trips. I could hear or spot a bird and my father would identify it. I remember the sparkle in his eyes when I pointed out a *kerfuffle* in the Okefenokee Swamp and identified it as an *American swampthingy* bird. He saw what I was trying to describe and identified it as an American Bittern, patted my shoulder and gave me a high-five. Actually, I think he lightly whacked my shoulder with his hat in his excitement.

I don't speak German fluently and I will never know All The Birds. My Dad, a.k.a. The Bird Man of Blue Ridge, a.k.a. Birdman Tom, a.k.a. Bird Nerd, humbly tells us in this book that even after formal education, decades of self-training in books and in the field, eyes always to the sky, to become a birder is not about knowing All The Birds. It's about who you become as a person. Perhaps one of the best gifts he could have ever given me will last my lifetime, every day. It's a quiet gift, one many in this world will never know, but those who see birds are already birders, no matter how fluent they become.

My father wrote this book and, even though he ignored my pleas to title it *Birdshit*, or *Learning to Bird in 7,362 Easy Steps*, I still commend and honor his title of *Never Bird in the Road*. However, at a recent writers' conference in Blue Ridge, Georgia, we had, perhaps, our greatest father-daughter bonding moment. This is huge to say since we have shared so many moments walking the world together, learning all the while.

I have thought a lot about what writing this book means to my father and how much his effort has affected my motivations in life. While quiet and stoic, he is a dreamer and this book is yet another dream come true. He battled the corporate rat race and won. He battled cancer twice and won. He battled the perils of owning a small business and won. He battled two near-fatal heart episodes and won. He has set several major goals in life and accomplished each one, and writing this book is the ultimate success of combining birds, the Forest Service, BellSouth and an MBA into his own bird store business and living every day to take care of his family, work hard, and see another bird. He never stops birding because that is his life blood, his passion, which has inspired so much happiness and joy for himself, and for others.

What we discovered at the writers' conference, in a gush of words that flowed straight from my heart is that the title of this book should not be *Never Bird in the Road*, but instead, *Always Bird in the Road*. The road is his life and birding is his passion; no matter the circumstance, one should always pursue his or her passion. My father didn't let road signs stop him from birding in the road. He didn't let doctors stop him from birding from his hospital bed. He didn't let corporate America cage him longer than was mutually beneficial. As long as his heart is chirping, he will look for birds and find joy. Every time I hear birds chirping, I know there is life and I am reminded of the man who taught me patience, persistence, and diligence, three qualities necessary for success in birding and quite transferable to attaining life goals!

Perhaps birding is not your passion. Maybe it's poetry or art, tennis, photography or jogging. Whatever your passion, I hope the biggest take away from reading *Never Bird in the Road* is inspiration. No matter what life throws at you, no matter how far off the path you think you've gotten, there is always the potential to make your dreams come true.

# NEVER BIRD IN THE ROAD

# PREFACE

The "birding bug" bit me in graduate school while I was studying to become a naturalist. Although demanding jobs and a growing family often limited my birding time in the years since college, I have found myself behind a pair of binoculars frequently for nearly 50 years.

Birders of all plumages write books. You don't bird for 50 years without gathering some stories. It might be in the birder's DNA to try to share the joys of birding, the almost spiritual experiences, the disasters, the funny stuff and the quirks of other birders. I have the added incentive of sharing some of the "how-to" knowledge I've gathered as a long-time birder and bird store owner that can make attracting birds more successful and fun for you.

I chose *Never Bird in The Road* as the title for this book because it captures the serendipity of birding, the essence, the gestalt. Birders are thoughtful of others and very safety conscious. Yet the classic birding situation that innocent non-birders come upon while driving somewhere is one or more cars stopped in the middle of the road with all the doors open, headlights on and the motor running. There's either nobody in sight or a bunch of khaki-clad birders in goofy hats standing on the yellow line in the middle of the road with binocs up. Somebody saw a bird, the driver hit the brakes and the car emptied in three seconds.

This book is about my path to becoming a birder, the education, events and people that got me started and taught me along the way. It's also about some of the bumps in The Road, if you will. My daughter, Lynda Striker Robinson, is an emerging author of children's books, and has been a companion and cheerleader at writers' conferences as we struggled together with the written word. Her thoughtful insight into what *Never Bird In The Road* is really about, shared with me and a roomful of fellow writers at a recent conference, brought tears to my eyes.

Lynda described it as *a dream come true* book, suggesting that *The Road* is my life and Birding is my passion, and that continuing to bird and share my passion with others despite bouts with thyroid cancer, non-Hodgkin's lymphoma and a variety of near-fatal heart problems confirm that birding in the road can be powerful therapy.

When I started this book, I wanted to pull together all the birding information and teaching tools I developed as bird store owner and teacher, clean them up and put them in a useful and consistent form for others to use. Another goal was to share my birding experiences with other people, especially just-getting-started birders. I hope they'll see that birding can be a window into the natural world, that wonderful things await them and, finally, how much fun it can be.

So, this book is about special birds, birding trips and companions, about yard lists, birding patches, and random birding stories, some of them mostly true. It details some of the things you can do to learn to identify birds in ways that are more focused and more efficient than thumbing clumsily through your field guide. Finally, it's about making backyard birding more fun by doing the right things to attract birds, buying the right feeders and seed, dealing with squirrels and bears, and learning what all those numbers on your binoculars mean.

I've been writing my whole life. Most of the writing in my early careers as forester and finance guy could be termed business writing - land management plans, environmental impact statements, memos, letters, technical reports and finally business plans. I did write a nature column called *A Northwoods Journal* for the Park Falls, Wisconsin *Herald* in the mid-70s, before the kids came along. Unpaid, of course, and worth every penny.

During my third career, as co-owner of Blue Ridge Bird Seed Company, I wrote monthly newsletters filled with bird stuff, and prepared handouts for my frequent Saturday Seminars. I did a lot of research as I prepared for those seminars; the customers who invested an hour of their weekend deserved useful and accurate information about things like bird feeding; winter bird identification; attracting hummingbirds, bluebirds, and purple martins; tree identification; dealing with critters; choosing binoculars; and the wonders of migration. I invited local experts for things I knew less about, like black bears, butterflies, ladybugs, dragonflies and wildflowers. I did my homework for those seminars as well and learned enough to put together handout materials and help the speaker with questions.

Customers liked my seminars. After all, they were free, and we followed the old tradition that leads to successful meetings: put out coffee and doughnuts in some form and people will show up! There was also our Seminar Survivor Coupon for buying some of the things we'd talked about at the seminar. You will recognize this as a transparent retailing tactic. Customers said nice things as they left, thanked me for the handouts, spent a few bucks in my shop and came back again and again. Customers told me that my seminar materials could be useful in a book about birds and birding.

Teaching bird identification to adults reinforced that feeling. I call my teaching approach *Thinking Like a Birder & Seeing like a Birder*. The idea is that bird identification is both complex and simple, using a combination of a brain full of book-learned information (*Thinking Like a Birder*) and field experience of how birds look and behave under a variety of conditions (*Seeing Like a Birder*). My approach to teaching is built on the fact that thinking like a birder and seeing like a birder are not divine gifts, but rather the result of studying your field guide, keeping lists, reading birding magazines and adventure books, and working hard while actually birding to learn how to see and what to look at.

Combining this hard-earned mental framework of information with birding every chance you get leads to an understanding of birds beyond the field marks, pulling together location, season, likelihood, habitat and behavior. When it comes together, when you are beginning to see like a birder, then all you'll need is a flick of white outer tail feathers at the edge of a thicket to know that bird is a Towhee (or a Dark-eyed Junco if it's smaller and it's winter).

Sometimes you have to bird in the road – that's where the birds are. If you don't mind a little sarcastic humor and a touch of rueful reminiscing along the way, grab your binocs and your ugliest hat, get out of the car and join me on the center line of my road.

Fifty years later, my favorite feeder in the background.

Career #3 – The Right Job At Last!

# PART ONE: How'd I Get Here, Anyway?

*I didn't set out to be a birder, but it snuck up on me over a period of years, as I traveled the bumpy paths of education and careers. The Birding Bug followed me and finally bit me when I wasn't watching, and the sting has lasted until today. After spending a good part of 50 years looking at, caring about and talking about birds, it may be interesting to look back at some of the trips and side trips I took while becoming a birder.*

*Part One is personal history, but it includes my experiences with some unique people, places, and projects that flavored my birding education and are interesting on their own merits. Forestry Summer Camp in an old Civilian Conservation Corps camp in Minnesota gave me a taste of the history of conservation. Managing Kirtland's Warbler habitat in Michigan gave me a first-hand view of the benefits of prescribed burning and the tragedy of a 25,000 acre burn that got away. Helping restore the magnificent Peregrine Falcon to a historic nesting cliff in Vermont exposed me to the pervasive damage of DDT and the recuperative power of the environment when people get out of the way. I wound up owning a bird store, teaching and writing about birds. These events were much more than personal adventures. I think you'll agree.*

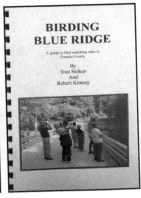

# 1

# The Birding Bug

*Memories of noticing birds as a kid, going to forestry school and learning to identify trees and wildflowers in a way that transferred later to identifying birds. Forestry Summer Camp near Blackduck in a historic Civilian Conservation Corps (CCC) camp, one of only three preserved from the Great Depression. Taking ornithology in grad school, discovering the joy of birding and finally feeling the sting of The Birding Bug.*

I was 21 when the birding bug bit me. The swelling is long gone but I can still feel the itch. By my definition, I've been a birder for almost 50 years. I'll never be a really good birder, but that's okay. I'm still working on it, I've had a lifetime of fun, and I'm comfortable with that. Although I may have reached <u>my</u> peak, I find myself a long way up the hill of learning and have found gratification and joy in helping other people learn about birds. That's what this book is about.

I'd had lots of experiences with birds when I was younger, but I didn't really sense what birding was all about until I was in grad school. I made a lot of little and big decisions that put me on the path to birding - going to forestry school, then training to be a naturalist in grad school, becoming a broad-viewed natural resource manager instead of a timber beast in the Forest Service, bailing out to go to business school, and, eventually, focusing my entrepreneurial energy on owning a retail shop that sold bird stuff.

My birding education went into overdrive on my first day in that sparkling new bird store. I quickly learned that my customers *expected* me to know the answers to their questions. I did everything I could to make that happen for 14 years, and it continues today. Despite stuttering as a kid, I taught my customers about bird feeding, bluebirds, binoculars and bird ID in Saturday Seminars and the teaching thing eventually spilled over into real classes for real birders. My wife,

Sonja, calls it *birding for old people*.

There are categories of birders, based loosely on the personality or philosophical leaning of the individuals involved. There are overlaps and phases and one person can move between categories over time. There are *bird watchers*, mostly restricted to the backyard or kitchen window; *listers*, whose goal is to see and identify as many birds as they can; *chasers*, (or, in the UK, *twitchers*), who take listing to extremes by chasing every rare bird that comes close; specialists, who may be experts on a particular species or bird family; and *ornithologists*, the overall experts with PhDs who do research, unravel DNA, teach, write learned articles and publish field guides. They're all birders in their own way, and while some in each category may read and enjoy this book, none fit my definition of a birder exactly.

My definition of *birder* fits the person who is, or wants to be, beyond *bird watcher* but nowhere near *ornithologist* in terms of formal education. A combination of field time and serious study by a *birder* will have generated a knowledge of migration and seasonality, geographic range, field marks, habitat, behavior and songs. An advanced birder's education and experience may include ornithology classes or Master Birder programs, regional and national festivals, and birding trips with professional birding tour companies. Birders get up early, wear strange hats, keep a pair of binocs in the car, have too many bird books, and learn to somehow stay in their lane when windshield birding. Birders may keep lists, chase rare birds, guide other birders and often teach informally, but the primary identifier is that birds and birding are part of their everyday lives.

I had pet parakeets as a kid, in a cage in our Sacramento, California kitchen. The real name for these cute green or blue parrots, native to Australia, is *Budgerigar*. Mine eventually escaped, when their cage blew over in a breeze while sunning on the porch. They disappeared into the suburban wild, as did many others in California and elsewhere. Some of these escapees bred successfully and flocks of thousands flew wild until the 1980s, in California and southwest Florida.

According to the American Birding Association (ABA), Budgerigars are established in North America and may be counted on your Life List for the ABA Area. Numerous earlier, budgies are scarce today in North America; only eleven were counted in January 2011 in the Hernando County, Florida, Christmas Bird Count. Competition for nesting cavities with European Starlings and House Sparrows may have caused their decline. My friend Dave Tickner, who keeps a monthly yard list on his mini-farm near Epworth, Georgia, had a budgie in his yard for a few days in 2011. Dave's bird was probably an escaped cage bird, like my childhood pets, and not technically countable, but Dave makes his own rules for his yard list and that little parakeet is on his list. I went over to take a look myself and it's on my list as well.

My childhood friends and I chased Ring-necked Pheasants in cutover corn fields near Chicago before they were converted to subdivisions. We were armed with cheap archery equipment, and, predictably, there were no fatalities. The same friends helped me steal Rock Pigeons (then called Rock Doves) from nearby barns, and we built all manner of pigeon coops to hold them. We didn't know what we were doing and never got them to nest successfully. Our mothers finally laid down the law and the pigeons were gone.

I found an early-fledged American Robin in my Illinois backyard one day and rescued it over the protests of its mother, who screamed threats at me from the maple tree. I kept it a few days, fed it worms, and released it when it wouldn't stay in the box any longer. It somehow survived my care.

I remember watching Common Grackles splashing in rain puddles and was fascinated by their glossy and iridescent feathers. Someone had told me that they were classified as two species then and I tried to separate Bronzed Grackles from Purple Grackles. Again, one flock in a puddle, one afternoon in 1962 maybe. Fun, but no momentum to do any more, no plans to make birding a part of my very existence.

Perhaps some of these early bird experiences, combined with my love of fishing and camping, pushed me toward an education and career in the outdoors. My grades were pretty fair in high school, despite a low interest in studying, and I enrolled in Forestry at the University of Illinois. I was a city kid, with no real knowledge of what I was getting into, but I took to it with a bunch of similarly wide-eyed guys from Illinois towns and farms and decided early on that it was the right choice.

Foresters are trained to manage forest lands, with short term objectives inside what is necessarily a long view. The best ones have a holistic understanding of what makes up their forest, and the natural and human influences on the land they manage. They need some tools and some special knowledge, including the names and habits of the trees they look after.

As a sophomore, I took my first real core forestry course: Dendrology, which is basically tree identification. Here's what Wikipedia says about it:

*Dendrology: The science and study of wooded plants (trees, shrubs, and lianas), specifically, their taxonomic classifications. Dendrology, as a discipline of industrial forestry, tends to focus on identification of economically useful woody plants and their taxonomic interrelationships. As an academic course of study, Dendrology will include all woody plants, native and non-native, that occur in a region.*

Right out of the gate, I was over my head. I didn't understand the basic structures of leaves and twigs and couldn't relate the patterns to tree families like maple, oak and ash. I flat failed the first field quiz. The teaching assistant was a patient guy and took three or four of us slowpokes out for some extra study. His teaching style was different than that of Doc Lorenz, our professor, and that remedial afternoon got me on a new track of learning. Looking back, I see that learning to identify trees had elements of what could be called *Seeing Like a Forester*, similar in many ways to the approach to birding I use in my classes. It taught me to look for the meaningful details, or field marks: opposite vs alternate leaves, simple vs compound leaves, branching patterns, crown shapes and bark characteristics. A couple of focused hours looking at trees on campus, lots of field notes and some study time in the dendrology textbook, and I had the basics of tree ID.

One of the keys to tree identification is learning the tree families – oaks, maples, ashes, hickories, birches, poplars, pines, larches, firs and spruces. Once you've learned to put a tree in its proper family, you're just sorting out family members.

Sonja had a less scientific approach to tree ID in her own college Botany class. On field trips, she memorized landmarks near each tree to help her remember: *The tree next to the motorcycle rack behind the Student Union is a Basswood.* Of course, the field quiz took her nowhere near the Student Union, that motorcycle rack or her own personal Basswood.

We also learned the scientific or Latin names of all the trees (Sugar Maple, for example is *Acer saccharum* and White Pine is *Pinus strobus*), and even that was easier after my tutorial. I recovered enough to ace the course but, more importantly, I knew my trees! Knowing a little about tree ID is useful for a birder, so you can help another birder find the bird you're looking at. The scientific names have stuck with me and I still slip one in sometimes when on a bird walk or birding class field trip.

*The Blackburnian Warbler is at one o'clock in the top of that Tulip Poplar, the very straight tall one with the tulip-shaped leaves!* (Tulip Poplar is *Liriodendron tulipifera*, in case you were wondering.)

Perhaps the biggest test of my decision to be a forester was Forestry Summer Camp, between my sophomore and junior years. It was eight weeks in the middle of the North Woods, immersed in forestry tools and management principles, most of it spent in a rustic camp in northern Minnesota originally built by the Civilian Conservation Corps in the 1930s.

On the way to Camp Rabideau, near Blackduck, we stopped for a week in a similar camp near Cloquet, Minnesota. A few miles southwest of Duluth and Lake Superior, Cloquet was a center for mills and factories that turned raw wood into consumer products. We visited and reported on sawmills and other facilities that made paper, cardboard, high density particleboard used for clipboards, matches, wooden crates and pressure-treated posts.

After a week of wood chips, chemical smells, machines marked **DANGER**, hard hats, flow charts and after-dinner softball, we loaded up for seven weeks at Camp Rabideau. Our time there was to be filled with forest ecology, silviculture, soil pits, peat bogs, Jack Pine, Black Spruce, Paper Birch and Aspen, forest measurements, and lots of tree, shrub and wildflower identification.

See – there's that identification thing again, and wildflowers will drive you crazy until you sort out the families. Put an unknown flower in a group of similar plants, though - asters, lilies, orchids, roses, violets, goldenrods, buttercups or peas – and then you're just working through the family members. For me, it worked with trees, so wildflowers came along more easily. I would find that it works for birds as well.

Regarding northern Minnesota in the summertime - have I mentioned what Camp Director Doc Lorenz referred to as the state bird of Minnesota? Not the Common Loon - the ubiquitous mosquito!

**The Original Black Duck Statue**

**Education Building – Camp Rabideau**

There's a lot of history behind Camp Rabideau. It was built in the 1930s, one of 2,650 camps built by the U.S. Army to house the Civilian Conservation Corps (CCC) as part of a program initiated by President Franklin D. Roosevelt during his first two months in office. The CCC was established to revitalize the economy and end the Great Depression. The camps were managed jointly by the Forest Service and the U.S. Army. By the end of the program in 1942, more than three million young American men had earned money and learned valuable skills. Many finished high school as part of Roosevelt's "Tree Army." They built roads and trails, bridges and fire towers. They fought fires and built firebreaks. They planted trees and developed picnic areas and campgrounds. Some 80 years later, their work is still visible – some of the best examples are the bridges and stone walls in Great Smoky Mountains National Park.

The Army went to Europe to fight World War II, and the Forest Service put Camp Rabideau in mothballs where it sat idle until 1945. The University of Illinois leased it from the Chippewa National Forest for use as a summer camp for engineering and forestry students. After clearing out the chipmunks, bats and raccoons, the engineers added sewer and sanitation lines and a pressurized water system and rewired the buildings. They installed roof supports, replaced wood stoves with oil burners and surveyed roads and property lines for miles around. The foresters moved in later and learned to do all the things that I studied when I was a camper in 1968. Based on my summer there, I'm sure those other hard-working engineering and forestry students found time to drink Grain Belt and Schmidt beer and discuss politics with the local blond-headed Scandihoovian girls.

The University of Illinois leased the camp until 1973. I am certain that the nearly 30 years of maintenance and improvements provided by the university preserved the camp and its buildings far beyond the level at other CCC camps. Most CCC camps were abandoned after World War II and most had been razed or burned by the mid-70s but Camp Rabideau survived. It was placed on the National Register of Historic Places in 1976 and is one of only three CCC camps that remain to shed light on this phase of American history. Thirteen of the original buildings remain, and much of Camp Rabideau has been restored. My wife Sonja and I visited Camp Rabideau on a 1999 nostalgia tour of our old Minnesota haunts that included Duluth, Isabella, Bemidji and Blackduck. The Forest Service had begun a three-year restoration program, and the Education Building, our old classroom, already had a new foundation. I studied there at a good time, and it was a memorable time for me.

Another memory of that trip is a Black-billed Magpie sighted during a brief stop at Sax-Zim Bog as we drove west from Duluth to Bemidji. Birders will recognize Sax-Zim Bog, named after two nearby ghost towns, as a wet but bird-rich hotspot where Great Gray, Snowy and Northern Hawk Owls may be seen in winter. Sax-Zim Bog is the most reliable eastern outpost for Black-billed Magpie, normally a flashy bird of the semi-open West.

Forestry Summer Camp was the most intense, interesting and fun educational experience of my life, and I've spent a lot of time learning. Twenty-six guys, plus our Teaching Assistant, Stan Sipp, lived in three big open dormitories with minimal furniture and swampy shower rooms. We ate breakfast and dinner in the Dining Hall, and packed PB and J and bologna sandwich fixings into coolers for lunch in the field almost every day. Morning and evening, we waited on the steps of the Dining Hall for the dinner bell to ring, under a huge Basswood tree (*Tilia americana*) that was fragrant with thousands of bell-shaped flowers and buzzing with honeybees in June 1968.

The classroom was similar to classrooms everywhere but had a pioneer flavor with big wooden tables that served as desks, an ancient chalkboard, creaky floors and wavy glass in the windows. We used those big adding machines with the pull lever on the right for the big jobs, and pencil-and-paper arithmetic for the little ones. Field days were the rule, with the red University of Illinois vans taking us to aspen, pine, spruce and mixed hardwood stands to study and measure, dig holes to look at the soils, and endlessly swat mosquitoes, black flies and no-see-ums.

**Recognize this guy? He has that Pre-Birdman Look...**

In late afternoon, after class, we swam in cold, crystal clear Lake Benjamin, and after dinner we fished for northern pike in Carl's Lake at the other end of camp. Birds were there in great variety, but most of them didn't register with me. Common Loons nested on Lake Benjamin, and Black Terns were common. Bald Eagles and Osprey made frequent flyovers, and I saw and heard my first Baltimore Oriole from a leaky rowboat while fishing Carl's Lake with Jim Baughman. This kind of birding was fun, but – no heat, not yet. The Birding Bug was circling but hadn't bitten me yet, unlike the ubiquitous mosquito.

**The Camp Rabideau Class of 1968 (I'm third from the right, back row)**

Summer camp cemented my decision to become a forester, and the last two years of undergrad work flew by, with a summer job in 1969 at Hardin Ridge Recreation Area, a big Forest Service campground on the Hoosier National Forest in Indiana. I was a straight "A" student by then and was elected to the Xi Sigma Pi National Honorary Fraternity for Foresters. I was good to go, looking forward to getting married in June of 1970 and anxious to get a permanent job with the Forest Service.

As graduation neared in the spring of 1970, it was evident that the US economy was underperforming, government budgets were tight, and the Forest Service wasn't hiring full-time foresters. So, I applied for grad school, married Sonja in June, and went back to Hardin Ridge Recreation Area for another idyllic summer. I wore my USFS uniform and badge and manned the gate, collecting entrance fees and selling camping permits. On other days, I mowed grass, picked up trash and cleaned bathrooms. Not quite the same as working at Arches National Monument, but I felt at least a little like Edward Abbey. One of the highlights of early summer was watching a Tufted Titmouse land repeatedly on the head of a Beatle-haired teenager to pluck hair for its nest.

I didn't set out to become a birder, but my forestry education and Summer Camp got me started and, after the Birding Bug caught up with me, my Forest Service career put me together with biologists and other birders and took me to birdy places. The combination sharpened my interest and honed my skills.

Sonja had landed a teaching job in Tolono, Illinois, close to the U of I campus. With no forestry jobs on the immediate horizon, I went to graduate school for a master's degree in forestry, but I structured my classes to train me to become a naturalist. In the first of a long series of *pulling the wool over their eyes performances*, I found myself in a teaching assistant position in the Forestry Department that covered tuition, helped out with home expenses and provided a few bucks for beer and books.

Ironically, my favorite class as teaching assistant was Dendrology, which you will remember as the tree identification course that had frustrated me as an undergrad. Teaching really reinforced the value of learning tree families to narrow down identification of sorting out the family members using specific field marks and natural clues like habitat. Later, as a working forester, I learned how to identify a tree at any season, using geography, topography, tree shape, bark, flowers, fruit and twig structure, in addition to leaf shape. Call it *Seeing like a Forester*. The second time around, as teaching assistant, I was able to pass on some of what I had learned to young forestry students.

My self-designed forester / naturalist master's degree included lots of botany, biology, and natural history – I even took a weather course. Just ask me: I can tell you today if it rained yesterday. On the way, I met some people who changed my life. I took *Natural History of the Vertebrates* during my first grad school semester, taught by Dr. Mary F. Willson, a young and enthusiastic professor who knew her birds, her mammals, her fish, her snakes and lizards, and was a very skilled field botanist to boot. When we weren't rolling over logs, hoping to find snakes underneath, I learned a lot about birds from Dr. Willson.

Turned out I was taught by one of the best. Dr. Willson, now in her late 70s, continues to push the boundaries of ecology and natural history from her home in Juneau, Alaska. She is perhaps the world expert on the American Dipper, a North American songbird that walks <u>under</u> water! She has published over 150 scholarly articles, most dealing with the interaction of plants and animals in their natural environment, and written several books. Perhaps best known are *Vertebrate Natural History* and *American Dippers, Singers in the Mountain Streams.* Looking back, I'm very pleased to have learned from her, both in the classroom and in the field.

Knowing the birds seemed like an essential part of a naturalist's training, so I took Ornithology (the study of birds) the next spring. I got the hang of things a little in the classroom, but what trapped me forever was the time outside during a spectacular spring migration.

In Ornithology, I saw right away that birds followed some of the same identification rules as trees and wildflowers; that is, they could be sorted out into families of similar-looking or acting birds and showed distinctive behaviors and preferences for habitat that helped narrow down their identification. Still, birds challenged me with their variety and sheer numbers, their spring colors, bright males and drabber females. They sang distinctive songs and chose places to perch, feed and nest that suited their food preferences. Ducks and wading birds were bigger and didn't move as much, but still required knowledge of behaviors, habitats and field marks. Vireos and warblers traveled the treetops. Sparrows and shorebirds needed a decoder ring to sort out at first, but it could be done. Of course, there was one big difference from tree ID: trees just stood there, waiting for me to say their name, while birds moved. They moved, all of them, all the time, twig-to-twig in local flight and over enormous distances during migration. A single tree held different birds today than it had held yesterday and different winter birds replaced summer residents.

Anyway, I got it, this birding thing, and birding made me happy. It seemed easy to me, while my fellow students griped about early morning field trips and junk binoculars and slapped at mosquitoes instead of marinating their eyes and brains in birds. Weekend field trips to wildlife refuges for ducks and cranes were great, flocks of spring warblers were the best, and even the quizzes were fun.

The Ornithology final exam was outdoors, in an ungroomed spot near campus, with open fields, brushy thickets and shaggy forest edge, even a few old apple trees. The May morning was perfect, sunny and cool and the air was filled with the scents of spring blossoms and the songs of migrating birds. The teaching assistant pointed out each bird, gave it a number and said, "Write it down." About thirty species in an hour, most perched in song or overhead in flight. I missed one; it turned out I was looking at a Black-throated Green Warbler, next to the Yellow-throated Warbler (it was still called Sycamore Warbler in 1971) the TA was pointing at. Imagine being surrounded by brilliantly colored birds in full song on a sparkling May morning! And that's the test! Visions of that day will be kept forever, in the video library in my head.

Later that spring, I went back to Forestry Summer Camp at Black-duck, this time as teaching assistant. You may recall that there is a huge wooden black duck in the center of town, hence the name. I had been there as a student in 1968, complete with a ratty beard, a $2.00 thrift store hat, and 26 other guys. Straight A's that summer, and a con-viction that I was on the right path to a life outdoors.

The job as teaching assistant at Forestry Summer Camp was a serious coup; eight weeks in the woods, all expenses paid, with Son-ja along to relax, read, hand feed chipmunks and wear her bikini. Housed in that refurbished but still slightly shabby Civilian Conser-vation Corps (CCC) camp left over from the 1930s, Camp Rabideau's mission was to take a bunch of farm and city kids away from TV and girlfriends for eight weeks and show them what working in the woods was all about. Hold back on the sympathy, though, about being in the boonies. It turned out they sell cold beer in Blackduck as a token gesture to culture and civilization, and there was a terrific bookstore in nearby Bemidji, near the statues of Paul Bunyan and Babe the Blue Ox. We got by, and those city kids survived, as they did every summer.

The real deal was that it was fabulous birding, and I was finally ready for it. I was surrounded by nesting birds that were brand new or that I had only seen poorly in migration: Common Loon (complete with nest and two nestlings which rode on Mom's back), Bald Eagle, Osprey, American Bittern, Ruffed Grouse, Black Terns, Yellow-bel-lied Sapsuckers, Black-billed Cuckoo, Least (*chi-bek*) and Willow (*fitz-bew*) Flycatchers, Connecticut and Yellow Warblers, Baltimore Oriole (which was to become Northern Oriole for a while, conspe-cific with Bullock's) and Evening Grosbeak! One after-dinner hike around Carl's Lake brought me within four feet of a pair of Spruce Grouse, the tame chicken of the north woods. A life bird and a life view that lasted five minutes or more! That Ornithology class, that never-to-be-forgotten field quiz, and Forestry Summer Camp got me into birds. The Birding Bug bit me and bit me hard, and the welt would stay with me the rest of my life.

**Male Kirtland's Warbler (Stan Tekiela)**

# 2

# Kirtland's Warbler
# Bird of Fire

*A personal side trip to explore the life of a beautiful but finicky bird restricted to the sandy Jack Pine plains of central Michigan, nearing extinction in 1980. My experience with the disastrous Mack Lake Fire, which burned 25,000 acres in a single afternoon and killed a young Forest Service fire plow operator but created the conditions to save the bird of fire.*

I spent two grad school summers as Teaching Assistant at Camp Rabideau. A lot of our field work for the Forest Measurements and Forest Ecology courses took us to a big, open Jack Pine (*Pinus banksiana*) stand, on sandy soil with bracken fern ground cover. Easy walking, long sight distances, and dry enough that a cubic yard of air contained less than 10,000 mosquitoes. A careful sawyer might cut a couple of two-by-fours from a Jack Pine log if it was straight enough, but most of it winds up in the pulpwood pile.

Jack Pine is a scrubby northern species, with twisted needles in bundles of two, bearing smallish cones that are naturally sealed with resin until heated enough by sunshine or fire to release the seeds. Sunlight is a damned poor source of cone-opening heat if you're a Jack Pine, while fire opens 'em right up. Ecologically, Jack Pine is a fire-dependent tree, and reproduces very sporadically unless and until it is swept by fire. The fire kills the adult trees but releases millions of seeds to germinate into a new stand of Jack Pine.

Kirtland's Warbler is another fire-dependent species whose very survival depends on fire-swept Jack Pine for suitable nesting habitat. It was named for Jared Potter Kirtland, an Ohio doctor and naturalist, who first identified the bird. This husky bird is often called the "Jack Pine warbler" because it always nests on the ground beneath young Jack Pines. While the range of Jack Pine is extensive in North

America, the Kirtland's Warbler nesting range is confined to Jack Pine growing on a particular soil type called Grayling Sand, which occurs in an eight-county area in central Lower Michigan. Ninety percent of the nests of this warbler have been located on Grayling Sand soils within the watershed of the Au Sable River. Most of the habitat is on state and national forest lands.

By the late 1960s, strict fire control measures and limited timber harvesting had shrunk the range of the Kirtland's Warbler to the point that only a couple of hundred pairs persisted in the sandy forests around Grayling and Mio. The Kirtland's Warbler was nearing extinction. It was declared an Endangered Species in 1967 and an annual census of singing males was begun, to be carried out by the U.S. Fish & Wildlife Service, the Forest Service and the Michigan Department of Natural Resources. The counts bottomed out in 1974 and again in 1987 at 167 males, total for the planet.

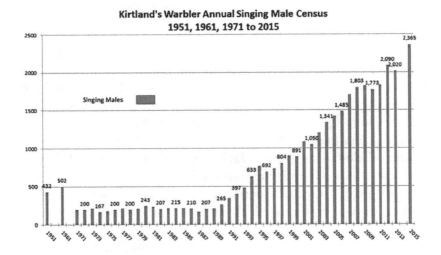

**Kirtland's Warbler Annual Singing Male Census 1951, 1961, 1971 to 2015**

**Source: U.S. Fish & Wildlife Service, Midwest Region – Endangered Species Program**

The Kirtland's Warbler Recovery Team, made up of federal and state biologists, was established in 1973 to "reestablish a self-sustaining Kirtland's Warbler population throughout its known range at a minimum level of 1,000 pairs." Increased harvest of Jack Pine, followed by prescribed fire, was the primary management tool recommended and used in the battle to keep Kirtland's Warbler from extinction. Mature Jack Pine was harvested in areas ranging from 10 to 250 acres, fire lines were plowed in, and the remaining treetops and logging slash were burned by professional land managers under carefully controlled conditions, typically in the spring. Despite the best efforts of the managing agencies, populations remained very low and apparently stagnant until 1990, when the count increased by 58 males, an increase of 28 percent over 1989. The 1991 count was 397 singing males, an increase of 132 birds, an almost 50 percent gain over 1990. The population increased steadily for more than 20 years and exceeded 2300 singing males in 2015.

***Clearly something happened to change the status of this tough and beautiful bird.***

**That something was the Mack Lake Fire.**

The Mack Lake Fire began as a controlled burn on the Mio District of the Huron-Manistee National Forest on the morning of May 5, 1980. The intent was to carefully burn the 210-acre Crane Lake unit, on the west side of Highway 33 in southern Oscoda County, to remove logging slash and prepare the site for replanting with Jack Pine. Following a nearly snowless winter, May 5th was warmer than usual for early May, with relative humidity of 24 percent and light winds. It had been five days since measurable rain. The afternoon forecast predicted movement of a cold front through the area with wind gusts of 25 miles per hour, cooling the air and raising the humidity, but bringing little rain.

These were not ideal burning conditions, but District Ranger Ven Bosman and Fire Boss Tom Bates felt conditions were manageable and began burning at 9:45 a.m. Small spot fires were handled routinely until a larger spot fire entered an uncut Jack Pine strip along Highway 33 and climbed to the tree crowns. Almost immediately, windswept embers carried across more than 150 feet of highway clearing and ignited several spot fires on the eastern side of Highway 33. At this point, the prescribed burn was out of control.

Before days' end, the fire had burned 25,000 acres of public and private forest land and damaged or destroyed 44 homes and summer cottages, most of them in a small community on Mack Lake. Tragically, the fire also took the life of Jim Swidersky, a young Forest Service wildlife technician and part-time fire plow operator who was trapped by the fast-moving fire.

The Mack Lake Fire was personal and I'll never forget that dry day in May. I was working for the Forest Service on May 5th, 1980, assigned to the Harrisville Ranger District, adjoining the Mio District to the east. I was on light duty, back to work after some minor surgery a few days earlier. I was checking dispersed camping sites in the western part of my district near Mack Lake, driving a rental Chevrolet sub-compact, poorly suited to recreation management work and sandy roads, and equipped with just a shovel. I did have my fire pack with me, loaded with fire-resistant Nomex shirt and trousers, gloves, hard hat and a folded aluminum fire shelter in a belt pack. I also carried a portable radio and was monitoring the radio traffic from the Crane Lake burn on the Mio District.

Shortly after noon, it became apparent that the Mio crew needed help, and I radioed my availability to Tom Bates, the Fire Boss. He asked me to help evacuate the Mack Lake community. I quickly changed to fire-resistant clothing and drove to Mack Lake. Although still a mile or more away, the fire was already huge and very visible. Residents were quickly gathering family members, pets and precious items and leaving their beloved homes and cabins behind. A few optimists were standing outside with shovels or garden hoses. I firmly instructed them to leave immediately and travel east or south until they were well away. Angry words were directed at me, the Forest Service and "that damned bird," and more than a few tears were shed. It was a terrible afternoon that I will never forget.

Jim Swidersky was caught by the fast-moving fire, overcome by the terrific heat and smoke. Typical of career Forest Service personnel, Jim did his best to contain the growing spot fire, realizing too late that he should abandon his tractor and run. His body was found within a hundred feet of his tractor. Everyone else got out safely, the big fire made its run, and the cooler temperatures and higher humidity of the early May evening brought it out of the treetops, allowing the night crew to cut some fire line and burn out hot spots. The Mack Lake Fire was not declared under control until noon on Wednesday, May 7th, but it was really all over by 7:00 o'clock on Monday night.

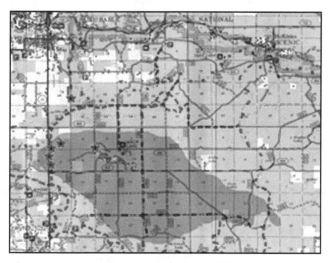

**The Extent of the Mack Lake Fire (Each square is 1 square mile, which is 640 acres)**

A top-notch fire investigation team was assembled, headed by Dale Gorman, who had been the District Ranger on the Isabella Ranger District, Superior National Forest in Minnesota, where I started my Forest Service career in 1973. I knew him well and he was an excellent choice to lead the team. At the time of the Mack Lake Fire, Dale was Deputy Forest Supervisor on the White Mountain National Forest in New Hampshire. He headed a nine-person team that produced a very thorough 100-page report, noted for its frank language. The report was critical of the staffing level, quality of pre-burn planning and judgement of key personnel. Significant recommendations were made that resulted in additional training requirements for prescribed burning personnel, a program for creating hardwood fuel breaks to break up extensive Jack Pine stands, and additional research into Kirtland's Warbler habitat requirements. Prescribed burning was described as a valuable management tool and would not be stopped or banned, but would be carried out under specific, carefully controlled conditions in the future.

The Mack Lake Fire occurred in 1980, but there were still only about 250 singing males ten years later. Why did it take so long for the Kirtland's Warbler population to respond? The answer is in the very narrow range of habitat conditions that meets the needs of this beautiful but finicky bird. In addition to its dependence on Jack Pine for nesting, the bird's nesting requirements are very specific. The nest is built on the ground beneath the protective shelter of pine limbs that reach or nearly reach the ground, a condition limited to Jack Pines from six to about twenty-two years old. Trees younger than six years don't have long enough branches to hide the nest; after 15 years or so, the lower branches die. The Mack Lake Fire area took several years to replant, and pines grow slowly in dry, sandy soils, so it was nearly ten years before adequate areas of Jack Pine of the right age were ready for nesting success. When conditions were finally right, the response was dramatic! Current population exceeds 5,000 birds!

Ironically, Kirtland's Warbler nests were discovered in the Upper Peninsula of Michigan in 1995, and three nests were found in Wisconsin in 2007. A few birds nest regularly in Canada. Kirtland's Warblers are rarely seen in migration, but one found its way into Central Park in New York City in May 2018. The news travelled quickly through the large birder community around New York, and the bird was not alone for long! The picture below, published by Ed Gaillard on his blog www.warblersandrumorsofwarblers.com shows the birder turnout on May 14th.

In May 2018, the U.S. Fish & Wildlife Service formally proposed that the Kirtland's Warbler be delisted, taking it off the Endangered Species list. A detailed post-delisting monitoring plan was released for public comment, including confident statements that ongoing habitat management activities would keep the warbler population at or above the 1,000 pair minimum set in the original recovery plan. Recovery of the bird was attributed to four decades of collaborative habitat management, Brown-headed Cowbird control, research and public education.

**_No mention was made of the Mack Lake Fire._**

**Red-eyed Vireo (Suzanne Zuckerman)**

# 3

# Beginning to Think
# Like a Birder

*Nighttime lab work as a grad student, study-
ing my bird books while the campus slept,
learning to think like a birder. A peek at my sur-
viving handwritten notes, a testimony to the value of focused study as an important part of bird
identification.*

We'll revisit the Kirtland's Warbler later to understand its relationship to the Brown-headed Cowbird, a brood parasite species that
leaves its eggs in the nests of other birds, its young to be raised by the
unwitting foster parents.

In the meantime, let's return to Blackduck and Camp Rabideau,
our Forest Measurements course, and that big stand of Jack Pine we
were working in. Our task as student foresters was to really get to
know those trees and understand the ecology while learning the tools
and management concepts we would later use as practicing foresters.
We could easily drag surveyor's two-and-a-half chain trailer tapes (a
chain is 66 feet, so these tapes were 165 feet long) behind us to measure distances, use Suunto Relaskops to measure tree heights, and use
little glass prisms to estimate the square footage of trees-on-the-stump
per acre, which could be converted to board feet or cords per acre. I
know - this all sounds like some kind of cult, but we were serious forestry students. They used to burn people at the stake for witchcraft, but
our forestry work didn't qualify, mysterious as it sounds.

Since we were already in the woods, measuring things, the Ecology professor assigned each team of students the task of laying out a
two meter-square plot with string and identifying and counting all the
plants in it. More ground-cover plots were assigned later in other forest types on moister soils – aspen/birch, northern hardwoods, spruce/
fir and White Pine stands. Later, we would dig soil pits in each of these
forest types and relate the soil characteristics to the plant life we found

there. Serious forestry, or more witchcraft? Trust me, digging soil pits is nothing but hard work, and the Witches Union wouldn't allow it.

As the god-like Teaching Assistant, I walked around answering questions, untangling trailer tapes, identifying north woods wildflowers and clubmosses and generally looking wise. On several mornings, I heard a strange, haunting call floating through the Jack Pine, something like "coo-coo, coo-coo-coo." I had no idea what it was. I finally gave it my best shot with an imitation of the call. I kept it up, despite the whispers and snickers coming from the scruffy students around me. Amazingly, we were soon joined by a long-tailed brown bird with a dark curved bill and white spots on the underside of its tail. Curious about whatever was invading its territory, it drifted to within 10 feet and cocked its head at me. I had spent enough time in my Golden Field Guide to recognize it as a Black-billed Cuckoo, a life bird for me!

Cuckoos are generally shy and secretive, but this beauty had come right in! I was able to call the Cuckoo out of hiding several more times; most of the students missed the specialness of those meetings with the Cuckoo, but a few sensed the same magic that I did. Of course, I would never repeat the feat in the future, except with a recorded song. It was a typically spectacular birding experience. I simply didn't know how special it was at the time.

We wrapped up Summer Camp and headed back to Urbana, Illinois, still with no forestry job in sight. I took advantage of an opportunity to fritter away another year at the university, this time as a Forestry Research Assistant. My job was growing potted red oak seedlings in the forestry greenhouse, adding carefully calibrated solutions of lead, and finally grinding them up to be analyzed to see how much lead they had absorbed. The objective was to identify how much lead could be tolerated by trees before dying of lead poisoning. All this, of course, was about the time that unleaded gasoline was introduced. Useful and timely work, right?

I administered my poisons at night, in an otherwise deserted building. I used the idle time between doses studying birds and making detailed notes. I still have my notes, hand-written on three-by-five inch cards tucked into a masking tape pocket in the back of my Golden Birds of North America. Thinking about it now, I had stumbled on a key part of Thinking Like A Birder, the part that requires reading about birds and studying the field guide when you're not out birding.

*My Vireo Notes*

**VIREOS — WITH WING BARS & SPECTACLES.**

| SPECIES | RANGE OR HABITAT | FIELD MARKS | SONG |
|---|---|---|---|
| SOLITARY (Blue-headed) VIREO (244) | Common — N. mixed forests | 4¾"; Lge size, Prominent blue-gray or gray head, white throat, spectacles, wing bars, large. Tame. Yellow sides | Robin-like phrases; 2-3 notes per phrase. Slow-slurred. Higher, sweeter than Red-eyed. |
| WHITE-EYED VIREO (246) | Common. — dense-moist decid. thickets, margins, hedgerows. | 6" - white iris; bright yellow sides Spec's, large wing bars. Yellow-green head | "PICK UP THE BEER CHECK QUICK. 5-7 slurred notes. |
| Yellow-throated Vireo (246) | Uncommon Near H₂O. Moist Forest. Clearings | Only spectacled vireo w/ yellow throat & breast. wide wing bars. 5". (Yellow) | Hoarse; 4-5 slurred phrases, repeated. also ee-yay or three-eight |
| Bell's VIREO (246) | Moist thickets wood margins, & mesquite (Western) | w. counterpart of wh-eyed. EYE BLACK. Narrow wing-bars. white spectacles 4¼' | Cheedle cheedle chee. " " chew. |

**VIREOS — NO WING BARS**

| SPECIES | RANGE OR HABITAT | FIELD Marks | SONG |
|---|---|---|---|
| RED-EYED VIREO (248) | Deciduous Forest (Very Common) | RED IRIS, Prominent white eye stripe, blue-gray cap. 5" | Robin-like, separate phrases by brief pause. Very long & monotonous. |
| Philadelphia Vireo | Wood margins & Decid. scrub (uncommon) | Yellowish breast, unmarked wings. 4¾' | LIKE RED-EYED. Higher pitched & slower. |
| Warbling VIREO | Tall decid. Shade trees. Common | Very drab. Unmarked wings; whitish breast Head inconspicuously striped | Long & warbling, like Hoarse Purple FINCH. |

The numbers in parentheses in the first column are the page numbers for each bird in the 1966 hardback edition of my Golden Birds of North America. I really studied the book during those late-night hours. The details on song pitch and cadence that I captured still serve me well in the field. Interestingly, the note in parentheses under Solitary Vireo suggests that the name change to Blue-headed was expected.

Without knowing it at the time, I was already learning to "think like a birder" by studying specific groups of birds and jotting down notes. A lot of the detail wrung so painfully out of my field guide during those long nights has stayed with me over the years and has been useful on field trips and in my birding classes.

Shield of the best organization in US government!

My first USFS job – two summers worth!

My last and best USFS job, District Ranger

# 4

# A Forester At Last

*A look back to 1973 and a summer job as a naturalist at Lake Tahoe, and finally getting that long-awaited job offer from the Forest Service. A peek at the Forest Service, a summary of my career and the decision to resign to go to business school. A look at the life of a naturalist, idle time at the nearby casinos and a recounting of the nearly famous Legend of Falling Rock.*

Let's go back in time for a moment. It's 1973, I'm 24 years old, waiting for my forestry career to start, and hooked on birding, but I'm running primarily on enthusiasm and the energy of youth. I bird alone most of the time. I'm finding birds by accident because I don't yet understand habitat and migration schedules. My identifications depend on luck and haphazard page-flipping in my Peterson or Golden Guide. I use my field guides only after I see a bird; they sit on my shelf between birding trips. Lots of guesses, lots of wrong IDs, including a bunch of rare birds that weren't really in the places I was birding at the times I was there. Don't get me wrong:  I was having fun and seeing lots of new birds, but I was clumsy and short on skills.

Meanwhile, I was working as a summer naturalist at the Forest Service Visitor's Center in South Lake Tahoe, California, leading bird and wildflower walks and doing evening campfire programs. We always had a great slide program or movie, but we "Rangers" were expected to sing a song or tell an Indian Legend to warm up the audience. It's funny how things stick in your memory; I still know most of the words to *My Hat It Has 3 Corners*, and I've included one ever-popular "Legend" to give you a sense of our campfire programs. This was my favorite:

### The Legend of Falling Rock (With Apologies)

Before the arrival of the white man, it was the custom in many Native American tribes to send young men out into the wilderness as a rite of passage into manhood. Members of the Blackfeet people, Running Wolf and Falling Rock had been friends since infancy and their time to become braves came in the same summer, when they were 13 years old. When the *Buffalo Come* moon was full in July the Chief told them solemnly of the importance of their quest, gave each a sharp knife made of obsidian and asked them to return when the *Leaves Falling* moon was full in October. The Medicine Man blessed them and their journeys to manhood began.

It was a hard summer with storms and cool temperatures. The wild fruits were few, fishing in the high water was poor, and the buffalo did not come. As fall drew near, the tribe waited anxiously for the return of their young braves. Running Wolf returned when the *Leaves Falling* moon was past full; he was strong, but his ribs told of his hunger, and his eyes told of the hardship he had faced.

Falling Rock did not return that fall. He did not come during the *Deer-Mating* moon (November) or the *Moon of Wolves* (December). When he had not returned by the *Ducks* moon (April,) the Chief sent scouts to search and to tell neighboring tribes.

As time passed, Falling Rock became part of legend, and the white men were told of his loss. Until today, he has not returned, but his tribe remains hopeful and the white people have honored their faith with vigilance. Perhaps you have seen the signs on mountain roads that say:

Sonja and I were having a great time, enjoying the sunny mountain weather, swimming in Lake Tahoe, and gambling a little at the Harrah's Casino across the state line in Nevada. We'd read a how-to book and taught ourselves to play blackjack, using pennies and a genuine Harrah's deck at our kitchen table in the decrepit Forest Service trailer that served as summer employee housing. Crappy as it was, the government rent was only $8.00 per two-week pay period and it was worth every penny in a resort town with ridiculous summer rates, although Sonja insisted they should have paid us for living there.

People just starting out in outdoor careers – forester, wildlife biologist, soil scientist, hydrologist, and ichthyologist – are very likely to live in less-than-glamorous housing for a year or two. Sonja was incredibly patient with the series of trailers we lived in while we were getting my Forest Service career started. Our first house in Isabella was a retired Job Corps single-wide trailer built for Alabama that wound up in Minnesota. Tiny bedrooms, frozen pipes and all, it was a big step up from our Lake Tahoe tin can. At least you could shut the bathroom door.

While in Lake Tahoe, we'd go down for the $3.00 Friday Buffet at Harrah's Casino, which offered salads, fried chicken, roast beef, fried shrimp, desserts, and free jug wine. The highlight was steamer trays of lobster tails! Lobster was a new treat for Sonja, and one she savors today. Predictably, we haven't seen "all-you-can-eat" lobster anywhere since 1973.

After gorging, we'd hit the $1.00 blackjack tables until our table stakes of ten bucks each ran out. We felt like wizards, knowing when to hit, when to split pairs and when to double down. We generally lost our ten dollars anyway, but it was cheap entertainment. Have you seen a $1.00 blackjack table lately.....

I was seeing a lot of new birds, and even spotted a pair of Pine Martens while hiking into the Desolation Wilderness. But the future after this idyllic summer was uncertain. I didn't yet see birding or wildflowers as a career and working in the skiing industry or the casino held little promise. I planned to return to Illinois and perhaps find some hanger-on job in the University of Illinois Forestry Department while Sonja continued her already successful career as a teacher.

Then one day in late July, the mailman brought a thick envelope with a Milwaukee return address and a lot of forwarding stickers. It was from Ted Thomas in the Personnel Department of the USDA Forest Service Regional Office, and contained the long-awaited job offer! It was a permanent full-time position, as a GS-7 Forester on the Superior National Forest in Isabella, Minnesota, with a reporting date of August 1st. The offer had been delayed by our move to California, and I was afraid I had missed my opportunity. I called Mr. Thomas at 6:00 AM the next morning – we were on West Coast time – and he reassured me that the offer was still valid and when could I get to Isabella?

We were elated with the news and, after offering apologies to my boss at the Visitor's Center (his name was Dick Pine, a perfect fit for a Forest Service guy), we packed up and headed east to start my career as a forester and natural resource manager, an adventure that was to last 15 years, and maintain my momentum with birds and birding.

The Forest Service is part of the U.S. Department of Agriculture and in 1973 was one of the least bureaucratic agencies in government. Most of its employees are career professionals, and the chief forester has always come from the ranks as well. Established in 1906 by Gifford Pinchot, it is charged with multiple use management of 190 million acres of public land, made up of 154 National Forests and 20 National Grasslands in 43 states. Headquartered in Washington, D.C. the Forest Service is organized into nine Regions, each headed by a regional forester. Each Region oversees a number of National Forests, headed by a forest supervisor. Each Forest is broken up into ranger districts, and the district ranger has one of the best jobs in the world. I know – I <u>was</u> one for five years.

While a typical career with the Forest Service was a lifetime commitment, mine was only 15 years. Except for that brief summer in California, all of my assignments were in the eastern United States – Indiana, Minnesota, Wisconsin, Michigan and Vermont. Despite the limited geography, I had tremendous variety in my assignments and had the opportunity to be involved in some exceptional events.

A brief summary of my Forest Service career might provide some useful perspective.

### Summer Jobs

- *Recreation Technician*, Hardin Ridge Recreation Area, Wayne-Hoosier National Forest. Summers of 1969 and 1970 - Hardin Ridge is a big campground on Lake Monroe, a little south of Bloomington, Indiana. I worked the entrance gate, sold camping permits, cleaned toilets and mowed lots of grass. I worked the just-opened Visitor Center in 1970, which was boring but gave me a resume line that helped land a similar but much better job at Lake Tahoe in 1973.
- *Visitor Information Specialist*, Lake Tahoe Basin

Management Unit, Eldorado National Forest. Summer of 1973, cut short by my acceptance of that permanent job in Minnesota. Lake Tahoe Basin Management Unit is a unique National Forest, responsible for managing and protecting the spectacular Lake Tahoe watershed in a very busy environment. It's headquartered in South Lake Tahoe, California, with major gambling casinos in nearby Stateline, Nevada, several ski resorts, the 63,000-acre Desolation Wilderness and numerous other recreation sites around the largest alpine lake in North America. I worked a regular shift in a very busy Visitor Center, led nature walks, guided a boat tour on Echo Lake and co-starred in evening campfire programs. Despite my eastern training, I quickly became the staff expert on birds and wildflowers.

### Professional Positions

-    *Forester*, Isabella Ranger District, Superior National Forest. August 1973 – October 1974. Isabella was one of the two most remote ranger districts in the Eastern Region of the Forest Service. The Potosi District, on the Mark Twain National Forest in Missouri, was equally remote but it was warmer. Isabella had only a couple of hundred residents, scattered along 10 miles of Highway 1, midway between Ely and the north shore of Lake Superior. Vast forests of spruce, fir, pine, white birch and aspen were crossed by a few gravel roads. Moose, black bears and gray wolves shared the landscape. The vast Boundary Waters Canoe Area Wilderness bordered the district to the north, and Canada was only 20 miles away. I marked timber for timber sales, inventoried thousands of acres of forest doing what we called Compartment Examination, trained as a fire fighter and helped with prescribed burns, and served as Camp Director for a Youth Conservation Corps (YCC) program that brought 40 city kids to the forest for a summer of outdoor work and education. YCC was my introduction to the special work programs that have been a part of the Forest Service for many years. Success with YCC and similar programs was an important criterion for promotions and career growth. I learned to cross-country ski and snowshoe, chased black bears out of campgrounds and saw some great birds.

-    *Forester,* Timber Survey Crew, Chequamegon National Forest. October 1974 – May 1976. I was a member of a four-man crew, headquartered in Glidden, Wisconsin and

charged with completing many thousands of acres of Compartment Examination on all five ranger districts of the Chequamegon National Forest. Good weather meant outside work on
foot, snowmobile or snowshoes, recording timber type, age,
density and quality of timber stands. Bad weather brought us
indoors to complete management prescriptions, draw maps and
work with aerial photos in preparation for the next compartment. Sonja and I bought our first house in nearby Park Falls, a
great little town compared to Isabella. Sonja taught school, we
went to real restaurants, and we played golf. I did my first few
Christmas Bird Counts and wrote a weekly nature column, *A
Northwoods Journal*, for the Park Falls *Herald*.

   -   *Forester*, Glidden Ranger District, Chequamegon
National Forest. May 1976 – August 1977. After completing
the Timber Survey work, I accepted a position on the Glidden
District which gave me more experience without having to
move again. Compartment Examination (it never ends,) timber
marking, timber stand improvement (TSI) and tree planting. I
had a crew of three local men working in the Older Americans
program who did the TSI work, mostly tree pruning and removing fast-growing aspen sprouts from areas recently planted
with slow-growing pine and spruce. Working with those reliable
and responsible guys added to my already solid reputation with
work programs. One of the challenges was cleanup from the
tremendous storm in November 1975 that sank the *SS Edmund
Fitzgerald* on Lake Superior and blew down thousands of acres
of timber in northern Wisconsin.

   -   *Assistant Ranger*, Harrisville Ranger District, Huron-Manistee National Forests. September 1977 – December
1980. I was finally promoted out of the timber track to manage
recreation and fire programs in Harrisville, Michigan, on the
shores of Lake Huron. Steve Chandler was the district ranger,
the best I ever met in the Forest Service, and he and Natalie
remain friends to this day. I had responsibility for two campgrounds, a swimming beach and picnic area and lots of trails.
Lower Michigan is Jack Pine country, home of the Kirtland's
Warbler, so fire was serious business, and I was involved in the
Mack Lake Fire. I also had responsibility for Special Uses, including permits for underground power and telephone lines, and
acoustic prospecting projects by oil and gas companies looking
for underground petroleum reserves. The economy was in poor

shape, with high unemployment, so I had a big daytime Young Adult Conservation Corps (YACC) work program for local kids age 18 to 24. I spent most of my time planning and developing two large Foot Travel Areas, Hoist Lakes and Reid Lake. They were closed to vehicles but webbed with hiking and cross-country ski trails. Not wilderness, but off-limits to the pickups, jeeps, motorcycles, four-wheelers and snowmobiles that characterized outdoor recreation in the Motor State. Run a Google search – both areas are still there and heavily used.

- *District Ranger,* Rochester Ranger District, Green Mountain National Forest. January 1981 – June 1986. One of the smallest districts in the Forest Service, Rochester was also one of the busiest. Located in the heart of beautiful Vermont, it featured two major ski areas under Special Use Permit, portions of the Appalachian Trail and the Long Trail, a salmon restoration program on the White River, an experimental grazing program for sheep, a Peregrine Falcon reintroduction site, many Native American and early settler archeological sites, hundreds of vacation homes, steep terrain, shallow soils and green mountainsides that were highly visible to visitors expecting pristine forest and brilliant fall colors. My small but dedicated district team managed all this beauty and conflict under my direction. I learned on my arrival that delivering the 1981 Capitol Christmas Tree to Washington was to be our privilege and responsibility. Governor Richard Snelling manned one end of the two-man saw when the 60-foot Balsam Fir was cut, and Senator Patrick Leahy met us at the Capitol. I took over the preparation of an Environmental Impact Statement for the proposed expansion of Sugarbush Valley and Sugarbush North Ski Areas when the consultant hired for the task quit to go to work for the developers. I attended one of the first gender sensitivity programs developed to address the rapidly growing number of women in the Forest Service and eventually organized and directed two additional sessions. I helped moderate public hearings about the creation of the Breadloaf Wilderness as part of a huge national "instant wilderness" program. Finally, and perhaps most importantly, I was heavily involved in development of the forest plan that would dramatically change management direction for the Green Mountain National Forest for the next 10 years.

My Forest Service career was busy, educational and successful by most measures. So why did I leave? My experience with trying to manage timber on highly visible Vermont mountainsides with steep slopes, shallow soils and expensive roads underscored my belief that timber management should no longer be the driving force in managing most National Forest lands. Nationwide, the public's unhappiness with clearcutting and growing interest in wilderness, visual quality, clean water, non-game wildlife and trail-based recreation was evident in verbal comments at public hearings and written comments to draft forest plans. My own dabbling in economic analysis told me that the investment required to build adequate roads for modern logging of second-growth timber could rarely be recouped, and the new roads changed the character and use patterns of the forest.

When I asked the Forest Service to send me to business school to explore these concepts, I was turned down politely but firmly. I was frustrated by the refusal, and the Forest Service job opportunities I considered seemed to be either in Washington, DC or a regional office where living expenses promised to outpace my salary. Determined to get an MBA, I took the GMAT (Graduate Management Admission Test) on my own, scored in the top 2 percent and landed a Goizueta Fellowship at the Emory University Business School. Sonja and I took a deep breath, told Smokey goodbye, put our Rochester house on the market and moved to Atlanta.

I unknowingly left at a critical point, where the next career decision and transfer would have locked me into one of two paths: 1) ignore my management concerns, pursue an ambitious series of staff positions in the Chief's Office in Washington D.C. and one or more regional offices, and eventually become a forest supervisor; or 2) continue my quiet resistance to the timber beast culture, bureaucracy and relative poverty of a staff job in a big city, remain a district ranger as long as I could and finally get old, dusty and forgotten as a recreation or timber staff officer on a National Forest in the boonies somewhere.

I have no regrets about leaving when I did. Either you keep going or you get left behind, and my strong counter-culture beliefs about what the national forests were for in the modern era made the traditional path to Forest Supervisor unlikely despite my capabilities. Ironically, the Chief of the Forest Service was fired in the early '90s for allowing or encouraging policies that gave too much leeway to timber, grazing and mining interests.

Business School was an eye-opener and a challenge, but I did very well and moved on to a very different career in finance and strategic planning for BellSouth as it was emerging from regulation after being broken out of the telephone mother-ship, AT&T.

Surprisingly, the amount of time I spent playing in the woods – hiking, camping, canoeing and birding – increased dramatically during my time at BellSouth. Burned out by teaching, Sonja went to secretarial school and also went to work for BellSouth. My parents lived in Atlanta and our daughters were finally able to spend time with their grandparents. My Dad, always my favorite golf partner, forgot all the grief I had given him as a young man and rejoined me on the golf course. I did a lot of birding when time allowed but focused on an oddly satisfying alternative career in corporate America, ran the Peachtree Road Race 15 times and watched / helped our wonderful daughters grow up. It was a special time for our family.

**Peregrine Falcon**
**(Suzanne Zuckerman)**

**Dr. Lynn Rogers at Lily's Den**
**(Jim Stroner)**

**Brown-headed Cowbird Trap**
**(Wisconsin Dept. of Natural Resources)**

# 5

# Learning While Working

*Wildlife experiences with the Forest Service – a winter day with bear expert Dr. Lynn Rogers examining a hibernating black bear and her cubs, watching drumming Sharp-tailed Grouse in Wisconsin, and helping restore Peregrine Falcons to a historical aerie in Vermont. Background on the devastation wrought by DDT on Peregrines and other top-of-the-food-chain birds, and a peek at Brown-headed Cowbird nest parasitism on Kirtland's Warbler.*

That Forest Service job offer was life changing in many ways. It put me into a career that fully utilized my education, firmed up my personal philosophy of careful and intelligent use of natural resources and sharpened my people skills. It took my family and me to small towns where living was affordable, safe and wonderful. The people I worked with were intelligent, thoughtful and professional. Without any planning on my part, my Forest Service years took me to great birding places in Minnesota, Wisconsin, Michigan and Vermont. We lived in houses with birdy yards and I worked in four beautiful national forests, roaming thousands of acres of diverse habitat, eating my peanut butter and jelly sandwiches beside beaver ponds and undeveloped lakes and enjoyed the solitude and beauty of working in our National Forests.

I met wildlife biologists who were delighted to help me learn since my strong birding interest and growing knowledge made me unusual; although most foresters love the outdoors and spend time hunting and fishing, they are not birders. They notice the birds when they're outdoors, but the birds are just part of the outdoor environment and not a focus. I asked for, and received, invitations to work on projects that involved birds.

<u>Black-backed Woodpeckers</u> - We often burned branches, tops and other logging debris on recently cutover tracts on the Superior Na-

tional Forest in Minnesota. I was sent to check for leftover hotspots the day after a spring burn in 1974 and found half a dozen Black-backed Woodpeckers working toasted insects in the bark of blackened tree stumps. Once called Black-backed Three-toed Woodpecker, this unique bird does have only three toes on each foot, and a yellow cap instead of the more standard red found on most woodpeckers. They were very tame and seemed intent on flaking away burned bark in search of the insects beneath.

Black Bears & Gray Jays - I was fortunate to accompany Dr. Lynn Rogers, famous black bear biologist, on a winter retrieval of a snoozing female black bear from her den in northern Minnesota. Dr. Rogers truly loved the woods and knew the birds well. He was especially fond of Gray Jays, known locally as 'camp robbers' because of their bold forays into camps and backyards in search of bright objects. During our chilly lunch break, he easily coaxed Gray Jays to our feet with scraps of sandwich. More about Dr. Rogers when we talk about dealing with black bears and bird feeders.

Sharp-tailed Grouse - Howard Shelton, wildlife biologist on the Chequamegon National Forest in Wisconsin, took me out early one spring day to watch Sharp-tailed Grouse on their booming grounds. Most of the grouse species use a similar booming ground, or lek, year after year where the males gather at dawn to perform their mating displays. I had seen Greater Prairie Chickens in southern Illinois while in grad school and was fascinated by the elaborate ritual displays of spread wing and tail feathers, colorful inflated throat pouches (purple in Sharptails, orange in Greater Prairie Chicken,) rapid foot move-ments and quill rattling. The Wisconsin Sharptails were spectacular, although the hens seemed oblivious to the males' romantic efforts.

Kirtland's Warbler & Brown-headed Cowbirds - Getting involved with Kirtland's Warbler management in Michigan was another great opportunity to meet biologists I could learn from. Before the annual population census, the Fish & Wildlife Service biologists gave us the details about life history and habitat requirements of the little Fire Bird and played recordings of the song we were to listen for. After the census, I was invited to visit one of the Brown-headed Cowbird traps set up in prime breeding habitat of young Jack Pine near a known Kirtland's nest location. I learned first-hand a little about cowbird be-havior and how dangerous the Brown-headed Cowbird is to Kirtland's Warbler survival.

The Brown-headed Cowbird is native to North America and rang-es throughout the continent. It is a brood parasite, laying its eggs in the nests of other species, usually smaller birds. According to Christopher Leahy, author of *The Birdwatcher's Companion to North American Birdlife*, the Brown-headed Cowbird female is not picky about where she lays her egg; cowbird eggs have been found in the nests of 220 species, including shorebirds and ducks. At least 144 of these victim species have reared cowbird young.

**Male Brown-headed Cowbird**

**Female Brown-headed Cowbird**

A single cowbird female may travel several miles through woodland and open habitat to lay dozens of eggs in other nests each season. While a particular female cowbird typically lays only one egg in a single nest, other female cowbirds may parasitize the same nest, resulting in an invasive "clutch" of up to eight cowbird eggs. During breeding season, courtship and parasitic activities generally occur in the morning, with feeding and resting in the afternoon. The cowbird sometimes lays its egg before dawn, when both host parents are away. She may return later that day to remove one of the host's eggs, piercing it with its bill and often eating the contents. The cowbird incubation period is unusually short, and the nestling is fast-growing and larger than the host hatchlings, giving it a better chance for survival.

How did this unsavory but amazingly successful behavior come about? The original range of the Brown-headed Cowbird matched the range of the American Bison. The bison herds stirred up insects from the plain's grasses, and the cowbirds took advantage of the food supply by following the bison. The problem, from the cowbird's perspective, was that the bison didn't stay in one place long enough to allow the cowbirds to nest successfully. Somehow, cowbirds learned to drop an egg in the nest of another bird and move on with the pantry, and the survival value of this parasitic behavior was high for the species as a whole. The evolutionary expectation is that the parasitized bird will hatch the larger cowbird egg and raise the young cowbird to fledge. In most cases, that is exactly what happens, and I have seen the results myself: a begging baby cowbird being fed by a towhee or warbler.

**Successful Kirtland's Warbler Nest – No Cowbird Eggs! (Stan Tekiela)**

Once confined to the wide open prairies where the bison roamed, Brown-headed Cowbirds expanded their range, taking advantage of the openings created by logging and agriculture. The first instance of cowbird parasitism of a Kirtland's Warbler nest was reported in 1908. While some species of birds victimized by cowbirds are able to recognize the foreign egg in their nests and either roll it out or build a new nest over it, the Jack Pine warbler is unable to identify the danger. Prior to the initiation of cowbird control in 1972, parasitism rates ranged from 48 to 86 percent of Kirtland's Warbler nests, and fledging rates were less than a single warbler per nest.

So, 200 nesting pairs of endangered warblers, decreasing acres of suitable young Jack Pine, and thousands of cowbirds primed to create havoc in every nest they could find. What to do? The answer was to build large traps of lumber and chicken wire, baited with corn and other grain, and with a single funnel-shaped entrance that was easy to find for the hungry cowbird, but nearly impossible to find when the cowbird wanted out after feeding. Fish & Wildlife Service staff checked the traps frequently during nesting season, removed the cowbirds and humanely killed them using exhaust from their official pickups. It sounds ugly, but things were desperate for Kirtland's Warblers, and the method was very effective. As a result of cowbird trapping, warbler success tripled from less than one to more than three fledglings per nest attempt. In short, cowbird traps helped keep the Kirtland's Warblers in charge of their own nests, raising warbler babies, until the Mack Lake Fire came along to create enough habitat to stave off extinction.

Peregrine Falcon Reintroduction - I had another opportunity to meet interesting people and get involved with an endangered bird while working on the Green Mountain National Forest in the early '80s. The Great Cliff on Mount Horrid, near Rochester, Vermont, was a nesting site for Peregrine Falcons for many years before man-made chemicals came into widespread use as insecticides and herbicides. Historic estimates of Peregrine Falcons nesting in Vermont suggest that as many as 32 pairs nested in the state. The last wild adult in the East was observed in Vermont in 1970. By that time, the falcon's numbers had dwindled to the point that no nesting pairs had been found in the entire eastern United States for more than a decade.

DDT (Dichloro-Diphenyl-Trichloroethane) is an insecticide that is very effective in killing insects, especially mosquitoes, until the mosquitoes develop immunity to its effects. It was widely used to control mosquitoes that carried malaria in the tropics and was used

as a body dust to control insects on soldiers during World War II. It was used extensively in suburban neighborhoods for mosquito control well into the 1960s. You may remember following the spray truck on your bicycle as it drove slowly through your neighborhood on a summer evening, dispensing a fine mist of DDT to make your backyard more pleasant. It seemed cool at the time but was foolish and dangerous. Most Moms threatened death if they caught you in the spray.

This "miracle" insecticide was banned in the United States in 1972, but not before wreaking havoc on the reproductive capabilities of many birds, especially those that ate fish or other birds, to the extent that extinction was an ominous threat to falcons, eagles and pelicans. The chemical was used heavily after WWII in North America and was washed by rain into lakes and streams where it became highly concentrated in the tissues of fish. Osprey, Bald Eagles and Brown Pelicans feed heavily on fish and accumulated high concentrations in their bodies, sometimes enough to cause death outright. A less visible but more damaging long-term effect was to create an imbalance in the production of magnesium and phosphate in these birds, making it more difficult to produce calcium. The result was thin shells on their eggs, so weak that the eggs collapsed during incubation. Peregrine Falcons, effective predators of fish-eating waterfowl, soon felt the same ill effects. Populations of these beautiful birds plummeted, with extinction on the horizon.

An American marine biologist named Rachel Carson published Silent Spring in 1962, a book that opened the world's eyes to the dangers of widespread and persistent use of chemicals like DDT. It took some time, but DDT was banned in 1972 in the US. Sadly, it continues to be used in less developed and less environmentally aware countries. In North America, the recovery of the affected species, while slow to start, has been dramatic.

Bruce Flewelling, Assistant Ranger on the Rochester Ranger District, and an avid birder, showed me The Great Cliff shortly after my arrival in 1981. As I looked at the cliff and walked the trail to the top of the massive rock face, I could sense its emptiness without the falcons. Bruce told me that Cornell University intended to bring them back to Mount Horrid, through the Peregrine Fund and the Peregrine Falcon

Recovery Project.

Cornell University is the home of the Cornell Laboratory of Or-nithology, perhaps the finest teaching and research center for birds on the planet, and a world leader in the study, appreciation and conserva-tion of birds. Wearing their conservation hats, biologists at the Cornell Lab set about re-establishing Peregrine Falcons in their native nesting locations as soon as the devastating effects of DDT began to subside.

Cornell professor Tom Cade, director of research at the Cornell lab in 1970, spearheaded the recovery program with the formation of The Peregrine Fund. His falcon research in Alaska was instrumental in proving that DDT was causing thin eggshells and was a major factor in the banning of DDT in 1972.

The objective was to breed Peregrine Falcons in captivity and re-introduce them across the continent using a process known as 'hack-ing' where young birds are placed in a protective wooden box at the release location until they're old enough to fly. The screen-front hack box allows the birds to see and adjust to their environment as they mature while protecting them from raccoons and other predators. The young birds are monitored and fed by human volunteers who remain out of sight to avoid imprinting and keep them wild.

Cade built a large "hawk barn" to house the spectacularly suc-cessful captive-breeding project. Birds for the breeding program were taken as chicks from successful nests and raised specifically to be breeders. To increase egg production, Cade experimented with a tech-nique called "double clutching" – taking the first clutch of eggs from a captive pair soon after they were laid, to be incubated artificially. Thankfully, the pair often produced a second or even third clutch.

Some of the eggs taken from wild falcons in the early days were thin-shelled. These vulnerable eggs were often successfully hatched in humidified incubators. The Peregrine Fund took captive breeding beyond the limits of anything ever done before. Over the course of the program, over 6,000 captive-bred falcons were released in 37 states and Canadian provinces.

Contact with humans was kept to a minimum until the young hatchlings were ready to be taken to hack boxes on traditional cliffs or placed in hack towers – platforms built high above the ground in otherwise suitable locations without cliffs. The hack box placed at Mount Horrid was made of plywood, with a screened front. A plastic feeding pipe was added the second year to reduce human contact with the birds. Volunteers or grad students stayed with the birds for several weeks, monitoring their progress and providing fresh meat through the feeding tube. The Mount Horrid birds were fed whole young chickens, kept frozen in a cooler until needed.

The Mount Horrid volunteers worked hard, under primitive conditions. They lived on the cliff in backpacking tents, and water and supplies came up on their backs. Toting the hack box, in pieces, up the Long Trail to the top of the cliff, was brute labor. The frozen chickens, packed in ice-filled coolers, were heavy loads for these physically fit ornithological backpackers. Forest Service employees and local folks helped out, brought meals, kept extra chickens in their home freezers and provided moral support for the long haul. I don't know what accommodations were made for getting these brave folks into a shower once in a while. I think Bruce Flewelling and others took them home to clean up periodically and just never mentioned it. These dedicated volunteers were critical to the Peregrine Fund's success nationwide.

**Top of The Great Cliff on Mount Horrid, Vermont**

**Typical Hacking Box. Note the feeding pipe at left.**
**(Courtesy National Park Service)**

## *Timing Can Be Important – One Scary Moment in 10,000 Years*

I got a peek at the great forces of nature as we were preparing for our falcons, with a nearly disastrous example of the importance of timing. The Green Mountains are very old, and the Great Cliff has been exposed to the elements for thousands of years. Over the millennia, house-sized chunks of rock have broken off and fallen into a jumble at the base of the cliff.

The young biologist from Cornell who came to check out the Mount Horrid hack site brought his dog with him. I don't remember the name of either biologist or dog, but they were both very relaxed and comfortable in high places. On their first visit, they wandered to the end of a point of rock to enjoy the view, and even sat down to en-joy a sandwich. Satisfied with Mount Horrid as a hack site, man and dog went back to Cornell.

When the biologist returned a few weeks later, we went back up to the hack site. He seemed unsettled or confused, so I asked him what was wrong. He said, "Where's the rock where we ate lunch last time?" The point of rock he had been sitting on with his dog two weeks before was at the bottom of the cliff. One wonders what might have happened if there had been three for lunch on that rocky point a few weeks be-fore.

---

The first Mount Horrid hacking was in 1982, with five young fal-cons 25 to 30 days old. They spent two weeks in the hack box before their release on July 3rd. No food tube was used that first year, result-ing in the birds becoming too familiar with their keepers which led to food begging later on. Honyo, a male bird and the oldest, fledged the first afternoon, and all five had flown within two days. The birds were fed daily while they perfected their flying skills and learned to hunt. The first kill was a swallow on July 24th. Daily feeding continued un-til August 3rd, and alternate day feeding continued until August 12th, when all the young falcons had left the hack site. The hacking process mimicked the development and fledging of falcons in the wild. Wild nestlings are ready to fly when they're five or six weeks old but con-tinue to be fed by the adults for another five weeks until they are able to catch their own food.

Mount Horrid was used successfully as a hack site each year until 1987. Thirty-four young falcons were successfully fledged and dis-persed. A food tube was used successfully, eliminating the begging problem. Interestingly, mature Peregrine Falcons visited the hack site each year. Their presence did no harm according to reports by the vol-unteers, and the mature birds probably helped sharpen flying skills as they flew with the young birds.

Adult Peregrines were observed at Mount Horrid annually for three years after hacking was suspended but did not nest. The first successful nesting was in 1991, when three birds fledged. A total of 51 wild falcons have fledged from Mount Horrid in addition to the 34 hacked fledglings. The Great Cliff of Mount Horrid has regained its historical place as a nesting site for these wonderful birds!

The reintroduction of the Peregrine Falcon to Vermont has been an astounding success. At least 51 wild pairs nested successfully in

2017, producing 63 young falcons. Similar results have been produced at many historic falcon nesting sites, including bridges and tall buildings in large cities. When I worked in downtown Atlanta in the early 1990s I watched Peregrine Falcons chase Rock Pigeons through the urban canyons, probably the offspring of a pair that has nested successfully on the Sun Trust Plaza Tower for many years.

As my Forest Service career took me from Lake Tahoe to Minnesota, Wisconsin, Michigan and eventually Vermont, I kept on birding. Without really knowing that I was doing it, I began to develop and practice some habits that have become the core of my teaching about birds. Those late nights in the research lab during grad school, making notes to stay awake, got me started. I read the field guides at home, studying families and looking at range maps.

I built a sizable collection of quality guides that used both artist drawings and photographs to provide comparisons of field marks. I bought and read birding adventure books, starting with *Wild America* by Roger Tory Peterson and James Fisher (1953). I took part in Christmas Bird Counts as near-polar adventures in northern Wisconsin and under more comfortable conditions later in Georgia. I started my yard list and kept my feeders full year-round.

Surprisingly, I spent more time playing in the outdoors – hiking, camping, fishing and birding – after I left the Forest Service than I did during my forestry career. In fact, birding became the focus whenever I was outdoors. Family vacations to the beach included early morning birding. I carried binoculars on the golf course and always kept a bird list on my score card, despite the chuckles from my Dad. My camping tent was birding headquarters for many trips to Florida and the Smokies. Binoculars joined boots, compass and walking stick as basic hiking equipment. Atlanta Audubon Society bird walks and Georgia Ornithological Society "meetings" (mostly birding field trips in great places) put me together with friendly people who were good birders.

As I did these things, my birding skills quietly increased. When we opened Blue Ridge Bird Seed Company in 2003, the full-time exposure to birds and people who cared about birds really focused my attention and my learning increased dramatically. I was the go-to guy for bird questions and I took it seriously. Eventually all these activities would become the core of my approach to helping people learn about birds.

Our bird store logo and newsletter heading

2003: The "young" shopkeepers, starting their third careers.

An honor to teach here!          A too-large Young Harris ICL birding class.

# 6

# From Cash Register
# to Classroom

*Opening of the long-dreamed-of bird store, Blue Ridge Bird Seed Company, in 2003 and the start of bird walks and Saturday Seminars. Walks and seminars led to invitations to teach bird identification in the adult education program at Young Harris College and at the renowned John C. Campbell Folk School in Brasstown, North Carolina. Two bouts with cancer and heart damage caused by the harsh treatments put some potholes and bumps in my birding road.*

Sonja and I opened Blue Ridge Bird Seed Company in February 2003. Recently retired from BellSouth, we were rookies at retail, with no experience in store layout and design, buying, inventory management, small business marketing, or bookkeeping. You name it, we were new at it. What we did have were people skills that translated to customer service, and birding knowledge, which quickly made us the local experts. We learned enough to recommend specific products for specific birds very quickly and found that the other stuff was learnable. This third career was to last almost 15 years, and I wouldn't trade those years for anything.

I became the go-to guy for bird identification questions from customers. E-mails with photographs contained the same exasperated query: "What bird is this...?" I was able to answer most questions, and often included tips about field marks, migration times, rarity and habitat. We quickly began to offer Saturday bird walks to local parks and nearby Lake Blue Ridge and added a series of Saturday Seminars about specific topics: bluebirds, hummingbirds, binoculars, bird feeding basics, black bears, wildflower and tree identification, butterflies, lady bugs and astronomy. Slyly, we offered "Seminar Survivor" discount coupons to entice customers to the bird store after seminars.

In a blinding flash of the obvious, we invited globe-trotting customers to share their adventure & nature travel stories as speakers at our seminars. Dave and Kathy Tickner took us to Ecuador and Costa Rica. We went to Africa with Skip and Pam Cook for big cats and Mountain Gorillas. Skip's tale of being literally brushed aside by the 300-pound dominant male gorilla added a little zip to that seminar. Reluctant to stay home for long, Skip and Pam later shared their November trip to Churchill, Manitoba for polar bears (stay on the bus!), followed by a July return to Churchill to swim with the Beluga Whales.

These seminars created the impression that we knew stuff about nature. In fact, we did know stuff about nature; I wasn't going to just do lightweight seminars, so I researched seminar topics and developed handouts and how-to guides for most of the topics. I improved and polished the information over the years. It dawned on me that my seminar materials would be useful to backyard birders and nature enthusiasts if I spiffed them up a bit. I've pulled them together in Part Four: Lessons From The Bird Store.

My teaching career was a natural extension of our bird walks and seminars and began with birding classes for retired folks. Young Harris College in Young Harris, Georgia, is a small liberal arts college in the beautiful mountains of North Georgia, more than 130 years old. It was a two-year college until 2008, when, guided by President Kathy Cox, Georgia's former Secretary of State, it finally shrugged its educational shoulders and decided to become a four-year school.

For the last 25 years or so, Young Harris College has hosted and supported an adult education program called Institute for Continuing Learning, or ICL. ICL is a diverse, ever-changing and well managed program, offering classes for adults through all four quarters of the academic year. A typical quarter's offering might include aerobics or yoga, poetry, music, western movies, Civil War or Appalachian history, computers, photography, contract bridge, genealogy, painting, languages and writing.

Birding classes have long been popular in ICL. Lou Laux, a professional ornithologist and Young Harris professor, and Dot Freeman, an outstanding amateur birder, handled the birding classes until Lou retired and Dot became seriously ill. My friend Kathy Tickner, an excellent birder you will hear more about, and a part-time literature instructor at the college, recognized the void and suggested to the ICL curriculum folks that I might be the new birding guy for ICL. They invited me to teach Summer Birding in 2007, and my teaching career was launched.

I had led field trips for years and done a series of hour-long seminars as a bird store owner, but this was a big step. I'd never done any kind of structured classes and wasn't sure I was ready for the challenge. I went ahead anyway, preparing myself to talk confidently about birding tools – binoculars and field guides – and then I asked the students in my first class about their experience level and their expectations.

My students were wonderful. They ranged from complete beginners to long-time backyard bird-watchers to seasoned birders with the right tools and strong field skills. They wanted to meet other birders, see birds beyond their backyard varieties, find local birding hotspots, and get better at this crazy birding thing. Some of the seasoned birders had taken some of the same learning steps I had, but none had followed any kind of structured approach to learning about birds. The backyard birders and rookies needed a place to start, and a path to follow.

My students don't get Roger Tory Peterson, Pete Dunne or Giff Beaton. Instead, they get a guy who cares a lot about birds, enjoys working with people, and has been doing both long enough to stay ahead of the class. I've found that I know enough, and share it well enough, that new birders often get the bug and intermediate birders learn a little bit, find more ways to enjoy birding, and often come back for more.

## A Bump in the Road

My young teaching career was interrupted in October 2007 by a diagnosis of non-Hodgkin's lymphoma (NHL). A funny bump was found in my colon during a routine colonoscopy; further tests uncovered a sizable tumor on my small intestine, which was surgically removed. I was able to arrange for chemotherapy close to home in Blue Ridge, avoiding many arduous trips to Atlanta. My treatment regimen was CHOP, involving four drugs, including Adriamycin, a strong drug used successfully to treat NHL. My treatment angels, the nurses who administered the drugs, called it "the red devil" because of the dangerous side effects that sometimes came with its use in cancer treatment. These side effects include congestive heart failure and arrhythmia, which were to appear as bumps in my road years later.

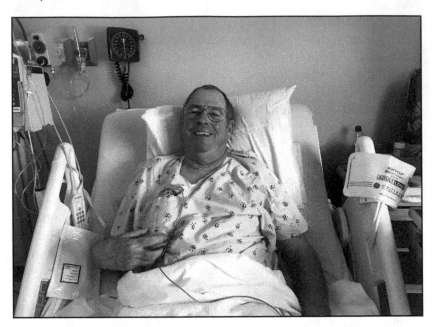

**This is from a later, less serious hospital stay. I had a lot less hair during cancer treatments!**

The nurses welcomed me for treatment every three weeks, sent me home with good wishes, said I'd start feeling puny in a few days and invited me to come back about the time I was feeling pretty normal again.

I put my binoculars on the shelf and started treatment right after Thanksgiving. My hair got a little loose, as predicted, and Sonja's favorite hairdresser gave me a really short haircut as a Christmas present. Six planned treatments became eight, and birding came to a standstill. I had no idea if I would ever be able to return to my shop keeping career or teach another class.

It was a long winter, with plenty of time to think about life and family and what was important. My recovery went well, my hair returned with only a little gray, and I went back to work in the store and in the classroom. My friends Dave and Kathy Tickner invited me to join them for a birding adventure to Ecuador, as their guest. We spent 10 amazing days in the Andes in January 2009, chasing birds, eating rice and chicken, and sharing the first healthy days of this next stage of my life. I kept an informal daily journal of my Ecuador trip; you'll find it farther along under Birding Adventures.

I was able to get back into the bird store full-time and returned to the classroom at Young Harris, teaching what Sonja called "birding for old people," but with a little more patience and heartfelt appreciation for the opportunity.

The Young Harris ICL classes proved to be popular, and my name eventually popped up at the famous John C. Campbell Folk School in nearby Brasstown, North Carolina. The Folk School was founded in 1925 to nurture and preserve the folk arts of the Appalachian Mountains. Traditional classes focused on music and art, with weaving, soap making, basket making, folk dancing, rug making, cane chairs and rockers and blacksmithing.

Outdoor activities and skills are also strong components of the Folk School program, ranging from trout fishing and fly-tying to gardening, beekeeping, wildflowers, geology, nature photography and, of course, birding. I was invited to teach a birding week in the spring of 2013, and several more week-long classes and a couple of weekends were to follow. The Folk School is well known and very popular and being invited to teach there is an honor.

A week-long class at The Folk School was very different from the weekly two-hour ICL birding classes. My ICL students ponied up about $20 for the six-week class and didn't mind an occasional rainy-day session inside. Folk School students were paying about a thousand dollars for their week and expected their money's worth.

I nervously prepared a detailed and meaty schedule for my first Folk School week with daily *Birding Before Breakfast,* indoor learning sessions, lots of birding in local hotspots, sack lunches, evening programs, movies, slide programs – whew! This marathon quickly evolved into what my somewhat senior students really wanted – optional pre-breakfast birding, refreshers on field guides and using binoculars, and as much on-campus and hotspot birding as we could cram in. They wanted to see birds but had little patience for lectures! I put bird feeders outside our classroom window two weeks before class, and we often interrupted class to watch the steady stream of resident birds and spring migrants that came to visit.

Our birding days were long enough so evening sessions were banished by popular vote, except for an Owl Prowl on Wednesday night, which brought Eastern Screech Owls almost within touching distance. We did a daily checklist session each afternoon, logging our birds to *eBird* and reviewing new or unique birds on the Cornell Lab's wonderful "All About Birds" website (www.allaboutbirds.org). Spring weather is often cranky, and my spring 2018 week featured rain every day. Not to be denied, my class of seven fired-up birders insisted on putting on slickers and ugly hats and chasing birds whenever the downpour lessened.

Less experienced birders in both ICL and Folk School classes logged lots of life birds. Many of the more experienced students were delighted to see old friends they hadn't seen in years and reveled in the variety of our daily checklists. We marveled together at the quality of the life views we shared, meaning the best viewing we had ever had of a particular bird.

Teaching has been a joy for me because of the energy, the enthusiasm and the excitement my students have brought to my classes. Patience, a sense of humor and a little structured guidance in the world of birds have been my teaching tools and I've enjoyed every minute.

**Watch out – Another Bump......**

What at first felt like just a cold got serious when I had trouble breathing one November night in 2012. Dr. Jack Roof listened to my heart the next day, asked "Can you spell atrial fibrillation?" and sent me to the hospital to get the fluid out. My heart was restored to normal rhythm with the first in a series of defibrillating electric shocks. They use hot-wired plastic pads instead of paddles these days, but the shock is real, and you do feel it. You also feel a lot better when your heart is trucking along as it should be.

The practice of cardiac medicine is incredible. I learned that there are specialists which I came to call *plumbers*, who deal with blockages and valves; *electricians*, experts in heart rhythm who install pacemakers and defibrillators: and *alchemists*, dispensers of medications for things like congestive heart failure. I've met them all and am grateful for their skills.

I was experiencing a series of impacts from the harsh chemicals used to treat my lymphoma. I was in and out of A-Fib and repeated efforts to shock me back into rhythm failed, including one scary morning highlighted by five unsuccessful shocking attempts. I'm pretty sure the lights dimmed in downtown Atlanta partway through.

2015 was a rough year, with two long stints in the cardiac unit at Piedmont Hospital in Atlanta. The first was triggered by a bout of ventricular tachycardia, which is much worse than atrial fibrillation and often fatal. I was home alone when it started but remained conscious and was able to call Sonja at the store. The EMTs arrived in short order and took me at rocket speed to the local emergency room. A technician named Josh cut my shirt off and shocked me into normal rhythm within a minute or two of my arrival. I know his name because he introduced himself and apologized for not giving me any anesthesia. The shock seemed to light up the room and nearly bounced me off the gurney, but I thanked Josh for saving my life.

I was shipped to Piedmont Hospital in downtown Atlanta, and many hours of tests and discussion ended with installation of an Implantable Cardioverter Defibrillator (ICD), a clever device that detects dangerous heart rhythms and delivers a restorative shock to bring things back to normal. Batteries need replacement every eight to ten years.

*My ICD has saved my life twice – so far.*

Needless to say, my birding was impaired for a while, although I remember watching Red-tailed Hawks soaring above the hospital one afternoon. When I was finally released, I joined a local cardiac rehabilitation program which I fondly refer to as Julie's Gym. Julie Shirah is the boss-lady, and her program delivers a combination of tailored physical exercise and a helping of Julie's strong non-denominational faith and warm human support whenever needed. Things are good today. I've slowed down but birding is a top priority and I'm in the classroom and in the field with ICL birders and at least one Folk School week every year. There's no guarantee how far my road stretches ahead of me, but I'm birding in the middle of it whenever I can.

In the ICL Classroom, sharing what I know about birds.

# PART TWO:
# BECOMING A (BETTER) BIRDER – LESSONS & TOOLS

*Like golf and tennis, birding is something that enthusiasts can enjoy at any level. My golf game has gone downhill and I always ran around my backhand on the tennis court, but I enjoyed both sports more when I was playing well. Birding is the same – once you get into it, it's both more satisfying and more challenging when you have some knowledge and the right tools.*

*Teaching got me organized about sharing my knowledge and helping other people get more involved with birds. I was able to separate the learning process into two parts – study time and field birding – and then integrate them into a specific and concrete set of activities that would lead to productive and enjoyable learning.*

*Birders need a couple of indispensable tools, besides the spark that burns inside them – binoculars and a field guide. Binoculars require an investment of a couple of hundred bucks or more and buying bird books can become an expensive obsession. Choosing the wrong tools is the source of a lot of frustration for novice birders and often leads to a premature retirement from a wonderful hobby. I start all my classes with a detailed introduction to binoculars and field guides – basic and indispensable birding tools – followed by a structured lesson plan that, if followed even a little bit, will dramatically improve birding skills.*

# PORRO PRISM BINOCULARS

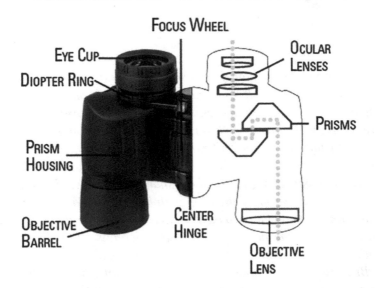

# ROOF PRISM BINOCULARS

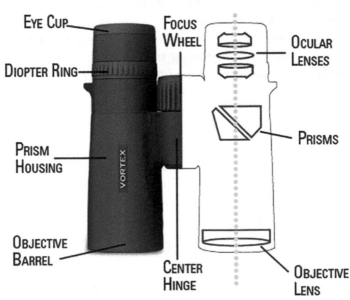

**Two Classic Binocular Designs (Courtesy Optics Planet)**

# 7

# Choosing & Using Binoculars

*A guide to choosing and using an essential birding tool – what all those numbers mean and how to make the simple adjustments that make binocular use comfortable and automatic. My friends at Vortex Optics said nice things about my treatment of this often confusing topic.*

---

**Binoculars let you peek – closely – at the natural world in a way that makes you appreciate our planet and who we share it with. Binoculars put WOW in your life!**

Pete Dunne - Director, Cape May Bird Observatory (from The Feather Quest)

---

A lot of birds are distinctive enough in flight and habitat that you can identify them a half mile away: Turkey and Black Vultures, Great Blue Heron, Bald Eagle. My favorite is the Blue Jay; there's something about the size, shape and flight behavior that clearly says "Blue Jay" to me at a distance. Sadly, most birds are not that distinctive, or hide out in the bushes, and a decent binocular comes in handy. I use the term "binocs;" the with-it crowd calls them "bins." They're sure not *"field glasses"* anymore.

I owned a birding and nature store for 14 years. Folks came into my little shop and stood quietly in front of the binocular case. When I asked if I could show them a pair, they'd get a little edgy. When I asked if they have a pair already, the answers came from all over:

*"I have my Dad's from the Navy. They're kind of heavy."*

*"I have a really cool pair of 8 to 20 power ZOOM binoculars. I can't get anything in focus."*

*"Yup; I have the best model of Nikons ever made. Got 'em as a wedding present in 1984."*

*"Yes, but the rubber eye things broke off, and one lens is cloudy."*

*"No. And I don't know what to buy..."*

Binoculars are a mystery to a lot of people (all those numbers...) but they're really pretty simple. There's a financial fallacy, too: a pretty good pair doesn't have to be expensive. In fact, you can buy a usable roof-prism binocular like the Vortex Crossfire or Diamondback for about $250 that is waterproof, easy to focus, clear from edge-to-edge, with durable twist-up eyecups. An excellent choice for women and young birders is the Vortex Raptor, a Porro-prism model priced at $140. It's lightweight and compact and ideally suited to a small or narrow face. You can spend a lot more, but you don't have to, and if you take care of your binocs, the cost per year of ownership is pretty low.

**Binocular Types**

- **Porro-Prism:** Traditional zigzag design – objective lenses are wider than the eyepieces.
- **Roof-Prism:** Newer design – objective lenses and eyepieces are in a straight line.

Porro-prism binoculars have been around a long time. They're what Dad had in the Navy. They're a fine design and shouldn't be ruled out, but they're getting harder to find. Most makers of birding quality binocs have moved almost exclusively into the roof-prism world. The internal mechanisms of a roof help ensure longer-lasting waterproofing and fog-proofing. Roofs tend to be a little lighter, they're hard to knock out of alignment, and they're more comfortable to hold. Birders prefer them, and most of the recent research and development money has gone into roof-prism binocs. Prices were high to begin with but have come down dramatically in recent years. I have a pair of Pentax DCF 8x42 roofs that cost about $600 in 1998. An equivalent (actually better) pair today is between $200 and 300.

The same investment will buy a better pair of Porro-prism binoculars than roof-prism. Roof-prism binoculars require phase correction and higher quality coatings to produce the same optical quality as Porro. For most birders, the slight difference in optical quality is offset by the lighter, more compact design of roof prism binoculars, and the lower chance of being knocked out of alignment.

**How Do Binoculars Work?**

- Light is gathered by the objective lens (the big end).

- Prisms correct the image so it's right-side up and right-to-left. They also keep the binocular small enough to hold by bending the light path that would otherwise be much longer without the compact "folding" properties of the prisms.

- The image is magnified by the lenses and eyepieces into your eyes.

**What Are All Those Numbers?**

For Example: 8x42 / 336 Feet @ 1000 Yards / 6.3°/ 16 mm Eye Relief / 5 Feet Close Focus

**8X**      The magnification (how many times larger the object will appear). More is better – up to a point. High magnification is hard to hold steady.

**42**      The diameter of the objective lens in millimeters. Bigger is brighter….. and heavier.

**336**      The width of the view, in feet, measured at 1000 yards. Wider is usually better but field of view narrows as magnification increases. (More about that 1000 yards thing in a minute…)

**6.3°**      Another way to measure the width of the view. One degree equals about 55 feet at 1000 yards, so 6.3° is 346.5 feet.

**16mm  Eye Relief**      The distance between the eyepiece and your eye. Optimum eye relief, between 15 and 20 millimeters, allows you to see the full view without darkened borders. This is especially important for eyeglass wearers. Properly designed eyecups provide excellent eye relief.

**5 Feet Close Focus**      Minimum distance to which a pair of binocs can be focused. Less than 10 feet promotes butterfly, dragonfly and wildflower viewing.

---

DID YOU KNOW? A fun fact about binoculars is that if you turn them around and look through the objective lens (the big end) they act like a hand lens or magnifying glass, allowing you to magnify the inside of a flower or look closely at the leaf scars on a twig. Try it on the hairs on your wrist or the face of your watch!

---

*Let's clarify a few more things while you're still fascinated by this brain-muddling stuff.*

Magnification - Seven or eight power (7x or 8x) is ideal for most birders. Ten power (10x) is popular with those who spend a lot of time with raptors and waterfowl. Anything stronger can be hard to hold steady and gets heavier with every tree-top warbler view. Be aware that field of view shrinks as the magnification increases.

The same thing applies to the size of the objective lens. Bigger is brighter, but weight goes up accordingly. A 10x42 is lighter than a 10x50. Imagine the difference after six or eight hours of moving from one spectacular singing spring male to the next at High Island, Texas, Point Pelee, Ontario or even Ivy Log Gap Road near Young Harris, Georgia. The same applies to raptors, sea birds and ducks overhead.

Brightness - A lot of experienced binocular users don't know this: you can measure the relative brightness of a pair of binocs by dividing the diameter of the objective lens (42 in our example) by the power or magnification (8). So, $42 \div 8 = 5.25$. The result, called the exit pupil, is the actual diameter of the column of light that reaches your eye, measured in millimeters. You can see the column of light as a white dot when you hold your binocs toward the light, well away from your face. The bigger the dot or exit pupil, the brighter the image.

*Now compare that with the brightness of a pair of 10x42 binocs:* [ $42 \div 10 = 4.2$ ] *or a pair of those cute 8x25 mini-binocs you take to the symphony:* [ $25 \div 8 = 3.125$ ]

I show this to customers in my bird shop by stacking 8x42s and 10x42s in my hand and holding them up to the light together. The difference in the bright spot of light is dramatic. For the best performance, the exit pupil should equal the diameter of the pupil of the human eye – about 7 mm at night and 3 mm during the day. A column of light larger than the pupil will be more than the eye can use; all of the binoculars in our examples deliver plenty of light to the eye on a bright day.

The *"so-what?"* in this is that all of these binoculars will give you a bright image on a sunny day, but take them into a dark forest on a cloudy day and the 8 x 42's will be much brighter. Dawn and dusk birding, dark habitat birding, and stargazing are all better with a brighter binocular.

Field of View - I've often wondered why manufacturers express field of view as so-many-feet-wide at 1,000 yards. A thousand yards is over half a mile! Unless you're looking at an aircraft carrier, it's a pretty meaningless statistic.

*So, let's divide those big numbers by 100 and see what happens:*

**336 feet ÷100=3.36 feet at 1000 yards ÷100=10 yards (or 30 feet)**

Now we're looking at a field of view that's 3 feet 4 inches wide at 30 feet, about the width of the shrub in which your Eastern Towhee is skulking. The wider your field of view, the easier it will be to keep that Towhee in view as it moves around in the shrub.

**Adjusting Your Binoculars**

Unhappiness with binoculars frequently happens because the user doesn't know how to adjust them properly. Three simple adjustments will make a huge difference in performance and satisfaction.

1. *Set the eyecups.*
Eyecups put the lens the correct distance from your naked eye. The eyecups should be "down" if you wear glasses and "up" if you don't. Until the eyecups are properly adjusted, you will probably see black crescents on the edges of the image.

2. *Adjust the "interpupillary distance."*
Open or close the binoculars on their central hinge until the eyepieces are directly in front of your eyes. You should see one field of view with no shadows or dark edges.

3. *Adjust the Diopter (to adjust for differences in strength between your eyes.)*
The right-hand barrel of most binoculars has a moveable ring below the eyecup. It has an adjustment scale with markings for + (plus)

and – (minus.) Set the ring on zero, cover the right lens and focus the binoculars on something about 50 feet away, using the center focus. Now cover the left lens and adjust the diopter ring until the focus is sharp. Make a mental note of the diopter setting so you can reset it after sharing your binocs with another birder or the grandkids. More expensive binoculars will allow you to lock the diopter setting.

*Note: keep both eyes open and cover the lens with a lens cap during this adjustment. Don't just close your eye; the pressure on your eyeball changes its shape and makes it focus differently.*

**Where's the Value?**

Binoculars should be viewed as an investment. Better binoculars will last many years and will give consistent service every year of their life. (I used my 1977 Bushnell binocs as backups until recently and my 1973 Bushnell SpaceMaster spotting scope still works fine). You will enjoy your hobby more with decent optics, whether it's birding, general wildlife viewing, hunting, boating, spectator sports or the theater.

As with most things in life, you get what you pay for. Quality binoculars are lighter, brighter, clearer, easier to focus and hold steady, and will withstand temperature changes, humidity and rain without problems. The twist-up eyecups will outlast those crummy rubber fold-ups 100-to-1. Well-designed binoculars are much less likely to be knocked out of alignment if they are dropped. Birders are moving rapidly toward the compact roof-prism design, and manufacturers are concentrating improvement dollars on roof-prism models. As a result, tremendous quality & price improvements have been made in the past five years.

**What Do I Need to Know to Understand What I'm Buying?**

Glass quality and coatings are the main drivers of a binocular's price.

Glass Quality - The quality of glass used in lenses and prisms varies tremendously.

- BK-7 (boro-silicate glass) is lower quality, used in cheaper binoculars.

- BAK-4 (barium-crown glass) is denser; used in better binoculars.
- High-end binocs contain proprietary glass (trade secrets).

Coatings reduce internal reflection of light and increase brightness enormously. Without coatings, about five percent of the light passing through your binoculars would be reflected away each time that light struck a lens or prism. Typical binoculars have 10 to 16 interior glass surfaces - without coatings, more than half the light entering the binoculars would be reflected away before it reaches your eyes! Magnesium-Fluoride coatings cut reflection at each air-to-glass surface from about five percent to less than one-half percent.

You'll see terminology like this about coatings:

- Coated - at least one side of one lens is coated with one layer.
- Fully-coated - all sides of all lenses and prisms are coated with one layer.
- Multi-coated – at least one side of one lens is coated with more than one layer.
- Fully Multi-coated - all sides of all lenses and prisms are coated with more than one layer.

### *Never buy any binocular that is less than Fully Multi-coated.*

Eyecups add comfort to binoculars. They also create proper eye relief that helps deliver a full view without dark crescents on the edges. In the past, even expensive binoculars had soft rubber eyecups that flipped up and down and eventually broke. Solid, twist-up eyecups are now standard on all but the cheapest binoculars. Despite the improvements, damaged eyecups are still the most often repaired part of today's binoculars, but they are easy to repair and replace under warranty.

Waterproof – A formerly expensive feature that is now affordable and essential in a birding binocular. Ordinary air is purged from the tubes during manufacture and replaced with Argon or Nitrogen. Rubber O-rings seal out moisture and dust and prevent fogging.

**Here's what to look for when buying binoculars:**

- Roof-prism design
- Rubber-clad housing
- Fully multi-coated lenses & prisms
- Waterproof & nitrogen purged
- Eye relief of 15 mm or more
- Close focus under 8 feet
- Twist-up eyecups

Match your investment to your hobby, your interest level and your budget. You can buy minis, compacts, full-sized binoculars, even monoculars. You can spend as little as $25 (Tasco 7x35 Porro-Prism) or as much as $2,850 (Leica Noctivid) for birding binoculars. Specialty hunting binoculars with weather sensors and rangefinders can cost $3600 (Zeiss Victory RF 10x54.) You pretty much get what you pay for, but the features and value have improved dramatically in recent years. $150 – 300 buys a lot of binocular these days, especially in the Nikon and Vortex lines.

Take your time choosing a binocular. You may eventually buy yours from an internet store, but it's important to hold them and use them before you write the check. A quality birding supply store will encourage you to try them out and may even loan you a pair for overnight or weekend use at no charge. My policy at Blue Ridge Bird Seed Company was to match a fair internet price to make the sale and to reward the customer for his or her confidence in me.

### *Practice, Practice, Practice!*

With practice, using your binoculars will become comfortable and automatic. Keep your eyecups in the correct position for you, and check the diopter setting frequently. Find excuses to use your binoculars while doing everyday things. Take them to sports events and watch whatever's moving the most, whether it's a ball of some kind or the running kids in their lime-green soccer uniforms. Shift the focus from the front to the back of the marching band. Try to lift your binoculars quickly and get them "on" a flying object like a soccer ball, football or Frisbee. Visit a farm or pasture where you can change focus quickly between a cow that's close-by to one on the other side of the field. These somewhat artificial practice activities will serve you well when watching birds.

**A simple technique will make it easy for you to get on a bird or other target – focus on the bird with your naked eyes, then lift the binoculars into place. Your bird should be instantly in view!**

**A Few of My Field Guides - The Pile Grows While You're Not Watching!**

**A Few Other Birding Books You Might Need.....**

# 8

# Selecting A Field Guide

*F*ield guides are your second essential birding *tool. Six full-spectrum guides are reviewed along with simpler, less comprehensive guides, and a number of out-of-print classics still available at used book stores. A brief overview of digital field guides for smart phones and tablets.*

An up-to-date field guide is an essential tool for birders. Many excellent field guides are available in book form, while the growing number of digital applications for smart phones and tablets makes it possible to carry and use detailed birding information wherever you go. You should choose and use a field guide that is comfortable for you.

Modern field guides are updated frequently to (1) reflect changes in our understanding of the evolutionary relationships between birds, based on DNA studies; and (2) to show changes in where birds are found during the year. The American Ornithologists' Society (AOS) (formerly the American Ornithologists' Union) and The British Ornithologist's Union (BOU) work closely together to incorporate new DNA information, create naming standards and ultimately determine what is a species and what's not. Professional research and organized citizen science activities like Breeding Bird Surveys, Christmas Bird Counts, eBird (www.ebird.org ) and The Great Backyard Bird Count generate data used to update range maps. Field sightings reported to eBird make a huge contribution to seasonality and range knowledge. *More about eBird later.*

It's hard to keep up using an outdated field guide. You may have heard the terms lumpers and splitters. These are slang terms, but they fit. Lumpers are people that want to lump similar birds into a single species. Officially, this sometimes happens as a result of the work done by the AOS. Lumping is what happened in recent years with orioles, flickers and juncos. Baltimore Oriole (east) and Bullock's Oriole (west) were somewhat similar in plumage and interbred where their ranges overlapped, so in the 80s the wizards lumped them together into a single species, Northern Oriole. Later DNA studies showed them to be different enough to be split back to two species. Yellow-shafted Flicker (east) and Red-shafted Flicker (west) were lumped into Northern Flicker and remain a single species in 2020. Interestingly, the similar Gilded Flicker found in the desert southwest and Mexico has remained a separate species throughout the discussion.

And juncos, oh my, juncos: Slate-colored Junco, White-winged Junco, Oregon Junco, Gray-headed Junco and Pink-sided Junco, all readily separable by field marks and range, became Dark-eyed Junco with one cruel swipe of the lumper's pen. These little sparrows look different enough that even a novice can tell them apart. I had to scratch four of the five off my Life List and replace them with Dark-eyed Junco. Luckily, I'd never seen the Gray-headed, so I didn't lose that one. Similar to the case with flickers, the Yellow-eyed Junco (formerly Mexican Junco) of southern Arizona and Mexico, remains a separate species. I picked that one up on Mt. Lemmon, north of Tucson, in August of 2014. Revenge is sweet.

Keep an eye on your Life List when lumpers are in favor. We lost five ticks when our lumping examples happened but got one back when Northern Oriole split back to Baltimore and Bulloch's. And I heard recently that the lumper-combined Slate-colored Junco may be split again to add a new species. The proposed Carolina Junco is found only in the southern Appalachians, migrates only vertically (up and down in elevation with the seasons) and has a stouter, whiter bill than the original Slate-colored subspecies.

Splitters, on the other hand, are a life-lister's friend, tending to break a single species into two or more. Western Scrub-jay had a mainland population and another population on Santa Cruz Island, off the coast of California. The Santa Cruz Island birds are now Island Scrub-jay. And the brand-new (in 2017) Seventh Edition of the National Geographic field guide reports a further split. Western Scrub-Jay is no more, replaced by California Scrub-Jay along the coast and Baja, and Woodhouse's Scrub-Jay, inland through the mountain west and Mexico. Note that a third (now fourth) related species, the Florida Scrub-Jay, geographically isolated from the western species and found only in Florida, was left out of the skirmish. Similarly, the Black-crested Titmouse was split from Tufted Titmouse in the west-Texas part of the range.

Enough about DNA, lumpers and splitters. The other reason for updating field guides is the changes, sometimes significant, in the ranges of individual species. The best example I know of is the House Finch. The House Finch is native to the American West, and the 1960s-era Peterson range map shows it solidly in the west, but with a tiny spot in eastern New York. A small flock of House Finches was released in Central Park in the 1950s and quickly spread throughout the eastern United States. Legend has it that these pretty birds were for sale (illegally) in a pet shop that went bankrupt. The Seventh Edition of the *National Geographic Field Guide* shows the House Finch everywhere in the US except south Florida.

Introduced species like Eurasian-collared Dove show the same pattern, spreading from south Florida in the 70s to the Great Lakes and Great Plains by 2016. Similarly, well established native species like Northern Cardinal have expanded their ranges because of habitat changes, widespread backyard feeding and climate change.

Finally, the vast number of experienced birders in the field, combined with instant communication, have increased reports of supposedly rare birds that have turned out to be more common or more predictable than once thought. Rarities are reported, properly identified, and seen by birders enough times that they need to be added to field guides to make them complete. The 1983 edition of the *National Geographic* guide included about 800 species; the Seventh Edition covers 1,023 species.

Some excellent guides use photographs to display the birds. Other guides use artist's drawings. Photographs can be more realistic, while drawings allow the artist to highlight specific features and field marks. All quality field guides will have a thorough and detailed introduction explaining how to use the book, detailed illustrations of bird topography, detailed range maps, a complete index and a quick index tab on one of the covers.

Whatever field guide(s) you choose, spend time with it (them!). Read the introduction, test the quick index tab, study the range maps and read the family descriptions. Get familiar with the organization of the book and study the descriptive information about some familiar birds and some from your "most-wanted" list.

One of the frustrations for newer birders is finding their bird in the field guide. Currently, all guides that include all species are organized by family, requiring the user to have some understanding of both family characteristics and the sequence of families. The sequence of bird families in field guides followed the "Wetmore Sequence" until about 2000. This relationship between families was based on morphological characteristics such as skeletal features, toe arrangements, feather tracts, muscles and tendons. Newer guides increasingly incorporate the results of new DNA studies and the arrangement of families has changed dramatically as a result.

Two older, out-of-print field guides, (*All The Birds and Naming The Birds At A Glance*) described below, use color, behavior, bill shape and other visible characteristics to lead the user to an identification. Finding one of these in a used bookstore or online and adding it to your bookshelf might be useful for novice birders. I have both guides and still marvel at their simplicity and value.

Regardless of your choice of field guides, a general knowledge of family characteristics is critical to success in birding. Plan to spend some serious time browsing your guide, reviewing family characteristics. It's worth the effort and a one-time hurdle; once you have a grasp of families, you won't ever have to do it again!

**Modern Field Guides**

Choosing a field guide is an important decision – take your time! Go to a well-stocked bookstore and leaf through several guides to get a feel for layout and ease of use. Online booksellers often allow you to browse inside pages. Pay attention to what other birders are using on bird walks; ask them why they like a particular guide.

Think about how you will carry one in the field and consider size and weight. Your guide should be easy to pull out and look at! Birding vests with big pockets are available and very convenient. Cargo pants and shorts have big enough pockets for a hefty bird book. I like to tuck mine under my belt in the small of my back when I'm not using my vest.

If your birding interest is confined to your backyard and feeders, the state field guides (*Birds of Georgia*, for example) published by Adventure Publishing, are a perfect combination of simplicity and professional quality. The author, Stan Tekiela, is a well-known naturalist, author and wildlife photographer. Available for all states, they are organized by color, with color guides printed on the edges of the pages. Turn to the red section, and all the red birds are there, regardless of family! Each guide includes about 140 of the most common birds found in the state, with illustrations, seasonal range maps and interesting details about identification and biology. A bird song CD is offered as an option for many states.

***Peterson Field Guide to the Birds of North America***: First published in 1934 by Roger Tory Peterson, this guide changed birding forever. Illustrated with Peterson's art, it introduced the idea of "field marks" which are indicated by arrows on each bird. Complete and frequently updated, this is an excellent first guide for a new birder. The full-sized North American edition is too big for field use unless you use a vest. Smaller Eastern and Western editions are available.

*National Geographic Field Guide to the Birds of North America*: Favored by many advanced birders, this guide features excellent artist drawings and the most up to date detail on all species found in North America. The range maps are excellent. Currently in its Seventh Edition, this is the most complete and comprehensive field guide available. Regional editions are available; all are compact enough for field use. Many of my beginning birding students like this guide best.

The *National Geographic Field Guide* is by far the most aggressive in staying updated and has become the bible to many excellent birders. It is updated at five-to-six-year intervals, incorporating the most recent of the determinations of the AOS's Committee on Classification and Nomenclature of North and Middle America, known less formally as the North American Classification Committee. The Seventh Edition came out in 2017, with significant changes in the sequence of bird families. This latest edition reflects a new understanding of the evolutionary relationships of birds and varies dramatically from earlier editions and from other field guides. Besides requiring you to relearn what page to turn to for the Wood Warblers or Raptors, the changes in family sequence hint at the dramatic amount of new learning that DNA studies have brought to ornithology.

*Sibley Guide to Birds*: Another excellent and up to date guide, recently updated by David Allen Sibley. The drawings are simple and clear, with many illustrations of seasonal and juvenile plumages. Range maps are excellent. Sibley focuses on identification, so detailed information on habitat and behavior is limited. The full North American edition is too big for convenience; compact regional editions are available.

*Stokes Field Guide to the Birds of North America*: Updated in 2010, with regional editions, this may be the best and most comprehensive photographic guide to birds ever published. It includes photos of all plumages for most birds, including juvenile plumages. The range maps are excellent, showing migration routes as well as seasonal ranges. Detailed behavioral information is included. This guide uses numbers and proportions much more than other guides, comparing tail length to wing width on Cooper's Hawk, for example. The fine print and somewhat heavy weight make it unhandy for field use, but it should be considered as a study and learning reference.

*Crossley ID Guide: Eastern Birds*: An excellent study guide! Richard Crossley turned the birding world upside-down in 2011 with this oversized, photography-based field guide. A professional birding guide and outstanding photographer, Crossley has assembled photos of each species in a variety of plumages and poses and overlaid them on a background photo of typical habitat. A Guide to Eastern Birds was the first Crossley. It is too large for easy field use but has been seen spread out on the hood of many birding vehicles and should eventually be a part of any serious birder's library. Crossley's *Guide to Raptors* was published in 2014 and offers challenging quiz pages in addition to the standard Crossley format. *A Guide to Waterfowl* was published in 2017 and may become the standard for waterfowl.

## Some Old Classics

*Many classic guides are out-of-date and out-of-print but continue to deliver great value as reference books. You might stumble across one of these in a thrift shop or at a garage sale. Buteo Books (http:// www.buteobooks.com) and Abe Books (www.abebooks.com) are online booksellers that stock used field guides.*

*All the Birds of North America*: Published by the American Bird Conservancy in 1997, this guide uses a unique organization based on how and where birds collect food. Charts for *Waterbirds* inside the front cover and *Landbirds* inside the back cover guide the user to the right group of birds to start identification. Beautiful panoramic illustrations and a weather-resistant pocket-sized format are valuable features. It's available in used bookstores and worthy of a place on a birder's bookshelf because of the information about feeding behavior.

*Golden Field Guide to Birds of North America*: Published in 1966 and updated in 1983, this is still the favorite guide for many older birders. It was my go-to guide in college and for many years afterward. I once shrewdly traded a new Golden Guide to one of my Forestry professors for his 1938 Edition of the Peterson Field Guide. The illustrations by Arthur Singer are excellent and I use mine to re-fine identifications. Sonograms are a unique feature, visual representations of each bird's song that show pitch, quality, phrasing, tempo and changes in volume. The Golden Guide is available at used bookstores and is worth buying for the illustrations and sonograms alone.

*Kaufmann Field Guide to Birds of North America*: Published in

2000, and updated in 2005, this excellent photo-based guide is getting out of date. The introduction and family descriptions are very thorough, and the pages are color-coded to help you find family groups quickly. Kenn Kaufman liked photographs, but wasn't happy with variations in lighting, distances, backgrounds and even film types he found in other photo-based guides. Further, he was skeptical that even the finest artist could capture the subtleties that make a bird distinctive. His guide was revolutionary because of the work he did himself to digitize and edit over 2,000 photographs, correcting them for consistent color, size and lighting and removing shadows. Despite its age, a copy of Kaufman is a great reference to have. After looking at several guides, his edited photographs confirmed my identification of a female Cerulean Warbler I saw during spring migration in 2018.

*National Audubon Society Field Guide to the Birds of North America (Eastern Region & Western Region):* These pocket-sized all-photographic field guides were originally published in separate Eastern and Western editions. The first bird guide to be organized visually, this book groups all birds by color and shape. The photographs are grouped together in the front of the guide, separate from the detailed text for each bird. Descriptions of the range are provided instead of range maps. This compact guide is durable for field use but is out of date and the split format is not easy to use.

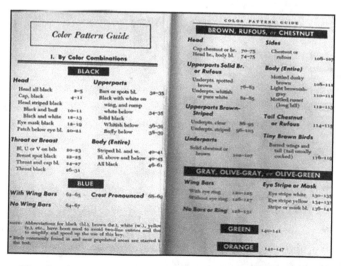

The simple and efficient front endpaper of Naming the Birds
at a Glance

*Naming the Birds at a Glance*: This is another unique field guide, designed to quickly lead the user to a short list of possible birds using a combination of color and other field marks shown on charts on the endpapers of the books. The method is unscientific but very efficient. Covering most of the Eastern United States, it was published in 1963, updated a couple of times and is still available in used book stores. I bought the book in the early 70s and was fascinated by the approach because it works. Look for it online at Buteo Books or Abe Books.

## Digital Field Guides

Many excellent digital guides or "birding apps" are available, including Peterson, National Geographic, Audubon, Sibley, iBird and Merlin. All are inexpensive, Merlin is free. Digital birding apps load to your smart phone or tablet and provide good to excellent photographs or drawings, range maps, descriptive information and samples of songs. Several, including Merlin, help you identify a bird based on details you enter: your location, the season, size, color, habitat, etc. You'll get a short list of likely candidates to speed your identification. Keep in mind that while digital field guides are portable, useful and fun, they are not substitutes for printed books or online birding resources for serious study.

## Other Resources for Birders

All About Birds                                          www.allaboutbirds.org

*A superb online field guide with an efficient search tool. All North American birds are described, with identification tips, similar species, range maps, life history and sample songs and calls.*

American Birding Association                              www.aba.org

*The American Birding Association (ABA) is the primary organization for birding in the US. Rare Bird Alerts, birding events, birding book sales, and a strong voice for conservation and bird protection in North America. Their monthly and bi-monthly publications are excellent reading for birders at all levels.*

Cornell Laboratory of Ornithology          www.birds.cornell.edu

*Headquarters for birding in North America. Species accounts, Project Feederwatch, online store, educational programs, live feeder cams.*

eBIRD                                              www.ebird.org

*A real-time, online checklist program launched by Cornell Lab in 2002. Allows birders to submit checklists by date and location and compiles the information for use by birders and scientists worldwide. I have about 1/3 of my lists posted and will load them all soon.*

Georgia Ornithological Society                    www.gos.org

*THE statewide organization for birders in Georgia. Great spring, fall and winter meetings (mostly field trips in great birding areas), publications, checklists, info about Christmas Bird Counts, Rare Bird Alert info, links to other birding organizations, birding festivals. Go to GOS to subscribe to Georgia Birders Online, a free list-serve where birders post bird sightings, trip reports, photos, etc. Great way to monitor migration, rare birds, great places to go.*

# WANT TO BECOME A (BETTER) BIRDER?

# LEARN TO THINK LIKE ONE....

# AND

# LEARN TO SEE LIKE ONE!

# 9

# Becoming A (Better) Birder
# A Lesson Plan

*A structured approach to improving your birding skills, used in my bird identification classes and student-certified (IF you do the work!) Two separate but related parts make it effective – focused study, allowing you to think like a birder, and lots of field birding, training you to see like a birder.*

**People are not <u>born</u> birders, they <u>become</u> birders by learning to do two things:**

1. <u>Think like a birder</u>, using a framework of knowledge developed through structured study and varied and frequent field experience.
2. <u>See like a birder</u>, looking for and recognizing the field marks, habitat cues and behaviors that help identify a bird quickly and accurately.

The whole idea is to immerse yourself in the world of birds and spend enough organized time at birding and learning about birds that the facts and impressions start to stick. The process applies to both new birders and experienced birders. New birders use the efficient structure to learn quickly, and experienced birders refresh old practices and add new habits and activities.

It's similar to the analogy about boiling a frog: put a frog in a pan of water, turn up the heat, and the temperature increase is so gradual that the frog doesn't realize it's being boiled until it's too late. Same thing with becoming a birder: start birding, read about birding, study the common birds, keep a yard list, take your binocs everywhere, bird with better birders, listen to bird song recordings, post your sightings to eBird, do the Great Backyard Bird Count and a few Christmas Counts. It sneaks up on you – you're a birder!

Once you start birding, you will have to face a crucial decision about what type of birder you want to be. It's not obvious at the start, but it will creep up on you over time. Your options:

Option 1: You can decide that it's fun to go with other people, especially to the really cool, "big-bird" places with lots of spectacular birds anxiously waiting for you to take their picture. You're happy to follow along and let the bird walk guide or expert birders identify the birds and e-mail you the list afterward.

Option 2: You can decide that you want to know the birds yourself, their field marks, songs, seasonality, habitat preferences and behavior. You want to identify each bird without being told what it is. You want to be the field trip leader.

### *Thinking Like A Birder* - **Building & Using Your Mental Framework of Knowledge**

Get a decent field guide and use it. Better yet, buy two: one for the field and one for the bathroom, bedside or arm chair. For your first guide, choose the new *Peterson Field Guide to Birds of North America* or the latest *National Geographic Field Guide to the Birds of North America*. Both of these offer smaller Eastern and Western versions. The regional editions are excellent and a little more compact in the field, but when you start traveling, you'll be packing both. Also, when it's time to update, you'll be buying two. I carry the full National Geographic most of the time.

Your second field guide should be one that adds to the information in your primary field guide. It's helpful to have one that uses photographs and another that uses artist's drawings. For a photographic guide, look at the Crossley *Guide to Eastern Birds*, the new Stokes or the brand-new Sibley Second Edition. Study both field guides and learn how to use them: *read the introduction twice*, understand the symbols and colors on the range maps, learn how to use the index, and understand how the book is organized. Most newer field guides include a quick-reference index inside the front or back cover.

Study the birds you already know – learning new birds is easier if you have a good foundation. Study the description, field marks, behavior, range map and song. Confirm what family they belong to. Then look at similar birds – related species or birds that may look or act similarly.

Some Eastern examples:

- Song Sparrow (streaked breast) – look at Fox, Savannah, Vesper and Swamp.

- Chipping Sparrow (unstreaked breast) – look at Field, Tree, White-throated, and White-crowned.

- House Finch – look at Purple Finch (east) and Cassin's Finch (west).

- Eastern Phoebe – look at Eastern Wood Pewee, Eastern King-bird.

- Indigo Bunting (blue) – look at Blue Grosbeak, Eastern Blue-bird.

- Cardinal (red) – look at Scarlet and Summer Tanager (east) and Pyrrhuloxia - (west).

- Downy Woodpecker – look at Hairy Woodpecker.

- Sharp-shinned Hawk (rounded wings, long tail) – Look at Cooper's and Goshawk.

- Mallard (brown female) – look at American Black Duck and Mottled Duck.

- Red-shouldered Hawk (banded tail) – look at Broad-winged Hawk.

Learn the major families or subgroups of birds, and how to sep-arate them in the field. If you can put a new bird in its family, you've really narrowed down the possibilities for identification. Spend some time in the books, reading family descriptions, reviewing field marks like body shape, neck length, bill size and shape, and habitat prefer-ences.

Further work will allow you to list the species in each family that are likely in your area, those that nest, those that winter and those that migrate through. I created *An Informal Guide to Bird Families in North Georgia* for use by students in my local birding classes. In addition to briefly describing each family, it lists the members of each family that are likely to be seen in our area, and in what season. You can develop your own written summary, but you'll find that, with enough study time and field experience, you'll have a mental version in your head!

When I was in Forestry grad school, I had a job that involved late night lab work, with a lot of idle time. I used that time to study my bird book and summarized what I learned about each family on three-inch by five-inch note cards that I kept in a pocket in my old Golden field guide. Looking back, I was already practicing the study part of Thinking Like a Birder. Here are my Thrush notes:

**Thrush Notes:** The numbers in parentheses in the first column are the page numbers for each bird in the 1966 hardback edition of my Golden Birds of North America. These notes were made in 1972!.

I also use some classroom activities to force the issue with students and show them the value of investing an hour in studying a particular family of birds. My in-class review of woodpeckers requires the students, using field guides, to list the woodpeckers they could see in north Georgia (Ha - Range Maps!). The next question for each species is: *"What are the field marks?"* Students shout answers and they are recorded on flip chart or white board by me or (preferably) someone who can write legibly. Then: *"Can you tell male from female?"* This is where I hear some murmurs of "Hmmm. I didn't know that!" and "Cool!" We move on: *"Downy and Hairy look a lot alike; how do you tell them apart?"* An hour in the classroom and we know more about how to use our field guide and have a solid handle on eight kinds of woodpeckers.

I've done similar exercises with Raptors and Swallows and plan to expand it to Vireos and Birds That Swim. The method works because it's focused on a particular family and it's local, so students have a good chance to find and identify those birds on the next birding field trip or bird walk. Each exercise is a compact example of *Thinking Like A Birder* and excellent preparation for *Seeing Like A Birder* the next time in the field.

Ask: ***Where am I and what season is it?*** The answer to this question is a critical clue in the identification process. Knowing if and when a species is likely to be where you are really narrows down the identification process. As you study similar birds, look carefully at the range maps. Is each bird likely to be seen in your "patch" and, if so, at what season? You'll soon develop a mental calendar that tells you what birds are resident year-round, which are winter visitors, which are summer nesters, and which are migrants that pass through. Knowing that the only brown-backed thrush found in the East in winter is Hermit Thrush really narrows things down on your Christmas Bird Count!

Get more involved with birds. Maximize the opportunities to see new birds and get better acquainted with familiar birds. Maintain a feeder and water source in your yard. Find a birding group and/or birding companion and go on field trips. Notice the birds around you wherever you are. This probably means keeping a pair of binocs and field guide in the car as well as at home and even in the office.

Start a "Life List," documenting where and when you saw each bird, with pertinent notes. Keep a monthly yard list or patch list of what you see in whatever you define as your yard or patch. It's more fun if you expand your yard to include nearby places you like with a variety of habitats. A great thing about a yard list is that it starts over each month, keeping you interested and alert. Your yard list will rapidly teach you what to expect at what season and give you a handle on arrival and departure dates. *Simply submitting your observations to eBird will automatically create and update a Life List that you can sort by county, state and country. Your birding observations, notes and photographs become part of the eBird global database, the value of which grows every day.*

When you see a new bird (a life bird or lifer), or one that you don't see very often, go back to your field guide and learn more about it – field marks, vocalizations, habitat preference, behaviors, range, seasonality. You won't remember it all, but it adds to your mental framework of knowledge and helps confirm identity the next time you see it.

**Life Birds** - It's part of birding tradition to celebrate a new life bird with a toast and a shot of brandy or other libation at the end of your birding day. That's fine when your life list is long, and you only add a new bird once in a while. It can get a little out of hand when you're just getting started in birding or when you have a great day in a new place as I did when birding in Ecuador. Ignoring tradition, we just had a beer to celebrate my 52 life birds on January 9, 2009.

Read Adventure Birding books. An artificial but entertaining way to learn about birds is to read adventure birding or "big year" books and check out unfamiliar birds in your field guide. Caution: owning two or more of these books is de-facto proof that you have the birding bug.

Some examples (from my bookshelves):

o Wild America (Two Great Naturalists on The Road) – Roger Tory Peterson & James Fisher (1955)

o Return to Wild America (A Yearlong Search for The Continent's Natural Soul) – Scott Weidensaul (2005)

o Adventures in Birding (Confessions of a Lister) – Jean Piatt (1973)

o Kingbird Highway (The Story of A Natural Obsession That Got A Little Out of Hand) – Kenn Kaufman (1997)

o The Feather Quest (A North American Birder's Year) – Pete Dunne (1999)

o Birders (Tales of a Tribe) – Mark Cocker (2001)

o Birding on Borrowed Time – Phoebe Snetsinger (2003)

o The Big Year (a Tale of Man, Nature and Fowl Obsession) – Mark Obmascik (2004)

o To See Every Bird on Earth (A Father, A Son and a Lifelong Obsession) – Dan Koeppel (2005)

o Birding Without Borders; An Obsession, a Quest, and the Biggest Year in the World – Noah Stryker (2017)

It can take a long time to finish one of these classics, if you read about each new bird when it is seen by the author. The bonus is that you become familiar with the names of birds you've never seen, understand what family each belongs to, and know at least the rudiments of how to identify it and where to find it.

### *Seeing Like A Birder* – Recognizing Physical, Contextual & Behavioral Features

A critical skill for someone who wants to be able to identify birds is to see as a birder sees, that is, to see *the features of a bird* that fit into an organized mental framework of knowledge. That mental framework (thinking like a birder) grows from our experience, focused study and the amazing ability of the human mind to take a few facts and come to a conclusion.

An excellent starting point is to review bird topography (the parts of a bird) in the introduction to your field guide. There's no need to get too detailed or technical – just the basics part of the head, wings and feathers to start.

### Physical Features That Help Identification

- Size (tiny, robin-sized, big)
- Shape & posture (long and slender, short and round, vertical or horizontal posture)
- Color (what color(s) and where they are on the bird; bright or muted)
- Bill size and shape (long/short, thin/conical, sharp/blunt, curved/straight)
- Tail length, posture, shape, color and markings
- Wing length and shape (wide, narrow, rounded, triangular, pointed, finger-tipped)
- Wing bars (or absence of wing bars)
- Breast markings (streaks or spots, or the absence of streaks or spots)
- Flight characteristics (fluttery, roller-coaster, soaring, hovering, flat vs up-tilted wings, rapid wingbeats)
- Neck and/or leg extensions in flight

- Voice (song or call, chips) – musical, repetitive, loud or soft, mnemonic phrasing

*Think of it as the physical description used to identify a person – sex, race, age, height, weight, hair & eye color, clothing. You can recognize a friend or family member instantly from a distance from their posture, gait and clothing (plumage) – you can do the same thing with many birds: "It flies like a Blue Jay!"*

## Contextual Features That Help Identification

- Physical Location & Season: "Where am I and what season is it?" is a critical question to ask yourself. The answer will often narrow down the possibilities and help identify your bird or rule out many birds that simply aren't where you are in that particular season. While rarities can and do happen, most of the time the odds are in your favor. Does that bird live here, nest here, winter here or migrate through here? Should it be here today?

- Habitat (heavy woods, brushy edge, pines vs hardwoods, suburban yard, open field, near fresh water, wetland or roadside ditch, on an ocean beach, at a feeder)

- Where (on the ground, in flight, perched, in a thicket, high in a tree, upside down on a pine cone, clinging to tree trunk, soaring overhead)

## Behavior That Helps Identification

Behavior is another factor that can narrow down the possibilities or lock down identification. General behaviors include: perching quietly vs moving actively, probing in tree bark, soaring vs flapping, hovering, hanging upside down, skulking, flying out and back to the same perch, alone vs in a flock, scratching with both feet, diving under water. Some examples:

- Very active feeding behavior (kinglets, gnatcatchers)

- Walking down a tree trunk, walking upside down (nuthatches)

- Walking or hitching up a tree trunk (brown creeper)

- Very large, soaring on flattened wings (bald eagle)

- Very large, soaring on <u>up-tilted wings</u> (turkey vulture)
- Tightly grouped flock of smallish birds in winter (cedar waxwing)
- Hovering flight (American kestrel, osprey, belted kingfisher, loggerhead shrike)
- Bounding, roller-coaster flight (woodpeckers, goldfinches)
- Perched, wagging tail (eastern phoebe)
- Walking on ground, wagging tail (palm warbler)
- Diving underwater (diving ducks, mergansers, grebes, loons)

*Context and behavior answer several questions and eliminate many possible identifications.*

*Could it be here, in the winter? Maybe it's a White-throated Sparrow.*

*It's too active for a vireo. It's pretty small, I think it's a warbler.*

*It's fly-catching and wags its tail when it lands. Might be Eastern Phoebe.*

**Rule #1: Look at the bird, note the physical features, context and behavior,**

**THEN look at the book!**

**Rule #2: When you're not out birding, spend more time with the book! With study and practice, you'll be thinking and seeing like a birder!**

Wing-Watchers at the Fannin County Park bridge (Robert Kimsey)

# PART THREE:
# LET'S GO BIRDING

*Birding requires optimism and patience. Experienced birders know that The Gods of Birding can be cruel. Occasionally, though, The Gods recognize your early morning efforts, your wet feet, your chigger bites and the time you spend giving bird talks to children and garden clubs and reward you with a special birding moment when you don't expect it.*

*Birding alone can be wonderful, but it's more fun and you see more birds when you go with other birders. Some birding companions stand out from the flock, either because they're incredibly good birders, they're wonderful company or because they're a little quirky.*

*Some birding trips are perfect, where the weather, your birding companions and the birds themselves combine to deliver a terrific experience and a great list. Other trips start with high hopes and detailed planning and wind up making you think seriously about a different way to waste your time. You live for the great birds, the great people and the great trips and learn to appreciate the contrast of the ones that somehow don't work out.*

*Now it's your turn. You've been schooled or refreshed on those essential birding tools, and endured my lectures on Thinking Like a Birder and Seeing Like a Birder.*

*You're ready to go birding!*

Becoming A (Better) Birder Was Published as a Booklet in July, 2019.
My First Book Signing!

# 10

# Favorite Birding "Patches"

*A field trip to favorite birding places. High-lights include 50 Evening Grosbeaks on a junk window feeder in Minnesota, a yard full of Rose-breasted Grosbeaks eating newly sown oats in my sandy yard in Michigan, displaying male Common Goldeneyes on the Flambeau River in Wisconsin, and my adult birding students torn between watching birds and taking pictures of the cows at Deerfield Pasture.*

Many birders have a "patch," a particularly birdy spot that they visit frequently. It might just be a backyard, but typically is a local woodlot, marsh or brushy field with easy access and little disturbance. Knowledge of your patch accumulates over time, and pretty soon you know what birds to expect at any time of year. A patch list helps organize what you've learned and becomes a useful reference. If you haven't found a patch yet, think about finding one.

My first patch was in Urbana, Illinois. Since my late-night research allowed some time flexibility, I spent my spring mornings birding at a trashy place owned by the University, with dirt mounds, brush, half-dead trees and an old oxbow lake. I rode my three-speed Schwinn from our little rental house in east Urbana to campus every decent weather day and this tiny birding patch was on the way. I don't remember the name of this place, if it had one. It might be what is now Crystal Lake Park. It wasn't developed at all in 1973, so there were no people, nobody mowed anything, and it was full of birds. A few memories from that patch:

My first Eastern Towhee, throwing up leaves with both feet, just the other side of that brushy thicket. It was called Rufous-sided Towhee then, but what mattered was the dramatic plumage of the spring male, and the energetic hop-scratch with both feet at once that sent the leaves flying. He never saw me, but I saw him - up close.

A pair of Wood Ducks nested in a dead tree next to the oxbow lake, arguably North America's most beautiful duck. The nest hole was about 35 feet up the tree, so I figured the little woodies would need parachutes or an elevator when they fledged. One morning I watched the pair of adults flying in a big circle around the nest tree, over the oxbow at full speed. One minute I was watching both birds, then suddenly only the drake was in view. I aimed my binocs at the nest hole in time to see the hen disappear inside; she had veered off and somehow braked quickly enough to enter the nest hole without harm. I didn't see the fledglings, but I had new respect for the flying ability of Wood Ducks. The edges of that old oxbow pond were also perfect habitat for skulking Green Heron, a fascinating bird that has more poses than a fashion model.

The place was full of warblers in early May. Singing males perched in the open and sang for me; females and year-olds were nearby often enough to help me recognize the muted field marks. The often bewildering brown-backed thrushes migrated through, along with flycatchers and vireos. I can still hear the wildly musical notes of a Warbling Vireo, another life bird. One male stayed around the same tree for several days and I listened in awe each morning. Like the Black-billed Cuckoo at summer camp, that was my best view and vocals of that bird, ever.

*I left Champaign-Urbana and my wonderful oxbow patch long ago but have always found a new local patch to haunt everywhere I've lived since then.*

I had a short-term patch at Lake Tahoe during my brief summer there as a Forest Service naturalist in 1973, and more permanent patches in Park Falls, Wisconsin (along the Flambeau River); Isabella, Minnesota (the USFS ranger station); Mikado, Michigan (my sandy yard next to a wetland); and Rochester, Vermont (a brushy floodplain along the White River.) There were memorable moments in all those patches:

*Lake Tahoe* yielded Steller's Jay in bunches, along with Band-tailed Pigeons, Townsend's Solitaire, Clark's Nutcracker, White-headed Woodpecker and Yellow-headed Blackbirds. I missed on the American Dipper, Dr. Willson's favorite. I saw the White-throated (European) Dipper in Germany in 2001, but the American version is still on my bucket list.

*The Flambeau River* wintered a lot of ducks, with great viewing from my pickup along the river road. Among the Redheads, Canvasbacks, Ring-necked Ducks and Common Mergansers, I watched male Common Goldeneyes, in breeding plumage, throwing their heads back and tooting their mating calls skyward. Nearby females paid no attention, of course.

**Common Goldeneyes (Wisconsin DNR)**

*Isabella* was a tiny town of about 200 people spread along 10 miles of Minnesota Highway 1 between Ely and the north shore of Lake Superior. Ultimate boonies! The young white spruce plantation behind the ranger station was a favorite place for American Woodcock to demonstrate their amazing mating flights.

**American Woodcock (Brian Lupa)**

Hunkered down behind a too-small spruce, I watched a male woodcock bob up-and-down, heard him 'ulp' and 'peent' 15 feet away, then lift off to announce his availability, climbing quickly, circling at the top of his flight, and finally spiraling down to land where he had started. Each phase of the flight was accompanied by a particular series of sounds. I've heard woodcock since but have never again seen the spectacular display of that evening.

A downed log, shielded by birder-hiding brush and young spruce, gave me my only look at a drumming male Ruffed Grouse. Early morning, mid-spring, and repeated drumming coming from the plantation across Highway 1 from the ranger station. I snuck across and watched this proud male drum three or four times from 20 feet away. He spread his tail, puffed out his chest and flapped his wings, slowly at first but too fast to count at the end. The drumming is felt as a pressure in your ears as much as a sound.

I did a lot of Compartment Examination (compex) for the Forest Service around Isabella, a form of 'timber inventory' done every 10 years to keep track of the age, species composition and condition of timber stands. A number of timber stands were organized into what we called compartments, bounded by roads and streams, that averaged a thousand acres or so. Most of the compex work was done in the winter, and I frequently flushed wintering flocks of Snow Buntings as I drove the snowy roads to my starting point. One memorable morning brought a view of two Gray Wolves that loped across the road in front of my green Forest Service pickup.

My compex work also brought me into contact with a couple of North Country specialties. While snowshoeing in a stunted Black Spruce swamp forest, I found my first Northern Saw-whet Owl in a small Black Spruce tree. I parted the branches to see what had caught my eye with a flick and a hop and found myself about two feet away from this secretive and tiny northern owl. My first and only Saw-whet to date.....

The other bird, Boreal Chickadee, was also a lifer and remains the only one I've seen. This cute little brown-capped dee-dee is primarily a bird of Canada and points north whose range sneaks into far northern Minnesota and Wisconsin. I heard its slow, nasal chick-a-day-day song and was able to clump close enough (on snowshoes, remember) for a close look.

The Minnesota Ornithologists Union (MOU) chose Isabella for its spring meeting in 1974, bringing birders from all over the state to the North Woods. A target bird for downstate birders was the Connecticut

Warbler, a hard-to-find yellow bird with a gray hood and white eye-ring that nested in wet spruce and tamarack stands. Intrigued by a loud *chippy-chuppy, chippy-chuppy, chippy-chuppy* song heard through my open truck window, I had located a nesting territory a week earlier, not far from the café-gas station-bait shop that made up "downtown" Isabella. I was able to show a singing male Connecticut Warbler to most of the MOU birders that weekend, a life bird for most of them.

I've always had yard feeders, and my most memorable was the ugly plywood tray fastened outside the kitchen window of our log cabin home at the ranger station in Isabella. The cabin was memorable as well, built of whole Red Pine logs by a Civilian Conservation Corps crew in the 1930s. It was stained brown on the outside and varnished to a golden glow on the inside. The chinking had shrunk and some of those big logs had moved or warped so it took about half my tiny paycheck to heat it in the winter. But in that same winter, covered with snow, the cabin was magical, as were the birds attracted to my ugly feeder.

---

**EVENING GROSBEAK**

*The Spruce Budworm was rampant in the Lakes States and Canada in the early 70s. This is one of the most destructive insects in conifer forests and epidemics occur every so often. The larva is a small caterpillar that eats the needles of Balsam Fir, spruce and sometimes hemlock and pine. About the time a strong budworm epidemic gets going, Evening Grosbeak populations boom as the birds feast on caterpillars. A year or two after the caterpillar peak, the Evening Grosbeak population crashes. The latest crash seems to have started in the mid-90s and populations remain low in 2020.*

*Spruce Budworm was decimating spruce and fir stands in northern Minnesota when we moved to Isabella. Loaded with sunflower seeds, my scrap plywood window feeder attracted hordes of Evening Grosbeaks and Common Redpolls, both life birds for me. Imagine a flock of 50 squabbling Evening Grosbeaks a foot from your kitchen window, shucking sunflower so fast you could hear the cash register ring at the feed store!*

**Female (left) and male Evening Grosbeaks (Vermont, photo by Joyce Twing)**

That house in Mikado, Michigan (pronounced my-kay-dough by the locals) was our first new home, a Wausau manufactured home that came in pre-assembled sections – floor sections, wall sections and roof sections, along with pre-built kitchen and bathroom modules. Ours came on a big flatbed truck in early December 1977, with a little snow already on the ground. That fall, I had cleared the home site of aspen and paper birch, starting with a tiny Craftsman chain saw I had bought from Sears years before. It was like mowing Augusta National with a push mower, so I set it aside and went shopping. My beefy new Stihl loggers' saw made me more efficient, and I was ready when the basement contractor arrived to take out the stumps, dig a basement and build the cement block half basement wall.

The house arrived on a cold clear day, with a big crane on another truck. The professional crew assembled the tinker-toy parts in one day, leaving us to coordinate the plumbing and electrical hookups with the help of the Wausau Homes representative. We got the furnace going and finished the inside paneling, a painful task. The goal was to be in by Christmas, despite the weather. Sonja was pregnant with our first child, due in late January. I worked early mornings and evenings, recruited my boss (the district ranger) and my brother-in-law Bob to help, and we celebrated Christmas in our new home. By the time we moved in, we had a regular parade of birds at the primitive feeder I had hung out back while watching the house parts come off the delivery truck. First things first. My daughter Karen's birding education began at that feeder; at age two, her first bird identification was a bright yellow and black, male "Gunshinch".

The first spring in Mikado brought a huge flock of Rose-breasted Grosbeaks to my new "lawn." The sandy soil was not ready to support a luxurious, deep-green golf course turf, far from it; it wanted to blow away after being disturbed by the construction equipment. I took the problem to Marilyn Wallace, the district clerk at the USFS ranger station, who reminded me of Donna Reed and was an experienced gardener. "It's easy," she said, "plant a mixture of annual Rye and oats." Oats? "Sure – they'll come up in clumps and hold the sand in place." Marilyn was right, of course; the mix stabilized my sand dunes, and the oats brought a nice bonus at the peak of spring migration.

Most of the time, I see Rose-breasted Grosbeaks in small numbers, both in migration and when they are paired up for nesting. My newly planted Mikado lawn was heavy to oats, and a flock of perhaps 80 Grosbeaks found them not long after sowing. My back yard was alive that spring with bright spring-plumaged birds, busily thinning out the soon-to-sprout oats. The oats were an accidental attraction, and I'll never forget the hour or so those birds spent in my yard. Like many bird sightings, it was brief; I just happened to be home. They could have come when I was at work, and I would have had no answer to the question "Why aren't there more oat sprouts?"

The other durable memory of a bird encounter in my Mikado patch involved a juvenile Great Horned Owl. I was poking around the edge of my property that bordered the shallow streamside marshland. It was early spring, before full leaf out. I was watching some crows over the marsh when I hear a harsh loud hissing sound, practically in my ear. I turned around to see a still downy but full-sized, puffed up owl with its wings spread and beak wide open at about eye level and eight feet away. If I had been a mouse or rabbit, I'd have been lunch! This youngster was telling me with all certainty that this was his patch and I had no business being there. Although the nest must have been nearby, I had never seen the adults.

I've lived in north Georgia for almost 20 years and have found several great patches to take my bird walk groups. The best is a local county park that is dominated by soccer and baseball fields and a paved walking path full of perspiring people and their dogs. Somehow, the wild edges and streamside brush of this manicured park have yielded 135 species over the years!

Another great patch is the Deerfield Estates pond and pasture near Young Harris that I found early on with my ICL birding classes. It's private property, so we have to bird from the roads (I told you!). Not a problem, except passers-by always stop to inquire about what we're doing. The cows sometimes wander across the pasture to check in with us as well. Invariably, the cameras come out and the cows pose for pictures.

Anyway, this is one of those patches that either bristles with birds or is nearly barren, depending on season, weather and time of day. In addition to a reliable Great Blue Heron, a pair of Belted Kingfishers and Eastern Phoebes nesting in the pond side gazebo, the two-acre pond has yielded Pied-billed Grebe, Canada Goose, Hooded Merganser, Bufflehead, Ring-necked Duck, Lesser Scaup, Green- and Blue-winged Teal and Mallard. One winter day, we counted over 100 Red-head Ducks on Deerfield Pond. That was during the winter of 2014, which was the Year of the Redhead in north Georgia. I don't know the reason, but these beautiful and seldom seen ducks were everywhere that winter and my students sure learned how to identify them.

One fall day, a student asked if we ever got any egrets in the mountains. I answered, "Sure, sometimes in the fall." Not 10 minutes later, four crisp white Great Egrets came into view against a perfect blue sky and circled the pond before settling into the marsh well away from the road. For a teacher, this is how reputations are built.

The land around the pond is marked out in building lots, with scattered trees among the emergent white plastic utility pipes. In the spring, those trees have held Indigo Bunting, Orchard Oriole, Blue Grosbeak, Yellow Warbler, Northern Flicker and Yellow-billed Cuckoo, along with Eastern Bluebirds, Red-winged Blackbirds, American Goldfinches and American Robins. Common birds, but often a first sighting and life bird for many of my students. Not every day, but often enough.

The Deerfield pasture is across Brasstown Creek Road from the pond and is well populated by Black Angus or Hereford cattle. It's pretty reliable for Eastern Meadowlark, whose numbers are declining in Georgia and elsewhere. The problem is habitat loss; they nest in hayfields that are mowed from fence line to fence line and right up to the creek, leaving no edge to nest in. The first hay cutting often happens in late May, when nesting activity is highest. Our pasture is unmowed, except by the bovines, and the meadowlarks are thriving.

**Male Blue Grosbeak**     **Northern Flicker (Photos: Suzanne Zuckerman)**

We can usually find Song and Field Sparrows, Eastern Bluebirds, European Starlings and American Crows in the pasture. Puddles have attracted Solitary and Spotted Sandpipers in spring. Eastern Phoebes wag their tails from the electric fence. A little creek winds its way thru the pasture, bordered by scraggly Sycamore, Red Maple and Hawthorn trees, offering just enough habitat to hold Brown Thrasher, Downy and Red-bellied Woodpeckers, Northern Flickers, American Kestrels in winter and the occasional Pileated Woodpecker.

One memorable class day at the pasture brought an American Crow into view, pursued by another large, all-black bird. The pursuer was a Common Raven, not so common in the lower elevations of north Georgia. The birds perched in a dead tree to continue their conversation, giving us the opportunity to distinguish the Raven's "croak" from the "caw-caw" of the crow, and compare body size, beak size and shape, and tail shape through the spotting scope.

If you don't have a favorite birding patch, find one and visit it often. Keep a patch list through the seasons and take the time to jot down notes about rare species, odd behavior (by birds AND birders,) the weather, and changes through the seasons. You can be diligent and meticulous, with sketches and detailed weather conditions, or you can keep a Spartan checklist on three-by-five cards like my friend Nedra, who ALWAYS follows-up by recording her lists on eBird. After all, it's YOUR patch.

**Crested Caracara (Suzanne Zuckerman)**

# 11

# Cool Birds & Cool Birders

*Encounters with interesting birds in inter-esting places, sometimes with interesting companions. Rare birds, hard-to-find birds and spectacular birds are the stars. Detailed peeks at Swallow-tailed Kites and Snail Kites, Greater Prairie Chickens on the booming grounds, and the birds found below sea-level near a birding hotspot caused by man's meddling – the Salton Sea.*

There's a lot of serendipity around "being there" for a birding spectacle, for an uncommon bird and for a common bird in an uncommon location. In this chapter I've tried to capture some of the delight and excitement of watching birds, especially being in the right place at the right time. If you've been birding a while, you know what I mean – five minutes early or late, looking the other way, being in the port-a-potty, can make all the difference.

## Canvasback at Fannin County Park

Male Redhead on left, Male Canvasback on right. (Brian Finnicum)

The Great Backyard Bird Count (GBBC) is a tremendously valuable citizen science activity and provides a lot of information about where birds are during its traditional four-day run each February. Launched in the United States in 1998, the GBBC went global in 2013, and its database has since been merged with eBird. My tour of the Blue Ridge birding sites during the 2018 GBBC took me to Fannin County Park (or Fannin County Recreation Complex as it is formally known), where we had a growing flock of Redhead Ducks on the little pond within the park. By Sunday, the Redhead flock had grown to 20 (13 males, 7 females) and a beautiful male Canvasback had joined the flock. A male Ring-necked Duck and a female Bufflehead had been there in recent days and were still there, providing additional eye candy. The Canvasback was new for Fannin County Park, where our since-forever species count is now 142. It was a new state record for one of our devoted birders and a life bird for another. Of course, the Canvasback was gone the next day.

### Sora In the Store

September 6, 2006 was a Wednesday, my day off from the bird store. About noon, I got a call at home from Betty, an associate who handled the store on Wednesdays:

*"There's a bird in the store. It's in the office and it's a shorebird or something."*

I came on in and eventually extracted the bird from the coziest corner of our office, under a corner shelf behind the FAX machine. Imagine my surprise to be holding an immature Sora in my hands. Actually, it was holding me with my finger in its bill. No telling how it came to our door, but come it did, perhaps attracted by the little running waterfall just inside the front door. We captured it, caged it in a cat carrier and released it soon after at Fannin County Park, our best local birding area, near the marshy end of a little pond. I hoped it would calm itself from its migratory hiatus and find something to eat. A group of customers peeked at it while in its cage and remarked how smart the bird was to pick a bird store to visit.

### Georgia Redpoll

I saw plenty of Common Redpolls on my window feeder in Minnesota. Predictably, while they do wander southward in harsh winters, they are extremely rare in the South. Imagine my surprise and delight to have one visit my tiny window feeder in north Georgia on a Saturday in late January 2016. The window blinds were down, of course, but open enough to allow me to watch through the slats as it picked at sunflower seeds and defended its position from a pushy Pine Siskin. I was able to take a couple of pictures through the blinds with my cell phone camera, barely good enough to send to Giff Beaton, an expert Georgia birder who serves on the Records Committee of the Georgia Ornithological Society. Giff confirmed my ID and shared the news with several birders who might have been interested.

**Lousy Picture of a Common Redpoll (Tom Striker)**

I instantly started getting phone texts and phone calls: *"Can we come see it?"* By noon on Sunday, I had four ace birders in my house, with binocs, scopes and cameras trained on all the likely feeders outside: Patty McLean, whom you'll meet again on Ivy Log Gap Road; Pierre Howard, great birder, southern gentleman and former lieutenant governor of Georgia; Mark McShane, birder, philosopher and inventor of the McShane Cable Tie Spotting Scope Sight; and Bill Lotz, serious birder and long-time field trip leader and officer in the Georgia Ornithological Society. There are natural rules about stakeouts like this, of course. The bird failed to show that Sunday, despite the vigilance of the watchers. I saw it one more time the following Saturday, with no witnesses. The diagnostic but lousy photo I took through my blinds remains my only evidence. But that's birding, eh?

## Golf Threesome - Swallow-tailed Kite, Dad and Me

My Dad was my favorite golf partner. He was polite when I kept bird lists on the margins of the scorecard and shared his pride about my hobby to his dinner guests: *"I always wanted a six foot-three bird-watcher for a son."* He got a really clear idea of how seriously flawed I was during a spring round of golf near Fort Walton Beach, Florida.

My rusty game was beginning to come around that day and my second shot to a long par-four had settled on the green about 15 feet from the pin when a Swallow-tailed Kite began to circle overhead, perhaps 100 feet in the air. I watched with the usual sense of awe that this spectacular bird demands, lost my concentration for a moment and hit my first putt about 20 feet past the hole. I won't forget his words after my first putt: *"You're still away."* Count 'em – four putts, but worth every stroke.

Dad's reaction? *"Nice bird,"* he said, *"I have the honor."*

## North Georgia Kite Show

The kites we see in north Georgia are usually made of paper and sticks and are attached to a kid by some string. Once in a while, though....

**Swallow-tailed Kite (Brian Lupa)**

Swallow-tailed Kites are unique birds. Their breeding range in the United States once spanned 21 states, including Nebraska, Minnesota and Wisconsin. The population declined drastically from 1880 to 1910 and is now limited to seven southeastern states: Texas, Louisiana, Mississippi, Alabama, Georgia, Florida and South Carolina. The US population may be as small as 2,500 breeding pairs. They are widespread only in Florida. The current range map is speckled at best in the other six states, indicating limited and scattered breeding. Seeing one in Georgia is a real treat.

The Mississippi Kite is much more common, especially in the southeast and the southern Great Plains. Scattered breeding has been noted recently in Missouri, Iowa and even the desert southwest. With luck and some planning, a determined birder can find them in central and south Georgia in summer. Sightings north of Atlanta are few and far between, although one turned up at Mercier Orchards near Blue Ridge on a Saturday bird walk about 10 years ago.

My friend Lisa is an excellent birder with lots of Florida experience with Swallow-tailed Kites. I tease her about being semi-retired from birding since she and husband Brian moved to north Georgia. Semi-retired or not, her sharp eyes picked up a Swallow-tail in flight one Tuesday in August 2011 near Davenport Farm Road, a few miles east of Blue Ridge, Georgia. She and her mother, Nola, diverted from their planned shopping trip long enough to confirm the sighting and immediately reported both Swallow-tailed and Mississippi Kites over the wet pastures along Davenport Farm Road.

We had known that Davenport Farm Road was a magical birding patch that somehow attracted some great birds, but this kite show was beyond giddy. Our kite flock contained three Swallow-tails and three Mississippi Kites, and they were in the air and visible every day. Local birders flocked to the site, and birders from neighboring states gathered to see these graceful birds, which found conditions to their liking and lingered for most of two weeks. Joe LaFleur, author of the *Better Birdwatching* DVD series, happened to live nearby and was able to capture excellent video footage for his library.

Serendipity is all about being in the right place at the right time. A birder from Rome, Georgia, captured the feeling for many of us in a September 3rd post to Georgia Birders Online:

*"Passing through Blue Ridge this morning, it seemed reasonable to give the Davenport Farm Road kites a shot, figuratively speaking. I pulled into the Temple Baptist Church parking lot and scanned the area for 15 minutes; vultures were rising, but nothing else. I drove*

*slowly along Davenport Farm – nothing, nothing, nothing.*

*My time was running out, so I turned north to have one last look back along the valley. As I came to a stop and looked up, there they were, almost directly overhead. A small kettle was rising and in it were Black and Turkey Vultures, a Red-tailed Hawk, two Swallow-tailed Kites and a single Mississippi Kite. The latter bird was already quite high, and the others were gaining altitude rapidly. In a matter of minutes all had vanished over the trees heading east. If I hadn't stopped for gas, I'd have missed them. Ah, those little decisions that shape our lives."*

## Aerial Duel on Lake Blue Ridge

Sonja and I were out on Lake Blue Ridge one summer Sunday morning with some friends. Barb wasn't a birder but loved the lake. Pete had joined me for many of my Saturday bird walks but had chronic and seemingly incurable trouble getting his ancient binocs on a bird. No matter - good friends, a beautiful day, and we weren't birding anyway, right?

Wrong – birders are always birding! I pointed out an Osprey perched in a dead pine. As we watched, its mate glided in, circled, then hovered over a fish. A graceful dive, a splash, and breakfast was in its talons. The Osprey flew to the pine where its mate was perched and began to tear at the fish. Within a minute, a Bald Eagle moved in and made a harassing stoop on the Osprey pair. Both birds flushed, with the fish held firmly in both talons of the successful fish hawk. The eagle stooped again and pursued in the age-old and sometimes successful tradition of stealing from Ospreys.

**Drop That Fish! Adult Bald Eagle (Brian Lupa)**

We watched the aerial drama for five minutes or so. The eagle was faster and quickly gained on the Osprey, but the Osprey repeatedly side-slipped in the air and regained its lead. The second Osprey joined the fray briefly, harassing the eagle, and the Osprey pair seized the moment and headed out across the lake in direct flight, with breakfast still intact. The eagle seemed to shrug off its defeat and landed nearby. We watched in awe, delighted with our near-spiritual experience on a perfect Sunday morning.

## Least Bittern

A rule in birding is that one bird will become your nemesis, refusing to be seen despite heroic efforts. Then, when you finally do see it, it becomes common and practically perches on the foot of your bed.

**Least Bittern – South Florida (Suzanne Zuckerman)**

My wife's parents retired to Hot Springs, Arkansas. We visited from Vermont one summer when the kids were small, and I took a couple days to bird on the Louisiana coast. Least Bittern was a target bird and I failed to see one the first two days, despite being in perfect habitat. On Day Three, the Gods of Birding finally blinked, and I saw 10 bitterns in about an hour. I had two or three in view at once and actually shot 8mm home movies. True to form, I've seen them since in Arizona, Florida and Georgia.

## Scissor-tailed Flycatchers

Back in Hot Springs, I heard that Scissor-tailed Flycatchers hung out at the airport. At the eastern edge of its range, this would be a new bird for me. Hot Springs airport was far from international class in 1985, and was quiet, empty and hot when I arrived. The pearly-gray flycatchers did not disappoint. Five birds were perched on the stylish chain-link fence near the airport office, taking occasional short flights to snap at insects. This was apparently a family, with three short-tailed juveniles. The long-tailed male was spectacular, the female only a little less so.

Scissor-tails wander from their normal range in the south-central United States after nesting and have even been reported from Alaska. A few wander east after nesting and winter in south Florida. A pair found its way to a giant high-tension tower near McDonough, Georgia a few years ago and nested there successfully for at least two years. The male, apparently widowed, but loyal to its territory, returned without his mate in 2009.

My most exciting Scissor-tail was perched on a wire near the new Recreation Building at Fannin County Park, my local north Georgia patch, one July evening in 2009. I recovered from my shock in time to alert several local birders about it. The Birding Gods kept it in sight for most of an hour. The sighting was complete serendipity – I NEVER take evening walks at that park, but I did that day and that beautiful Scissor-tail was my reward.

## Painted Bunting

I took a solo trip to South Florida in February 1999, after a phone conversation with Paul W. Sykes Jr., a Department of the Interior research biologist associated with the University of Georgia at the time. I had met him the year before during the Atlanta, Georgia Christmas Bird Count. When we met, I had no idea that I was talking with one of the great birders of the world, and the world champion participant in Christmas Bird Counts, with over 400 CBCs under his belt. He claimed to remember me when I called and was generous with detailed information about where to find birds in South Florida. He recommended a stop at the famous Corkscrew Swamp Sanctuary near Fort Myers.

There was a big wire cage out front of the nature center building with a tube feeder full of millet hanging inside. A flock of plain-looking, drab birds without wing bars visited the millet feeder. A few showed a hint of green on the back. I was stumped. I walked the board-walk, which was being converted from cedar planks to plastic lumber that winter and decided on the return trip that I had – <u>maybe</u> – seen immature Painted Buntings. They were nowhere to be seen, of course, when I got back to the nature center. A note on the trip list, but no tick.

After this near-miss, Painted Buntings continued to elude me until my first trip to Harris Neck National Wildlife Refuge on the Georgia coast in 2005. While driving slowly down the longish entrance road, I heard a few notes that could have been Indigo Bunting, but sweeter. I stopped (middle of the road, of course) and was greeted by a male Painted Bunting, singing lustily from the top of a short telephone pole. Several more welcomed me at the entrance to Harris Neck. Apparent-ly, the word gets around, and I had paid my dues.

**Snail Kite**

Another target species for my Florida adventure was Snail Kite. I asked Dr. Sykes for advice and his reply was quick and specific: 40-Mile Bend on US 41, the Tamiami Trail, near the Miccosukee restau-rant and airboat terminal. It's called 40-Mile Bend because it is a bend on an otherwise arrow-straight highway, forty miles west of Miami. And Paul had a good basis for knowing where to find them; a defin-itive species summary by the U.S. Fish & Wildlife Service cites Dr. Sykes in 13 research publications from 1974 to 1987.

Snail Kite is widespread in Central and South America, with an estimated global population of two million birds. Less than one per-cent of the population lives in Florida, the only place it is found in the United States, where it is considered endangered both federally and in Florida. It is vulnerable to pollution, hurricanes and artificial water level changes. The present-day system of canals, levees, and water-control structures has disrupted the volume, timing, direction, and velocity of freshwater flow.

It feeds almost exclusively on apple snails, freshwater mollusks found in the Everglades. Snail Kites glide head-down over shallow water, looking for snails that cling to emergent vegetation at or just below the surface. They swoop down and capture the snail in their talons, then transfer it to their bill in flight.

I was fortunate to find a large group of kites actively feeding on snails within 100 yards of the roadside parking area. The dark gray males were especially beautiful, with white rump patch, wide black tail band and red eyes and feet. I watched several successful snail captures, and it was fascinating to watch the smooth in-flight transfer of the snail from foot to bill. The kites perched to feed, using their curved bill to tear the snail from its shell. A spectacular bird on a beautiful winter afternoon, a life bird and a never-to-be-forgotten life view for this birder.

**Snail Kite (Suzanne Zuckerman)**

## Crested Caracara

South Florida again, same trip. I camped at Periwinkle Campground on Sanibel Island, where a patch of lawn, a rusty fire ring and a swaybacked picnic table cost just $27.00 a night, a bargain compared to the $200 rates at a local *We'll Leave the Light On* motel. To balance the ledger, the showers were hot, Eurasian Collared Doves (lifer!) were plentiful, and the raccoons came to dinner at no charge. I toured south Florida from my rustic Sanibel headquarters, ticking off lots of new birds.

I had Crested Caracara on my most-wanted list but did not expect to see one of the 300 or so left in Florida. Habitat loss and shooting have reduced the population, and their taste for road-killed carrion makes them vulnerable to becoming roadkill themselves. I cruised the open country between Sanibel and Lake Okeechobee for three days and had about given up when a Caracara finally glided across the road in front of me and perched in a treetop. I stopped to look, prudently parking off the road.

Part falcon and part vulture, Crested Caracara is a tall, bulky bird with a black crest that contrasts with the white neck and orange face. It's mostly a Central American bird, but ranges into Texas and southern Arizona, with an isolated population in Florida. They often perch on fence posts and treetops. True to form, once I found my Florida bird, it gave me long close-up views with binocs and spotting scope.

---

*Warning: Do not bird in the road in citrus country! Fruit trucks pause for no one.*

---

## Spectacles

*Spectacular gatherings of birds happen all the time, but most often during migration. The trick is to be there to see them. I've been fortunate a time or two.*

**Sandhill Cranes** winter in Florida and South Georgia and migrating flocks are overhead in Georgia in October and again in January. Watching and listening to a few hundred cranes in an afternoon is a treat, but a huge flock on its overnight roost is positively awe-inspiring. Their bugling is primitive and wild-sounding. Close your eyes and listen to be transported back to the Pleistocene Era!

**Adult (left) and Juvenile Sandhill Cranes (Suzanne Zuckerman)**

The spring gathering on the Platte River in Nebraska is probably the ultimate, with up to 500,000 Sandhills between mid-March and mid-April, about 80 percent of the world population. I haven't seen it – yet. But I have seen thousands of cranes coming to their evening roost in lower Michigan, between Lansing and Battle Creek, during the October Crane Festival, reported to be the second largest gathering in the US. Closer to home, I have taken my birding classes to the Hiwassee Refuge near Birchwood, Tennessee at the confluence of the Hiwassee and Tennessee rivers, where up to 12,000 cranes gather in January, along with one or two Whooping Cranes and several Bald Eagles. Similar gatherings and festivals can be found in Colorado, New Mexico, California and Wisconsin. Sometimes there are some Red-winged Blackbirds there as well.

**Hiwassee Crane Refuge – Male Red-winged Blackbird flock hides the cranes (David Fann)**

My most unique Sandhill Crane sighting was completely unexpected because it was so far out of normal range and the location of the sighting was so unique. While visiting Steve Chandler, my old Forest Service ranger, at his retirement home near New Gloucester, Maine, Sonja and I visited the Sabbathday Lake Shaker Village. It is the last active Shaker community, with two members remaining as of 2017. There were originally 19 such Shaker communities in the United States, but the total Shaker congregation probably never exceeded 200. Celibacy is a bedrock value in the Shaker world and an obvious hindrance to congregation growth. New members must be recruited from the outside and it clearly has not been going well.

Despite the tiny population, the Sabbathday Lake Village is in excellent condition and surrounded by lush farmland. I was shocked but delighted to see a pair of sandhills flying low over a nearby pasture, well east of their normal breeding range in Michigan and Wisconsin. I did a little research and learned that a few pairs have established breeding territories in Maine since 2000. Another taste of serendipity!

The Salton Sea, near Brawley, California, is located in a low spot called the Salton Sink, directly on the San Andreas Fault. Did I say, "low spot?" The surface elevation of this shallow, briny lake was 236 feet below sea level in January 2018. Subject to natural changes in flow in the Colorado River over time, what is now the Salton Sea has been alternately a freshwater lake, a saline lake and a dry desert basin. A 1905 project by engineers of the California Development Company, intended to irrigate the nearby and very fertile Imperial Valley, resulted in an accidental rerouting of the entire Colorado River into the Sink, which created the Salton Sea and took two years to repair. The Salton Sea enjoyed brief fame as a resort area after World War II but increasing salinity and the stink of dead fish and massive algal blooms eventually reduced the attraction. It remains a tremendously diverse birding area, supporting over 400 species including about 30 percent of the remaining White Pelican population, and is an important resting stop on the Pacific Flyway. It may be best known as the most reliable location for Yellow-footed Gull in the United States.

A February 1999 one-day trip to the Salton Sea area with my sometimes-a-birder sister Ann produced more than 50 Long-billed Curlews in the fields and at least 25,000 Snow Geese on the strange and briny Sea. While Brawley doesn't exactly overlook the Salton Sea, its official elevation is a heady 112 feet below sea level. It was fun to see the lines marking sea level high on the silos in this low-elevation agricultural area. A roadside colony of tame, yellow-eyed Burrowing Owls completed a spectacular day!

**Broad-winged Hawks** nest throughout the eastern United States, but most leave the continent in winter. Fall migration features large flocks, often called kettles, riding thermals for efficiency. I spent an hour one October morning flat on my back on the deck of my Atlanta home, watching hundreds of Broad-wings in several flocks as they circled and climbed in the thermals, then shot off to the south when they found a straight-line wind at the top.

**Burrowing Owls Using A Handy Culvert (Barb Hauer)**

**Greater Prairie Chickens** have declined dramatically with the conversion of native tallgrass prairie to farmland, but fair numbers remain in the Dakotas, Nebraska and Kansas, with small pockets in Wisconsin, Iowa and Illinois. They are officially extirpated from Canada despite a few reports from Alberta and Saskatchewan. Once numbering in the millions, the population is fairly stable at about 400,000 birds. A new threat to Prairie Chickens is the growing number of tall wind turbines in otherwise suitable habitat; the birds shy away from any tall object that may harbor a hawk.

The annual mating ritual is centered on dramatic displays by the males on communal leks or booming grounds. Up to twenty males gather in an area of short grass where they strut and dance with raised neck feathers and wings held stiffly downward. They may jump in the air with loud cackling and wing fluttering. Featherless yellow-orange sacs on their necks inflate; release of air from these sacs creates the eerie hollow moaning sounds that can be heard a mile away. The dancing and booming are intended to attract females; one or two dominant males may handle 80 percent of the mating chores.

Two small colonies persist in southern Illinois, barely 200 birds, down from perhaps 2,000 when I was in grad school at the University of Illinois in 1971. These colonies are monitored by the Illinois Natural History Survey, and I was able to wangle a guided visit to the booming grounds for a small group of fellow birders in April 1971. We arrived well before dawn and quietly entered the crude wooden blind without disturbing the few birds that were already there. Others arrived with the dawn and the show began immediately.

The focus and intensity of the displaying males was amazing, although the females seemed to pay scant attention. Dust and the random dislodged feather were in the air along with the loud and continuous symphony of booming: "whoo-whoo-whoo-whoo-whoom, whoom, whoom!" Specialized neck feathers called pinnae were raised like horns to reveal the sacs, and the tails were held high. The males scuttled back and forth, often facing off with each other and leaping into aerial skirmishes. The prairie ballet was reminiscent of Native American dance steps. The activity slowed as the day warmed and the birds dispersed into the nearby prairie. The watchers in the blind sat stunned and spellbound by the wild drama they had witnessed.

Spring trips to the Florida Panhandle beaches were a staple when my daughters were in high school. I took advantage of the early mornings to bird up and down the Gulf Coast, but the best memory is of a feeding frenzy of Northern Gannets and Brown Pelicans, glimpsed for a magical 30 minutes shortly after we arrived one April Saturday. The sky had been overcast, but the sun was finally breaking through and the water sparkled under a brisk breeze. A tightly bunched flock of Gannets and Pelicans was circling over a school of baitfish and diving repeatedly into it, then scrambling airborne to dive again. The whitecaps, shafts of sunlight, arrow-like dives by the Gannets and the clunky-but-graceful plunges by the Pelicans created a once-in-a-lifetime show.

## Young Guides & An Earful of Ruffed Grouse

One of the field trips for the 2018 Spring Meeting of the Georgia Ornithological Society took me to Brasstown Bald, the highest peak in Georgia, which looks like Canada for a bunch of nesting birds normally found much farther north - Veery, Canada Warbler, Common Raven, Dark-eyed Junco, Rose-breasted Grosbeak, Winter Wren and Ruffed Grouse.

Our leaders were John and Angus, a couple of young guys who

happen to be two of the best field birders I've ever met. Their hearing is incredibly sharp, they know exactly who is singing, and they can point the singer out with precision. Both John and Angus can do a near-perfect imitation of an Eastern Screech Owl call, which will draw otherwise shy birds out of hiding when done correctly.

We picked up Gray Catbird, Canada Warbler and Rose-breasted Grosbeak at the parking lot and then headed up the hill for our real target of the day, Ruffed Grouse.

Ruffed Grouse is a small chicken-like bird that is widespread in the northern US and Canada with a range extension down the Appalachians into the mountains of north Georgia, where it is hard to find. Brasstown Bald is a reliable location for this little grouse; in fact, the volunteer staff at this Forest Service recreation site tell me that you can easily see the female with chicks on the roads later in the summer. That's unlikely today and our goal is to hear male grouse "drumming."

Ruffed Grouse are part of the Partridge family of birds, which includes the Wild Turkey, several species of arctic-based ptarmigan, the Ring-necked Pheasant, Prairie Chickens and several other species of grouse found in the West. The family is well known for the elaborate mating displays put on by the males, which involve a gathering of several birds in a mating ground called a lek. The ritual is both territorial defense and an announcement that the male grouse is seeking a mate.

Ruffed Grouse are a bit less showy, instead finding a fallen log to perch on while they flap their wings more and more rapidly, making a drumming sound. A barkless log a few inches off the ground seems to have the desired resonance. I was fortunate to watch a grouse drum in northern Minnesota in 1974 and it's quite a sight. In truth, you feel the vibrations as much as you hear them.

This day on Brasstown Bald, John and Angus signaled for quiet a short way up the trail – they had heard a male grouse drumming. We waited and were rewarded with not one but a series of eight drummings, spaced four to five minutes apart. It was probably a single bird, in a rhododendron thicket just out of sight. Each time, the drumming seemed to start with a faint pressure in our ears, then became a series of audible wingbeats and ended with a rapid whirring. Truly a magical sound.

**A Mixed Flock of Roseate Spoonbills and White Ibis. (Suzanne Zuckerman)**

**Woody Pond Rookery, Harris Neck National Wildlife Refuge (Robert Kimsey)**

**On the way to Yanacocha Reserve in Ecuador (Kathy Tickner)**

# 12

# Birding Adventures

*More detailed birding trip reports, including a reprint of a 1975 article first published in the Park Falls, Wisconsin Herald. My Northwoods Journal column was weekly, one draft on an aging Smith-Corona typewriter. An "attack" by Gopher Tortoises hints at the goofy side of birding during old-guy trips to the Georgia Coast. Arizona trips feature the Paton Hummingbird Center and the world-famous Patagonia Picnic Table Effect. Trips to Brasstown Bald take you from Georgia to Canada in a morning, and Christmas Bird Counts can have grisly moments.*

Every birder eventually takes some longer birding trips, although they're sometimes disguised as family vacations or even business trips. Some are well planned; others are informal or accidental. A few work out as planned, some get washed out by rain or heat or uncooperative birds. A few deliver beyond all expectations and become the stuff of personal legend.

I've lived a lot of places, and almost always had binocs and field guide close enough to be useful, but there were several unavoidable lapses where other life priorities allowed dust to accumulate on my birding tools. Looking back, I missed some opportunities to chase great birds in northern Minnesota, Michigan and Vermont especially.

Time tends to balance things, though, and I've done some catching up since moving to Georgia in 1986, with lots of local birding and trips to Florida, North Carolina, and Arizona. In the bonus category, I picked up a few birds on a family trip to my wife's hometown in Germany in 2001 and many more during ten rain- and bird-filled days in Ecuador in 2009. Find your hat and binocs and join me in the memories.

**Arkansas Swampland**

*Note: A description of this adventure first appeared in April 1975 as an article in my <u>Northwoods Journal</u> column in The Park Falls (Wisconsin) Herald, a local weekly newspaper that came out on Thursdays. I wrote my articles on a manual typewriter, one draft, and dropped them off at the newspaper office on Monday morning on my way to work at the Chequamegon National Forest Ranger Station in nearby Glidden. There was an envelope waiting on the doorstep that contained a few sheets of typing paper, my payment for the article. Good value given and received, although with better compensation I might have hired an editor.*

Imagine, if you will, a deep, dark southern cypress swamp. As your boat winds into the depths of the swamp, your guide, a grizzled veteran, calls your attention to a huge log ahead. As you watch, the 'log' sinks out of sight, only to emerge again in your wake. "Gator," says the guide matter-of-factly, "'bout a 12-footer." Ahead, an enormous water moccasin slides into the water; as you pass into the open, a cloud of white egrets rises from the top of the 70-foot cypress. The stillness, the giant trees and the birds call to you from another time.

I said imagine because that is what I have to do. Such a place does exist in southwest Arkansas, but it is well guarded, and access is difficult. During a recent trip to the South, I made it a point to visit this place, a well-known mecca for birders. Guided by Olin Sewall Pettingill's *Guide to Bird-finding West of the Mississippi*, and a kindly postal clerk in Fulton, Arkansas, I was able to find the reserve, known as Grassy Lake, and talk to the caretaker.

Mr. Taylor told me that without the permission of the Hempstead County Hunting Club, I could go no farther. It seems that a group of wealthy men had purchased the area in about 1900 for a hunting area. The 5,000 acres of swamp and upland annually attract thousands of teal, black ducks, mallards, pintails and woodies because of the winter food and cover it provides. Since then, the area has been maintained and protected from logging and poachers and has become one of the prime examples of virgin swampland in the South. After talking awhile with Mr. Taylor, who was extremely courteous but firm, I sadly drove back to the highway, acutely aware of what I was missing.

My disappointment was so great that I nearly missed the sign announcing the Grassy Lake Fire Tower, about a mile from the Hunting Club entrance. I saw it in time, however, and turned in. I obtained permission to climb the tower from a very nice lady and soon was perched precariously about a hundred feet above the hilltop, with a tremendous view of Grassy lake.

Magnificent! Use your imagination again, but rest assured that it does exist, because I saw it! Hundreds of Little Blue and Great Blue Herons, Snowy and Great Egrets were nesting within my view atop giant cypresses standing knee-deep in green swamp. Black Vultures flapped and soared above me. A pair of Red-tails passed within a few feet. And, unbelievably, a flock of Anhingas was soaring above the swamp; as many as six were within the view of my spotting scope at one time! I was awed, as any naturalist viewing this spectacle should be; here, in 1975, was the South as Audubon and Bartram saw it.

As I carefully descended from my lofty perch, I vowed to return with permission to explore the depths of Grassy Lake. Next time, I'll write ahead and be sure. Such places are not easily forgotten. Nor do they exist by accident and here is the point of my spellbinding narrative. A small number of wealthy hunters (26 active members at last count; $20,000 admission fee,) by selfishly protecting an area for private exploitation of a huntable resource, had also created a priceless haven for many species of wildlife, crowded out of our modern world by logging, rice fields, superhighways and greed.

I do not know if the hunters know what they have, in terms of protection for endangered wildlife. I suspect they do know, and I hope that is part of the reason for excluding visitors. The only viable Arkansas population of American Alligators is thriving at Grassy Lake. The Anhinga and Least Bittern nest nowhere else in Arkansas. Small populations of the rare Purple Gallinule and Black-crowned Night Heron nest there, in company with the more common herons and egrets. A thorough botanical survey would doubtless reveal several rare plants. And a near-virgin 3,000-acre cypress-tupelo swamp is priceless in itself.

I don't resent the hunting club's reluctance to permit visitors to enter. If refused permission in the future, I would be sorely disappointed, but I would understand. Maintenance of such a precious area is a grave responsibility, for in places like Grassy Lake lie the hope and the future for much of our native wildlife. The soiled and crumpled hat of this birder is off to the Hempstead County Hunting Club.

## Georgia Adventures
**Brasstown Bald 5/14/2013** *(from a summary posted to Georgia Birders On-line)*

I led a field trip today to Brasstown Bald for my Young Harris College ICL (Adult Education) birding class. I've been doing these classes for four years or so, through all seasons. Class members are generally backyard birders, with some rank beginners and some with more experience. We spend one class period inside on basics (binocs, field guides, bird topography) and then go birding around Young Harris and Hiawassee, Georgia and into North Carolina a bit. Favorite spots are Ivy Log Gap Road and Brasstown Bald, but we've found some other hotspots with nice birds and low traffic.

Today was cool early but warmed up nicely and turned into a great day to be outside. Brasstown Bald was "on program," revealing lots of nice birds. Some of our relative veterans had seen some of them before, but most were life birds for most of the class. You hardened, hard-core birders may have forgotten the thrill of a close look at a new bird, but our group acted like four-year-olds at Christmas.

We heard but did not see Veery but had good views of a Gray Catbird. Everyone saw the dark cap and rusty undertail coverts. Brown Thrashers, Towhees and Wood Thrushes took turns scratching leaves on the trail ahead of us. Rose-breasted Grosbeaks sang on territory like robins with voice coaches. We had fabulous views of Black-throated Blue Warbler, and everyone saw the pocket handkerchief patch, noting that it's visible in all plumages. Chestnut-sided Warbler sang at close range at the first clearing on the Wagon Train Trail.

Canada Warbler popped up just past the gate marking Brasstown Wilderness, and we watched two males negotiating a territory boundary, grappling in the air and twisting to the ground. Such a battle was never seen before by this faithful guide, and much appreciated.

Recorded songs create a fuzzy point as educational tools for classes of learning birders. We often talk about the stress that recordings can cause for birds on territory, which can be more severe when recordings are repeated. On the other hand, judicious and careful use of recordings can bring a bird into view. The experience can turn a novice into a dedicated birder who is suddenly environmentally aware and who will become a staunch defender and supporter of habitat preservation and rare species management. Not to weary the point, but does careful use of a recording cause more stress than another real male singing?

Note: Georgann Schmalz, a friend and noted birder who served as Resident Ornithologist at the Fernbank Museum in Atlanta for over 20 years, responded to my post about the use of recordings: *"Don't apologize or justify using tapes especially when in a teaching situation. As*

*you said, if used carefully there is no true evidence that it is any more
stressful than a real male singing."*

**Carefully using audio of Prothonotary Warbler at
Savannah-Ogeechee Canal**

I bemoaned the fact that both Giff Beaton's *Birding Georgia* and
Ken Blankenship's online *Wings Over GA* reported Winter Wren to be
nesting at Brasstown Bald but that I had NEVER heard or seen them
in 20 or so visits to this birding shrine. "What does it sound like?" was
the question, so I played the song. My hearing sucks anymore, most
notably the high ranges, but I always travel with audio-capable bird-

ers, and one of them said "I hear it!" so I played it again (get out the ruler and rap my knuckles) and that little charmer came in and sang for us for at least 15 minutes! It flitted in the giant rhododendrons and was hard to see, but what a concert! The Canada Warbler was voted out of its earlier 'bird of the day' status, replaced by this so-cooperative Winter Wren.

My little class had a terrific day of birding and will be back for more. Several are already Georgia Ornithological Society members and monitor GABO-L (Georgia Birders On-Line, a wonderful tool for reporting bird sightings.) Others will become more active in the birding fraternity in the future. Sadly, the hikers and wildflower enthusiasts who shared the trails today seemed oblivious to the winged wonders that graced our day at Brasstown Bald.

## A Memorable Christmas Bird Count

I've done the Chattahoochee-Cohutta Christmas Bird Count since 2006, with a variety of excellent birders as companions over the years. Centered in the Cohutta Wilderness west of Ellijay, Georgia, this count is traditionally scheduled on a Sunday in mid-December and begins with an hour of owling before daylight. The Forest Service Overlook along Highway 52 is our first stop after sunup, where we sometimes find Ruffed Grouse, Common Raven and Barred Owl. The Overlook is always deserted early on a winter Sunday, except it wasn't on December 18, 2011, when Robert, Bill and I arrived. Here's what I reported in my summary of our results for that day:

*We "owled" from 6:15 to 7:15 a.m. along Forest Road 18, with four Eastern Screech Owls responding. We then headed to the USFS Cohutta Overlook on Highway 52, hoping to get a Barred Owl or Common Raven at this early hour. Instead, we found an old Chevy pickup parked there, with the driver's side window open and the young male driver inside, an apparent suicide, dead of a gunshot wound to the head. A gun was in his lap and there was a bullet hole in the rear window behind his head. We called 9-1-1 and the Gilmer County Sheriff's Department responded pretty quickly. We were questioned briefly, asked to wait for the detective from the Criminal Investigative Division to arrive, and eventually released after about two hours. It was pretty unreal, and we did not get our usual Eastern Towhee at the overlook.*

## May 2007 Georgia Coastal Trip
*Originally posted to Georgia Birders On-Line, the list-serve for the Georgia Ornithological Society*

Fellow birders Robert and Dave joined me for my annual trip to the Georgia Coast, May 20-23, 2007. Georgia birders will recognize many of the locations; others should plan to visit to sample the marvelous birding on the Georgia coast!

As I left my long rural driveway at 0400 hours to pick up Dave & Robert, the night sky to the south was filled with orange light from what turned out to be a house fire. I headed that way and found the one-lane gravel road that led to the burning house. I got close enough to feel the heat and realized there was nothing I could do but call 9-1-1. I was high enough on the hill for adequate cell phone reception and made the call. Mine was the first report. I realized that I was soon going to be an obstacle to fire truck access if I stayed where I was, and more importantly, was likely to be blocked in, so I retraced my steps to the main road and headed for Epworth to pick up two sleepy birders. Scuttlebutt after the fire suggested it was an arson fire, started by the builder for insurance purposes. A strange start to this birding trip, for sure!

Briefly, we visited the McDonough Scissor-tailed Flycatcher site, Bucksnort Road near McDonough, Central City Park and Ocmulgee National Monument near Macon, Savannah-Ogeechee Canal, Youman's Pond, Altamaha Wildlife Management Area, Harris Neck National Wildlife Refuge, Andrews Island Causeway and Jekyll Island. On the way home, we visited Big Hammock Wildlife Management Area, a new Bachman's Sparrow site nearby, and Beaverdam Wildlife Management Area. We listed 124 species, with notable misses on Swallow-tailed Kite, Reddish Egret, Roseate Spoonbill, Common Ground Dove, all the goatsuckers, all the owls, Gray Catbird and American Goldfinch.

*Have you noticed that (1) there are too few early morning hours and (2) it's hard to be in two places at once during those hours?*

McDonough – we found only one Scissor-tail, probably the male. No nest was visible and there was no nest-building activity. Could this be the end of a wonderful nest site? Ken Blankenship put us on to Bucksnort Road, a few miles south of the Scissor-tail site, for Dickcissel. We found none, but found Grasshopper Sparrow, Eastern Meadowlark and five Mississippi Kites over the huge wheat fields. Looks like Kansas – great site. Thanks, Ken!

Macon – Orchard & Baltimore Orioles cooperated immediately, mainly in the big Sweetgum tree 100 yards from the parking lot and along the levee. Central City Park is an urban park of mowed grass and giant shade trees, two minutes off Interstate 16, and the only reliable location for nesting Baltimore Orioles in Georgia. Look at your field guide and you'll see a spot in central Georgia indicating nesting Baltimore Orioles – that's Central City Park, and it's really only two or three trees. Pretty cool.

The Common Ground Doves were not in the usual places on Lower Poplar Street. Nearby Ocmulgee National Monument is full of birds; try to get there early. It's only five minutes from Central City Park. We saw Anhinga, waders, and Redheaded Woodpecker from the boardwalk, and Mississippi Kite on a nest near where the boardwalk trail meets the main road.

We angled southeast toward the coast, seeking Swallow-tails near Glennville and Ludowici without success. We found Loggerhead Shrike near the Glennville Sewage Plant.

Altamaha – despite the dry weather, the marshes east of Highway 17 were wet and had been recently drained and mowed. Visibility was the best I've ever seen there. We saw one Purple Gallinule and numbers of Common Moorhen, Black-necked Stilt, White and Glossy Ibis, Little Blue Heron, and Green Heron. Many Least Bitterns, some posing for photographs. A couple of Black Skimmers near the observation tower – rare freshwater location. Several Gull-billed Terns and Mottled Ducks. Close-up views of Black-bellied Whistling Ducks, feeding in pairs.

**Black-bellied Whistling Ducks – Altamaha Refuge, GA (Robert Kimsey)**

A flock of about 40 Whistlers wheeling overhead is a sight not to be forgotten. The back roads west of 17 were full of Painted Buntings and Summer Tanagers. A highlight was a flock of 150-200 Cedar Waxwings coursing back and forth across the road.

Youman's Pond – they've paved the road next to the pond and installed a new boardwalk and observation deck. Nice facilities but the number of birds was way down from 2006.

Andrews Island Causeway – caught on a rising tide. Clapper Rail, Sanderlings, Least Tern, Willet, Red-breasted Merganser. Black Vultures working on stinky dumped pig parts. A super highlight was American Bittern in the marsh on the right just before the gate to the fill site. We flagged down a fill-site employee and got permission to go to the top of the levee overlooking the fill area - White Pelicans (3), Dunlin, Short-billed Dowitcher, Wilson's Plover, stilts, etc. Lots of peeps. No Avocets as there were in 2006. No Ground Doves. The fill work is being done on the other side of the fill site – don't hesitate to ask permission to enter for a short time. I've been welcomed two years in a row.

*Note: I was chastised by several knowledgeable birders after I posted this, and told in no-uncertain terms that the fill site was strictly off-limits and the employees were not authorized to let me in. Oh, well – some say it's better to beg forgiveness than to ask permission, and we'd have missed the pelicans otherwise.*

Jekyll Island – Good beach flock at the south end near the wreck: Wilson's Plover, Ruddy Turnstone, mating Royal and Caspian Terns. Dave and Robert were amazed that the tame Gray Kingbird seemed to be on duty all the time across from the Convention Center. The sanctuary site at Jekyll Campground is wonderful and restful, even at 2:30 in the afternoon. Four male Painted Buntings in view at once; Northern Parula and Cardinals bathing all the time. It's a great example of co-operation between the campground owners and the birders on Jekyll, especially Lydia Thompson, who set up the sanctuary site. On the way back to the mainland, we visited the Welcome Center on a falling tide – terrific views of Whimbrel, a lifer for all of us!

Harris Neck – always wonderful. Take the time to walk and bird the entrance road under the spreading oaks if you can. A gorgeous early morning setting with lots of common passerines. Lots of gators at Woody Pond, many resting under the rookery. A highlight was watching a large gator swim 100 yards or more to harass a young Anhinga into dropping the catfish it had just caught. The Anhinga has to work its bill to widen the spear hole in the fish enough to allow it to flip the fish around for swallowing. It takes a while and the gator knew a low skill level when he saw it. No water in Snipe Pond; lots of water for a change in Teal and Greenhead Ponds.

Big Hammock – always reliable for Swainson's Warbler, a shy bird that nests in swampy canebrakes in south Georgia and in stream-side rhododendron in the mountains. A frisky male responded to a recording at the usual spot. We met Steve the Game Warden who told us about a reliable Bachman's Sparrow site within three miles: turn left out of Big Hammock, cross the Altamaha River, turn left (south) on 169 and go about two miles to a church on the right. Right past the church is a big pine stand with palmetto and shrub understory. If you see Silver City you've gone too far. Silver City is a homesite/campground with everything painted silver – trailers, fences, sheds, tractors, mowers – you can't miss it. Listen for the Bachman's; ours responded to a song quickly. A lifer for Robert and me.

North towards Reidsville and Lyons – many Mississippi Kites, no Swallow-tails. An early afternoon stop at Beaverdam Wildlife Management Area yielded Yellow-breasted Chat, Hooded and Kentucky Warbler, Louisiana Waterthrush, Eastern Wood Pewee and Acadian Flycatcher, but no Ground Doves.

Overall a fabulous trip. Every birder should make similar pilgrimages when time and circumstances allow. Georgia is a wonderful place to bird, with everything from salt marsh to Canadian Zone mountaintops.

**May 2008 Coastal Georgia Trip** *(Originally posted to Georgia Birders On-Line.)*

*Note: This 2008 trip was similar to last year's, but I include it because it was the first of many blessings that followed my encounter with cancer. I was diagnosed with non-Hodgkin's Lymphoma in October of 2007 after a routine old-man-over-50 colonoscopy revealed a bump under the lining of my colon that turned out to be part of a big tumor on my small intestine. Surgery was followed by a series of chemotherapy treatments that finished on May 1st as preliminary plans were being made for this pilgrimage to the coast. I took the diagnosis and treatments in stride at the time but am awed and humbled today as I look back on what might have been and grateful for the life-, love- and bird-filled years that have been a gift since then.*

Dave, Robert and I birded through north Georgia on our way to the coast for our annual coastal adventure May 18th thru 21st. I did this solo for two years; Dave and Robert joined me last year. Focused marathon birding is pure therapy – I recommend four consecutive 13-hour birding days to cure what ails you.

Last year we had no nightjars and no owls. To cure this, we started out in Epworth, Georgia at 0430 with I-Pod assisted owling stops and were rewarded with Screech Owl and Chuck-Wills-Widow. Barred Owl at Savannah-Ogeechee Canal and Common Nighthawk at Altamaha Wildlife Management Area were additions later in the week.

First stop was the E.L. Huie / Clayton County sewage treatment facility – Five swallows (Purple Martin, Barn, Rough-winged, Tree and the rare Bank), Yellow Warbler in the willows around the northwest pond, Semi-palmated Plover, Osprey, and possible Short-billed Dowitchers that may actually have been the Stilt Sandpipers Mark McShane posted later that day.

We headed to Piedmont National Wildlife Refuge for Red-cockaded Woodpecker and Bachman's Sparrow, but missed both due to our midday arrival. We did land our sixth swallow of the day with Cliff Swallow at the Ocmulgee River bridge at Juliette, along with Mississippi Kite. We did not have time to stop at the nearby Whistlestop Café for fried green tomatoes, the southern delicacy made famous by the movie with the same name.

Central City Park in Macon yielded Orchard and Baltimore Orioles and Eurasian-collared Dove, but, as usual, the Common Ground Doves on Lower Poplar Street were not to be found. A flat tire on I-16 added a little drama to the trip - those trucks are fast and close while one is struggling with a spare amidst the tornado debris. We short-circuited our typically aggressive itinerary and cut the corner thru Glennville, on our way to birding headquarters near Darien, adding several Loggerhead Shrikes.

We got an early start to Tybee Island on Monday, in time to be the first to plug the parking meters at North Beach; I can't imagine what that beach is like on a July Saturday. No Purple Sandpipers, but we did spot an agile Spotted Sandpiper leaping to avoid the waves on the rock jetty, along with the first of many Ruddy Turnstones in breeding plumage. Also, immature Northern Gannet, Royal and Sandwich Terns, and Whimbrels in the marsh along the causeway.

We visited Savannah-Ogeechee Canal after Tybee, and were rewarded with calling Barred Owls, and views of Yellow-billed Cuckoo, Northern Parula, Louisiana Waterthrush, and Pine, Palm and Yellow-throated warblers.

**Male Prothonotary Warbler (Suzanne Zuckerman)**

The owls were fabulous, calling repeatedly and eventually showing themselves. The Gopher Tortoises were running at high speed (for them) in their enclosure, putting on a dramatic display. This privately managed area is a little gem and worth a visit. Apparently, funding has improved – path improvements were evident, and a couple of engineers were compiling notes to support a rehab project that will restore the canal and towpaths to a condition resembling their past glory.

**Run, Dave, Run!! (Photos by Robert Kimsey)**

Gopher Tortoise just before            Charging Gopher Tortoise
*The Attack*

The Gopher Tortoise exhibit at the Savannah-Ogeechee Canal was the setting for a silly moment that became a part of the mythology of birding for Dave, Robert and me. I left it out of my report of our 2008 coastal trip, but Robert reminded me of it when he read my trip summary:

*"I can only think you must have blotted out the terrible incident of our last day on the trail when the band of hostile Gopher Tortoises attacked Father Dave. The poor fellow is still repulsed by the mention of the incident and is thrown off by the sight of an overturned bucket or a person's hat thrown carelessly on a chair, innocent shapes that remind him of the terror of that day. It is a sad memory to be sure and if we go back to that area next year we must ensure that he is well protected from any hostilities."*

Imagine three old guys stepping carefully over the foot-high fence to see the tortoises up close. After several minutes of absolutely no movement at all, one of the larger tortoises came out of its burrow at what may have been its top speed, but still sloth-like, right toward Dave.

Robert, a troubled Kentucky kid turned birder, poet and lay-minister, is known for his sense of the dramatic. He yelled: *"Run, Dave, run!"* and Dave backed up what Robert believes to be one life-saving step. Robert captured the moment in a later e-mail: *"I shudder to recall the fear in Father Dave's eyes, and the pathetic shuffling of feet that constituted his best stride as he fled for his very soul."*

You can't make this stuff up, but our wives roll their eyes when this nearly-true story is retold.

Harris Neck National Wildlife Refuge delivers from the front gate – Painted Bunting, Red-headed Woodpecker (posing for photos on the entrance sign), and Summer Tanager under the wonderful live oaks on the entrance drive. Woody Pond had hundreds of nesting Wood Storks, Anhingas, Snowy Egrets, Little Blue and Tri-colored Herons, with White Ibis flyovers, and a few Black-crowned Night-herons. Common Moorhens herded puffball chicks thru the duckweed. We missed Yellow-crowned Night-heron but picked up Black-necked Stilt thanks to a tip from Dan Vickers and Pierre Howard, who showed no signs of fatigue despite birding with GOS in Clayton the previous weekend. The population of alligators seemed to be much lower than normal.

Altamaha Wildlife Management Area is the best birding habitat on the Georgia coast. We encountered 27 Black-bellied Whistling Ducks on the ponds near the tower on the west side of the highway. The east-side ponds were cleaned of vegetation and drained last year; this year they were full of roosting egrets and herons, along with coots, moorhens, stilts and many Least Bitterns. A pair of Gull-billed Terns seemed to be considering nesting in the area. A Common Nighthawk spent Monday evening 'boom-diving' for us – falcon-like dives to within 10 feet of the marsh. Again, funding seems to be increased; mowed dikes, new signage and a new viewing tower were much appreciated.

We checked Marshes of Glynn on Highway 17 in Brunswick near the St. Simons Causeway minutes before a rising tide visit to St. Simons Island. Great views of Black Skimmers were matched by Clapper Rails walking <u>under our feet</u> as we stood on the boardwalk. There are *Life Birds* and there are *Life Views* of birds you've seen before – this was the latter, and every bit as gratifying as a lifer. No Reddish Egrets at Gould's Inlet, but good numbers of Ruddy Turnstone, Willet and breeding-plumaged Dunlin, along with the usual variety of gulls, terns and pelicans. More than 20 Whimbrel were in Bloody Marsh. Note – there's a new traffic circle / roundabout near the airport; stay to the right but pretend you're in England and you'll get through it OK.

Andrews Island Causeway was a little disappointing, but we had a great view of a Marsh Wren singing in the reeds. Another life view to be remembered for a long while. The Roseate Spoonbill roost south of the Jekyll Causeway held 16 spoonbills Tuesday morning. We didn't get a closer view anywhere but were delighted to see so many. The Jekyll Visitor Center had Orchard Oriole, Yellow-billed Cuckoo, a late Blackpoll Warbler, and breeding-plumaged Black-bellied Plover. Jekyll South Beach was loaded with Ruddy Turnstones, along with a beautiful Wilson's Plover (three beach plovers plus Killdeer for the trip!)

Giff Beaton's *Birding Georgia* almost guarantees Gray Kingbird at the Zachry's shopping center across from the Convention Center, but they were not to be found until we reluctantly played the call. Instant gratification – two kingbirds appeared within 10 seconds and settled on their accustomed wire-span at the south end of the parking lot. Zachry's Café has moved from the shopping center across from the Convention Center and is now Zachry's Riverhouse near the causeway. Find it - and get a Shrimp Hoagie!

On the way to Big Hammock Wildlife Management Area for Swainson's Warbler, we checked the pine stand north of Silver City on Highway 169 northwest of Jesup for Bachman's Sparrow. Silver City still isn't a city and it still isn't on the map; we visited it last year and everything is still painted silver. The pines yielded a furtive Bachman's last year; this year the sparrow was singing proudly from an exposed perch – another life view.

We found Swainson's Warbler at Big Hammock – it has been reliable about a mile from the entrance. Recent timber cutting has created open areas along the main road but reduced the buffer around some of the best Swainson's / Prothonotary swamps.

Gray Kingbird (Robert Kimsey)

The Famous Shrimp Hoagie
(Zachry's.com)

A tour of the Dublin Airport on the way home produced three Loggerhead Shrikes together on the boundary fence, Common Ground Dove (finally – it should be renamed Un-Common Ground Dove), and great views of Northern Bobwhite. No Bobolinks and no Grasshopper Sparrows. We had missed the widowed male Scissor-tailed Flycatcher in McDonough but got him on the way home on

Wednesday. Here's hoping he finds a date in South America in time to keep the McDonough territory occupied.

**Widowed Scissor-tailed Flycatcher near McDonough, GA
(Robert Kimsey)**

We listed 142 species in all. Significant misses included Swallow-tailed Kite, Bald Eagle, Reddish Egret and Yellow-crowned Night-heron. A fabulous trip, nevertheless!

## Arizona Adventures

*Finding Birds in Southeast Arizona,* published by the Tucson Audubon Society in 2011, is an essential tool for birding this region. Mine is only slightly dog-eared after three visits, and whole sections cry out for rereading in preparation for future trips. Gotta have it.

Arizona is a spectacular place to bird and I haven't spent nearly enough time there. Its 550 species of birds make it the birdiest state without an ocean coastline. Southeast Arizona, south and east of Tucson, may be the best single area to bird in the United States. Proximity to Mexico makes it a hotbed for wandering birds from south of the border, along with the occasional nester, including Black-capped Gnatcatcher, Five-striped Sparrow, Yellow Grosbeak, Eared and Elegant Trogon, Flame-colored Tanager, Streak-backed Oriole and a variety of hummingbirds and flycatchers.

Despite its reputation as desert, Arizona has a rainy season in the summer. Heavy, monsoon-like rains in July and August turn the desert from brown to green and produce wonderful displays of blooming cactus and wildflowers. Many birds wait to breed until the rains begin, creating a "second spring" of activity for birders. The Tucson Audubon Society has sponsored the Southeast Arizona Birding Festival in August for several years to take advantage of the spectacular birding opportunities.

The scattered but tall 'sky island' mountain ranges that dot the region contribute to the bird variety because of the biomes or life zones created as the mountains rise from desert floor to alpine forest. A simple explanation is that you travel climatically from Mexico to Canada as you go up, with accompanying changes in vegetation and animal life. Mount Lemmon, just north of Tucson, is the tallest at 9,157 feet and the most accessible. The 25-mile-long Mount Lemmon Highway winds from the Sonoran Desert with saguaro cactus and ocotillo through scrubby oak forest to montane forest with Ponderosa Pine, Douglas Fir, White Fir and Aspen.

Each mountain range offers at least one stream-watered canyon with names that stir a birder's heart: Madera Canyon, Chino Canyon, Ramsey Canyon, Cave Creek Canyon, Sycamore Canyon and Carr Canyon, to name a few. Miller Canyon, in the Huachuca Mountains, contains the famous Beatty's Guest Ranch, which may be the best hummingbird-watching location in the United States. As many as 14 species have been seen there in a single day.

Other areas offer outstanding birding. The riparian vegetation along the San Pedro River near Benson and Sierra Vista and the Santa Cruz River from Green Valley south to Nogales provide breeding habitat and serve as lush highways for migration in spring and fall. Both of these rivers may disappear during the dry seasons, but the habitat persists, and birding can still be quite productive. A favorite spot for me is the Santa Cruz River crossing on Santa Gertrudis Lane on the south edge of the Tumacacori National Historical Park, which protects the ruins of three separate Spanish mission communities. On the way south from Tucson or Green Valley, a stop at the nearby Tubac artist community is a must. Bring your checkbook.

The tiny town of Patagonia is another birder's mecca. It can be headquarters for visiting several nearby hotspots, including the Patagonia-Sonoita Creek Preserve, Patagonia Lake State Park, Sonoita Creek Natural Area, The Paton Center for Hummingbirds and the uniquely famous Patagonia Roadside Rest.

**The Stage Stop - Patagonia Birding Headquarters in 2000 (Tom Striker)**

I stayed at the Stage Stop Motel in downtown Patagonia in January 2000 with family and birding friends during my first-ever trip to Arizona and was awed by the variety and beauty of the winter birds. The Stage Stop was built in 1969 near the Patagonia stop for the Butterfield Stage Lines. Its original owners were friends of John Wayne and the Stage Stop housed cast and crew for several of his movies. It was still in near-original condition – a little shabby - in 2000, but new owners have refurbished it and TripAdvisor gives it four and a half owl eyes today.

The Paton Center for Hummingbirds, now managed by Tucson Audubon, is the former home of Wally and Marion Paton. It's located on the edge of town near the eastern entrance to the Patagonia-Sonoita Creek Preserve. Lovers of both birds and birders, the Patons opened their property to bird-lovers soon after moving to Patagonia in 1973. They put out seed feeders and hummingbird feeders and kept lawn chairs available for viewing. They soon installed a canopy for shade and provided bird books and a chalkboard for recording sightings. A simple jar with a note invited visitors to contribute to the sugar fund. A huge fountain was completed in 1996 and was still there when I visited in 2000.

Paton's Feeders, as they were then known, hosted one of the best hummingbird shows in America. Many years later, the Paton Center remains the best place to see Violet-crowned Hummingbird from April to September. Blacked-chinned and Broad-billed are common. Anna's, Costa's and Rufous are regular in season. Lucifer and Allen's are occasional. Super-rarities have included Plain-capped Starthroat, Ruby-throated Hummingbird and the first Cinnamon Hummingbird ever seen north of Mexico. I got my life-record Lazuli Bunting there in August 2014; the feeders were full, but the house was empty and showed signs of neglect.

Wally Paton died in 2001 but Marion kept the birder welcome mat out until her death in 2009. The feeders went unfilled for a while and the future of the famous yard was in doubt. But the birding community quickly pulled together to save this gem for future generations, led by 104-year-old Ann Cullen Smith, who told Victor Emanuel that the house was for sale. Owner of Victor Emanuel Nature Tours (VENT), and board member of the American Bird Conservancy (ABC), Victor worked with ABC to initiate an international fundraising effort.

The property was acquired by ABC in 2014 and Tucson Audubon agreed to manage it for the birding community. Initial funds for renovation and restoration of the property came in the form of generous donations by Dorothy Fitch and John Munier. Marcia Grand donated money to celebrate the life of her husband Richard, an attorney and avid birder. These gifts and small donations by thousands of ordinary birders sealed the deal and the Paton Center for Hummingbirds became a reality. Be sure to put a buck or two in the Sugar Jar when you visit.

The Patagonia Roadside Rest, four miles south of town, deserves special mention. A tiny rest area created long ago by a rerouting of Arizona Highway 82, it has a single picnic table and no rest room facilities. Yet, it's famous among birders as the origin of the Patagonia Picnic Table Effect (PPTE), something I first read about in Kingbird Highway, Kenn Kaufman's book about his 1973 Big Year, when he was 16 years old. According to Kaufman, a birder from nearby Nogales, Arizona named Bill Harrison found Rose-throated Becard here in the 1960s. Harrison visited again and found other interesting birds, including the first US colony of Five-striped Sparrows and the second nesting pair of Thick-billed Kingbirds. These Mexican birds were rare enough to be reported and other birders visited the rest area, where they found other rare birds – Yellow Grosbeak, Black-capped Gnatcatcher, Fan-tailed Warbler and Yellow-green Vireo. These rarities were reported, and other birders came.

This phenomenon of rare birds attracting birders, who then find more rare birds, attracting even more birders, became known as the Patagonia Picnic Table Effect. It's not unique to that roadside rest or even Arizona; it applies to lots of places that have become hotspots after a few rare bird reports. My own local wet pasture on Davenport Farm Road is an example. Flocks of wintering Ring-billed Gulls and Killdeer, far from rare, brought birders who found White-fronted Geese, Cackling Goose, and a Ross's / Snow Goose hybrid. Later birders found Sandhill Cranes, Wilson's Snipe, Greater Yellowlegs and both Swallow-tailed and Mississippi Kites.

**The Famous Patagonia Roadside Rest (Tom Striker)**

While researching the Patagonia Picnic Table Effect, I came across an internet blog called Model Birder, owned by Jody Enck, who is both an accomplished birder and a guy who likes to build models. He has modeled other birder behaviors, all starting with basic Bird-Birder interactions: encountering birds; deciding whether to try to identify them; and finally, making some identifications. In modeling the PPTE an addition to the basic model is identifying one of the birds as a "rarity." With thanks to Jody, here's the full model of the Patagonia Picnic Table Effect. The print is pretty small, but if you follow the arrows and think about what's happening in each step and in the minds of the birders involved, it flows pretty well. The loop that converts Inactive Birders to Chasers after hearing a rare bird report is especially intriguing.

## The Patagonia Picnic Table Effect

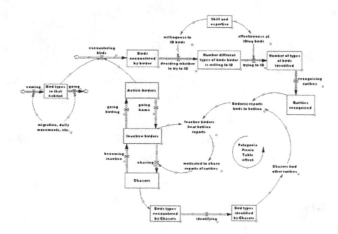

Here's the link to Jody's blog: http://modelbirder.blogspot.com/2012/

I told you birders are cool people. Jody is certainly a great example! Model on, Jody!

Jungle Birding (Kathy Tickner)     It's dry on the porch! (Kathy Tickner)

Amazingly fine dining – soup before the chicken. (Dave Tickner)

Andean Cock-Of-The-Rock          Chestnut-breasted Coronet

(Both Photos – Charlie Hesse)

# 13

# A Trip To Ecuador

*M*y daily journal from 10 days in Ecuador, a gift trip from my friends Dave and Kathy to commemorate my recovery from non-Hodgkin's Lymphoma. The flavor of out-of-the-country birding and the magic of the tropics, with Charlie (part super guide and part eating machine) and Juan Carlos (expert pothole dodger) and an endless stream of chicken & rice.

**"Ecuador - If you don't hurt and you aren't wet, you're not birding!"** - Dave Tickner

*A birding trip to another country is a special kind of adventure, delivering much more than a list of new birds: a different culture, different and delightful food, making change in a different currency, a new and sometimes challenging language, interesting accommodations and modes of travel, and the chance to meet other people in their world. Many birders travel world-wide to see new birds. I'm sure that some buffer themselves from the culture and the people and focus on the birds. I was fortunate to travel to Ecuador with good friends who truly value the full experience. Their appreciation of the differences was evident to me; their recognition of the commonality between people, the struggles, the joys, the strength, the optimism and the humor shared by people around the world added immensely to the magic of the experience for me. This daily journal captures some of the flavor of out-of-the-country birding and perhaps hints at some of the magic. I hope you can experience the magic one day yourself.*

**The Party:** Dave & Kathy Tickner
Tom Striker
Charlie Hesse (Guide)
Juan Carlos Cruz (Driver)
**The Dates:** January 8 – 18, 2009

**Background:** Dave & Kathy are experienced tropics birders. Prior trips included Panama in 2005 and 2006, and Ecuador in 2007 and 2008.

Charlie Hesse guided their trip in 2008, and Juan Carlos Cruz has been their pothole avoider before. This was my first birding adventure outside the United States.

It's relevant to know that Ecuador has nearly 1600 species of birds in a country the size of Arizona. It's also relevant that most of them don't want to be seen. If you had a name like Antpitta, Antshrike, Antthrush, Antvireo, Antwren, Bristle-tyrant, Chat-tyrant, Dacnis, Foliage-gleaner, Ground-tyrant, Guan, Leaftosser, Manakin, Metaltail, Peppershrike, Hemispingus, Piha, Plumeleteer, Pygmy-tyrant, Shrike-tyrant, Spinetail, Tapaculo, Thistletail, Thorntail, Tit-tyrant, Tody-flycatcher, Treehunter, Water-tyrant, Woodhaunter or Xenops, you'd keep your head down, too.

We saw lots of these Antcritters and Miscellaneous-tyrants and were amazed by their diversity, their behaviors and their skulking. We also met a number of proud, poor but not unhappy people, living their lives in a world of board huts, chickens, laundry, motorcycles, rain and beautiful children.

### Day 1 – Thursday, January 8, 2009

Departed Tickner Farm at 0545, in Kathy's car. Dave asked me to drive to preserve his good nature – he hates Atlanta traffic. The drive to Atlanta was smooth. The airport has changed since I last traveled (2001) and even since last year. We were surprised to see all the self-serve check-in stations. We tried our best, only to find that international check-in requires a person. Marcia was very helpful. We had no problems with security and settled in to wait a couple of hours before our flight to Miami.

Our otherwise smooth flight to Miami was filled with boisterous Oklahoma fans arriving for the NCAA BCS college football championship game. We arrived on time, with four hours to wait for our flight to Quito, Ecuador. There is a robust Hispanic or Cuban flavor to the signage, shops and people. Many speak Spanish, and PA announcements are in two languages. I was to learn that I no longer speak Spanish, despite four years of it in high school.

The first chore was to confirm the gate # for our LAN flight 517 to Quito, Ecuador (the capital city, located in an inter-Andean valley at 8500-foot elevation). The electronic scheduling boards didn't have our flight listed yet, so Kathy walked most of the airport trying to pin it down. It turned out Dave and I were already camped at the correct departure gate. We checked in early, got seats together and boarded at 4:30 p.m. I talked to Sonja on the cell phone, and then turned it off. The four-hour flight was smooth, with excellent service, a hot snack and free wine. The snack was chicken, rice and vegetables, served on china with real silverware. It was the first of many encounters with chicken and rice.

Quito's airport was quite busy. Getting through Immigration and Customs took only 45 minutes, partly because we used the *La Tercera Edad* line (The Third Age – meaning old people). Everyone's luggage was carefully dumped off the conveyor, but we found everything. A large crowd was waiting to greet incoming passengers, including Juan Carlos Cruz (our driver) with a sign reading TICKNER X 3. Juan Carlos loaded our stuff, somehow extricated his large van from an impossibly small space and took us to the Eugenia Hotel. The small, older hotel was nice enough but, per Kathy, "a far cry from the Hotel Quito," where they had stayed on previous trips. We were checked in quickly but told that no breakfast would be available at 6:30 the next morning as had been promised.

A partial unpacking and I was ready for tomorrow. I tried to call Sonja using my prepaid international calling card but had failed to download some critical information from the internet and got nowhere. I finally asked the desk clerk for the country code for the US (001) and got through for a brief call at $1.60 per minute. Ecuador uses US currency but has its own coins. I had a welcome shower and shave, and then searched the TV channels in vain for a football score. *CNN Espanol* did provide excellent soccer coverage and I absorbed my first weather *(el tiempo)* forecast in Spanish.

Tomorrow (Friday) we visit Yanacocha Reserve at 10,500 feet and higher. Cool temps and cool birds are in store. Target bird is the Black-breasted Puffleg, a rare and threatened hummingbird.

## Day 2 – Friday - January 9, 2009

*In keeping with daily journal tradition, I got lazy, so the following was written at the end of Day 3. It is a little less detailed (you're welcome). Resolved to get back on track from now on.*

Up at 5:30 a.m. The hotel kept its promise of no breakfast. Juan Carlos and Charlie Hesse, our guide, picked us up at 6:30. Dave & Kathy spotted a Great Thrush and Eared Dove in front of the hotel, our first official Ecuadorian birds. Of course, I saw neither, but got them later in the morning. JC took us through the city and stopped at his favorite bakery where we bought *pan dulce* (sweet bread), a chocolate bun and juice for under a dollar each. Peach juice is a treat!

We drove up through the steep and cloud-draped farm fields to Yanacocha. The farmers use green wood for fence posts; the posts sprout branches and put down roots, forming sturdy and leafy fences. Turns out the cows all have horns and when they reach through the fence for the green grass outside, they often hook those horns in the wire and pull down the fence on the way back in. Living fence posts reduce the damage. I registered Eared Dove in Quito's outskirts and Great Thrush and Chestnut-collared Sparrow in the farmed landscape, but missed on Tawny Antpitta, which is described by experts as "for an Antpitta, easy to see." An omen, perhaps?

We stopped several times to bird on the bumpy road from Quito to Yanacocha. I simply looked where Charlie pointed, and saw many new birds. The Black-chested Buzzard Eagle (would you name YOUR child that?) was spectacular. We parked, peed, and started our five-mile round trip walk up the Yanacocha road, which follows the ancient Inca Trail and happens to cover the pipeline that provides water to Quito. There are plants along this road with leaves big enough to bury your car. The leaves of the *Gunnera* plant are four to six feet across, and each plant has about ten leaves. The plants seem to prefer disturbed soil and are first to colonize the many landslide tracks down these steep slopes.

Hummingbird feeders are clustered at strategic locations along the road, and the hummers are beyond imagination. We saw 18 species on this day, most here at Yanacocha. The best were the Sword-billed Hummingbird with a four-inch-long beak, and the bold but unidentified hummer that took a sip of Kathy's pear while she was biting into the other side.

At day's end we drove and birded our way to Las Gralarias Reserve, headquarters for Mindo Bird Tours, where Jane Lyons welcomed us in her rubber boots. We enjoyed light to heavier rain on the way, which is what the weather is this time of year in Ecuador. (Wait until the RAINY season!) The new lodge is pretty and comfortable, with an excellent dining room. We enjoyed a feast of chicken (!), mashed potatoes and veggie slaw, with the first of our daily bird checklists afterward. I had a bout of digestive gas, but no turista, which is the modern term for Montezuma's Revenge. I was apprehensive about this continuing tomorrow, and a little sheepish about sounding like a trumpeting elephant, but it subsided, and no one complained.

65 species for the day, and 61 (yup – sixty-one) life birds. Tomorrow – we'll bird Las Gralarias for two to three hours, then drive and bird our way to Canande'!

## Day 3 - Saturday - January 10, 2009

Up at 5:30 a.m., breakfast at 6:00. Terrific breakfast – granola, yogurt (pink, liquid, in a pitcher, to be poured over cereal or fruit; not readily available in the US), fruit, scrambled eggs and coffee. We put on the rubber boots for a walk through the rejuvenating forest (Jane is planting trees where they once were and will be again). The weather? Cloudy, misty, with a light drip. The birds were fairly quiet; Charlie was surprised and disappointed. Not to worry – we will return on Thursday for two full days at this elevation and we WILL find the birds.

We left Las Gralarias about 9:00 or so, stopping often to bird during the 6-hour drive to Canande'. One of the best stops was on the three-kilometer access road to Las Gralarias, a timed 16 minutes in or out, over rough terrain. On the way in, uphill, Charlie abandons his shotgun seat for the jump seat in the back of the van to add ballast and traction. My first Woodcreeper, a Seedeater, and chickens grazing the hillside along the contour – this is steep ground.

Our route took us through several small towns with busy shops. These mostly concrete block buildings are cheek-by-jowl, each with roll-up garage doors in the front. Surprisingly, the shops have modern glass-front display cases and are filled with bright merchandise, plastic bags of corn, beverages, prepaid cell phone cards and rubber boots, the footwear of choice in the wettest place on earth. What an entrepreneurial adventure and challenge it must be to open a store!

There are very few cars but lots of small motorcycles. Most carried two or more people, sometimes as many as four, including tiny children. Kathy saw one child sound asleep on the front of the family conveyance. Most people seem very poor, but no one looked under-fed or unhappy. Laundry was hung everywhere (Why? It never has a chance to dry…), and we saw several groups washing clothes in streams, some kids swimming, even a pig bathing in a stream.

Ecuador is the Land of Tanagers. These fruit-eating birds, along with hummingbirds, characterize the birdlife of the country. But – while all animals are equal, some are less equal than others. I was introduced to 'the ultimate junk bird,' the equivalent of the starling or Mourning Dove in Georgia, the Lemon-rumped Tanager. You put it on your daily list because you have to, but you never mention it to a real birder. Of course not – this midnight black bird with a startlingly brilliant yellow rump is too common. To my taste, and Kathy's, it's a pretty awesome bird, and it doesn't skulk! Hell, no – it sits on top of a palm spike and lets you admire it as long as you want. Further, the somewhat less striking female is usually nearby, so you can review the field marks of both. The bill is a silver-blue, contrasting with the black body plumage. Next trip, I'll yawn, but this time it's a favorite bird each day. Other "better" birds today included a Pearl Kite, well north of its usual range, Masked Water Tyrant and Long-tailed Tyrant.

Lunch was at a wide spot in the road that had yielded a rare bird in the past, the Scarlet-breasted Dacnis, and, of course, Charlie found it again and got it in the scope for all to admire. The plastic shel-tered bench was a welcome respite from the seldom-seen sun, and Kathy captured our idyllic lunch on film for Sonja's benefit. A road-side bench is a typical, perhaps even luxurious, travel accommodation in rural Ecuador.

With the roads getting increasingly worse, we wandered through immense palm-oil plantations and eventually reached the ferry crossing on the Rio Canande'. The ferry was out of sight, having been sent to take the once-a-day bus upstream to another road crossing. It was back in 10 minutes or so, and Juan Carlos drove the van onto the floating platform. It was JC's first crossing, but he was very calm and competent. The ferry is a smallish steel raft powered by two long skinny johnboats with Yamaha outboards, perhaps welded to the stern. Four men operate the efficient little ferry, two in the johnboats and two more operating the chain hoists that raise and lower the ramps. The trip is short, perhaps 250 yards, passing a dugout canoe on the shoreline. As soon as the johnboat pilots put the bow on shore, the ramps are lowered, and you get the hell off. No time is wasted. *"Bien hecho!"* says Kathy (well-made or well done!), and we are underway again.

**Speedy crossing of the Canande' River (Kathy Tickner)**

The ferry is operated by the Botrosa Lumber Company, which also maintains the road and is steadily logging the primary forest of the Choco Lowlands. Primary forest means jungle. This company apparently is more selective than some, but the bottom line is that once the big trees are removed, the complex, multi-storied habitat is altered and the microhabitats of the antpittas, antvireos, and tody-tyrants can no longer support these specialized birds. The place we're heading for, *Reserva Canande'*, is a bit of primary forest that has been purchased from Botrosa by the Jocotoco Fundacion (pronounced Hoe-Co-Toe-Co) with the hope of preserving an island of pristine forest that can be added to in the future. I was a forester in an earlier life, and I'm glad I was never assigned to these steep and muddy mountains.

Another 11 uneven kilometers took us to the Reserve. We were greeted by five or six friendly souls, with less combined English than I had Spanish. They wished us welcome and carried our bags to the bunkhouse-style sleeping quarters – a new bungalow of four rooms with a wide covered porch, built entirely out of teak or mahogany. Take off your shoes at the top of the steps. Dave and Kathy were in *Quarto Uno*, with *'el matrimonio'* (a double bed). Let the honeymoon begin again, despite the minimal space around the bed, and never mind the cold showers and open-ventilated bathrooms. I was solo in Quarto Tres, furnished with a single and two bunk beds. One light bulb in the ceiling, another in the bathroom. Charlie and Juan Carlos were next door in *Quarto Quatro*.

A few minutes to revel in the luxury, then I unpacked, washed my delicates in the sink, threw them into the shower for rinsing, and bravely followed them in. Brrrrr – *Mucho frio*! Of course, the neighbors could hear every gasp and snort – the open ceilings connected across all four bathrooms. Despite the initial shock, the shower was refreshing after the hot and humid day of travel and birds. I strung a clothesline across the shower stall and started my open-air dryer.

We walked down the paved switch-backed sidewalk (44 steps, about 200 yards) to the sparkling new dining room for dinner, at the traditional 7:00 time. Our table was set for five, with cloth tablecloth and napkins, and beer, wine and soft drinks available. Kathy and I split a large Pilsener, the national beer, to celebrate our arrival. Excellent dinner - vegetable soup, chicken (surprised?) with rice and veggies. Over the five days we were at *Reserva Canande'*, the cloth napkins would be folded in a different shape for every meal.

Charlie, our guide, has had a storied life to date, but has sworn off alcohol and sugar. Perhaps this explains his amazing capacity for other foods. He mentioned his tour of the US as a younger man, centered on beer and baseball, including Wrigley Field. *Nothing* can explain his eating speed. At any rate, Charlie and Kathy re-established their mealtime ritual of last year, where Kathy would finish her normal half of a generous portion of food, and offer the rest to Charlie, who always accepted graciously. It took the kitchen staff a couple of meals to figure out that Kathy was not a clean-plate-club member, and that Charlie was part of the formula. Dave and I sometimes had extra provisions, which were never refused. Dessert was simple and sometimes sweet – the dining room girls always had a sugar-free treat for Charlie.

After dinner – checklist, orchestrated by Charlie, who had been taking microscopic notes in his notebook all day. For the record, Charlie's notebook has a drawing of kids' animals on the cover. He says, without blushing, that he has a big stack of them. I think notebook economics rather than art drives the selection. We recorded more than 100 species for the day, with 52 life birds for me. Then off to bed. Since the bed was equipped with mosquito netting, I pulled it down, perhaps trapping whatever was already in the bed. Read a bit, lights off at 9:30.

## Day 4 - Sunday - January 11, 2009

Up at 5:30, breakfast at 6:00. I slept pretty well and felt very good when I woke up. At breakfast, Kathy reported in good shape, but Dave had a touch of turista and opted out of the morning birding. Dave confessed later to a worry that this touch would continue and ruin the week for him and for all of us. Thankfully, that was an empty concern. He took a dose of Imodium and was considerably better by lunchtime. Perhaps the tea the kitchen ladies brought him helped; he was impressed and pleased by their consideration and care.

Charlie led Kathy and me on a five-hour "stroll" on the trails – a little muddy, sometimes rough, with many ups and downs. The trails were well maintained, with lots of good steps where needed. We crossed two streams, both quite scenic with crystal clear water. Note – it was not raining. The birding was slow early, but it picked up @ 8:30 or so. We heard Howler Monkeys several times – like a lion's roar. We did have good birds finally; some were quite hard to locate and harder to see well. Charlie is SO good (see my Charlie notes at the end of this journal). Highlights were a Great Tinamou, which we flushed at the second stream crossing. It's a big bird, and it flushed suddenly and loud, like a Wild Turkey launching into flight. We had heard Little Tinamou earlier (never saw one of these much more common little chickens) but didn't expect its big cousin. Another highlight was two or three Choco Toucans at the top of a large tree. Black on the huge bill instead of chestnut – my first look at one of the classic jungle birds!

One scary moment that could have been much worse: I was last in the group and spotted a tiny snake, coiled up in the path. I called out, "I have a snake," in a conversational tone. Charlie started back from his lead position, followed by Kathy. As Charlie retraced his steps, he almost stepped on a much larger snake that then started toward Kathy. She saw it and backed up, asking, "Where should I go?" Charlie identified it as a Bushmaster, a seriously venomous snake, and suggested she back up slowly, since it seemed about to cross the trail on its own. The snake did so, dragging its four-foot length and baseball-bat girth harmlessly across the path and into the forest. Charlie reported that it had brushed his boot as he walked past, although it did not strike.

Of course, no cameras leapt to hand to photograph this prize. After our heartbeats slowed, Charlie came back to my little snake, which slept through the festivities. After a nudge or two, this little guy, which turned out to be a young Hog-nosed Viper (also venomous) allowed himself to be photographed and then slithered way.

No harm, no foul, but we were reminded that we were in wild, remote terrain and far from medical help. We were perhaps an hour's walk from the lodge, and several more hours from the nearest hospital. Be assured that we kept a sharpened eye out for snakes from then on.

We dragged our muddy selves back to the lodge for lunch. A nice salad of lettuce, fruit and cheese, followed by a main course of grilled fish, rice, veggies and fried plantain. Dessert was a custard pudding with a mild grape flavor.

We went back to the porch and bunkhouse to bird and rest and left again at 2:30 to drive and bird the Botrosa Road. We stopped periodically for very good birds and spent an hour or more near the end of the road with five species of parrots, Swallow-tailed Kites, Scarlet-rumped Casique and Chestnut-headed Oropendola. These last two are spectacular blackbird relatives that missed the "We are drab" dress rehearsal.

We returned to camp at 6:25, with dinner set for 7:00. I brushed, shaved and did my laundry, then showered in the cool water provided. After hanging everything, my room looked like the local natives' yards, with ever-wet laundry ever-present. Dinner was chicken soup (for Dave), spaghetti with spicy meat sauce and flan for dessert. We were also served warm, cinnamon-flavored water, an interesting taste.

We did our evening checklist (125 species, a GREAT day, and 65 life birds for me) and made plans for the morrow. A change in routine — up at 4:30, owling at 5:00 on foot on the Botrosa Road! We would return for breakfast at 6:30 or so and then start a full day of birding the rest of the Botrosa Road. Rubber boots were the order of the day, since we would be venturing into the jungle for owls and Choco Poorwill, a relative of the Whippoorwill of Georgia.

## Day 5 - Monday - January 12, 2009

Sure enough, we went owling at 5:00 a.m. Whatever Charlie plans, happens. We walked the Botrosa Road to the right out of camp. After a side trip down a meager woods road, Charlie called a Choco Screech Owl to a tree a few yards away, and we got a great look at it with a flashlight. Back on the road, Charlie picked up the eye shine of a Pauraque, another nightjar cousin. We heard Choco Poorwill, but it wouldn't come in to the call. It was surprisingly light before 6:00 a.m., with large but harmless bats flying overhead. A non-scheduled highlight was a great look at three Howler Monkeys in a palm tree near the road. They were clearly watching us watch them.

Juan Carlos picked us up at 6:30, and we headed back for breakfast – fruit with yogurt, scrambled eggs, toast, juice and coffee. The coffee is strong and not particularly tasty. However, with two sugars and a lot of milk, it kick-starts the day.

We drove the Botrosa Road to the "logging concession" where active logging was underway. There is an understanding between the Botrosa Logging Company and Reserva Canande' that allows birding within the concession, and I expect there is a healthy economic tension between the loggers and the preservationists that will lead to periodic additions to the protected reserves of primary forest managed by Jocotoco Fundacion. I hope the additions are timely enough to protect the very specialized habitats of the funky little birds that make ecotourism work in this part of Ecuador. Otherwise, it's subsistence farming, soccer, laundry, Sunday pool, beer and babies for the local people.

The best birds were Black-tipped Cotinga, a snowy white bird with soft, delicate flight, and a pair of Long-tailed Tyrants on their nest snag. Both species were hanging on in disturbed habitat.

In keeping with any luxurious vacation, we were back in for lunch, highlighted by an interesting green soup, followed by grilled beef and mashed potatoes. We took a half hour break, then headed out on the nearby trails to bird. Since Dave was still recovering from his touch of *turista*, Charlie took us on what was known as the *flat loop*; it would have challenged Sir Edmund Hillary and Sherpa Tensing Norgay. It was long, muddy and by no means flat, plus we walked back the last hour in a steady, hard rain. All of us were wet and tired when the lodge came back into view at 6:10 p.m. Two highlights – a good look at a Crested Guan, which is a huge black/brown bird with a red throat flap, sort of a Jurassic Park chicken, and a decision NOT to force a hike to the top of the ridge to find the Golden-chested Tanager. It was rough and steep and not well suited to the birding wishes and physical capabilities of our group at this point.

We wrapped up a full day with another cold shower (you get used to it,) laundry, dinner and checklist. Dinner started with mushroom soup, BBQ chicken, boiled yucca, tomato & heart-of-palm salad, with an orange half for dessert. I had 20 life birds today! Tomorrow – up at 5:30, *el desayuno* (breakfast) at 6:00. We'll walk the road early, then drive & bird in the afternoon. It's daughter Lynda's 29th birthday tomorrow, the first one I've missed in, oh, 29 years.

## Day 6 - Tuesday - January 13, 2009 HAPPY BIRTHDAY, LYNDIE!

Breakfast of fruit, cereal and liquid pink yogurt. Everyone declined eggs, which seemed to disappoint our dedicated kitchen team. The size of the fruit bowl made eggs impossible.

We walked the Botrosa Road to the right from camp, setting an easy pace to recover from a hard day yesterday. Dave and I had sore legs, Tireless Kathy was OK except for her knees. There is *never* a complaint from these two – a little wry humor is as far as they ever go.

For example (Dave): "If it doesn't hurt, you aren't birdin'!"

After I mentioned that I had shaved last night before my 'cool' shower. I brought it up as we were hiking to lunch. Dave wondered why I shaved with cold water while on a birding trip. Dave claims to be a longtime member, perhaps the founder, of **BAS** (**B**irders **A**gainst **S**having.) Kathy chuckles more than most….

More from Dave, introducing an incredible new birding concept: "ROBE is an important measure for birding. That's **R**eturn **O**n **B**irding **E**ffort – how hard you had to work for what you got. In Ecuador, road birding has a high ROBE – lots of birds with little effort. Forest/trail birding has a lower ROBE – fewer birds, more mud, hills and rain."

ROBE was first explained and documented on this date, simple notes jotted down on a Cecropia leaf since no paper was available. The historic Cecropia leaf was smuggled out of Ecuador in my luggage, risking capture, long imprisonment and worse because of the incredible value of the ROBE concept to birding. My luggage was selected for inspection by the overweight Yellow Lab on security duty at the airport, but the search by dark-uniformed security guards with guns somehow overlooked the precious leaf. The Cecropia leaf is pictured below:

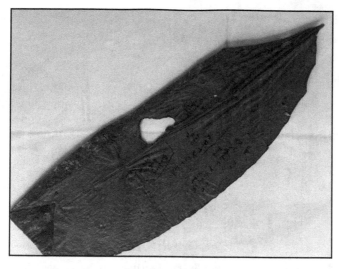

The Cecropia Leaf

## RETURN ON BIRDING EFFORT (ROBE) EXPLAINED

ROBE is an attempt to quantify the benefits received from a birding trip in relation to the effort involved. It was first verbalized by Dave Tickner, Birder Emeritus, on January 13, 2009 during a very long and wet birding day near the Rio Canande' in the Choco Lowlands of Northwest Ecuador. *Much work remains to refine ROBE, but the concept is valid and may transform birding.*

$$\text{ROBE} = \frac{\text{\# of Species X Quality of Birds X Quality of View}}{\text{Effort Required X Time Required}}$$

### Definitions & Values:

**# of Species**    The number of species of birds seen (Subjective Value: 1 to 10)

**Quality of Birds**    Specialness of the birds, including rarity, beauty, in or out of normal range, etc. Life birds are very high quality. Quality is somewhat subjective; Cerulean Warbler is higher quality than Pine Warbler, Green-breasted Mango in Macon, GA is VERY high quality. (Value: 1 to 10)

| | |
|---|---|
| **Quality of View** | How well you saw the birds, how many you saw, special behaviors observed, etc. A spring male Cerulean Warbler, 20 feet away at eye level for 30 seconds is a much better view than a five second vent-view of the same bird in the canopy. (Value: 1 to 10) |
| **Effort Required** | Measured in physical effort, dollar cost and quality of birding companions. Bad weather and physical danger dramatically increase effort. Cost of an expensive trip is ignored when rating individual birding events during the trip. An overall ROBE can be calculated for the entire trip. (Value: 1 to 10) |
| **Time Required** | Time is subjective; an hour waiting with a cup of coffee on your deck for a first-of-the-season hummer is much shorter than an hour shivering in a leaky blind in the rain waiting for Prairie Chickens to boom. (Value: 1 to 10) |

Naively unaware of the significance of the ROBE concept, we headed back to the lodge for lunch. The Cecropia leaf was safely tucked into a vest pocket. Back on the road at 3:00, after porch birding and a 30-minute nap! Juan Carlos took us way down the road to a spot with good forest below the road. There was something dead in the woods that smelled to high heaven, attracting several Black Vultures. Curiously, a dog wandered by and paid no attention to the stink while avoiding us. The best bird was a Crimson-bellied Woodpecker – rare enough in Ecuador to delight Charlie! Juan Carlos picked us up and took us back through an area of small farms. The road was blocked by a truck full of concrete culvert sections, being unloaded by a tractor with a front-end loader. Leaving Juan Carlos and the van in the traffic jam, we walked around the activity, intending to bird our way back on foot. Virtually everyone in the neighborhood had come out to watch, and loud music from huge speakers at a nearby house made it a festive event. We met several local folks walking down to watch, who responded to our gringo-accented *"Buenas tardes!"* with shy smiles.

One of the interesting roadside birds was the Smooth-billed Ani, a big blackbird-like bird with a huge beak and long, floppy tail. It's rare in the United States, but we saw many of them perched on fences in the agricultural areas in Ecuador. Their communal nest is built by two to five pairs, and the adults share incubation and feeding chores. They feed on termites, large insects like cockroaches, and sometimes pick the ticks off cattle. The locals call them *Garrapatero*, meaning tick-eater.

**Rural Ecuador – Happy people despite the poverty. (Kathy Tickner)**

Back to camp by 6:00, with a whole hour before dinner. Shaved (sorry Dave,) took another refreshing shower, and spent some time checking out our new birds in the ponderous but fabulous *Birds of Ecuador*. Dinner was excellent – asparagus soup, pasta w/ chicken and mushrooms (Charlie got mine) and fruit for dessert. I had a whole bottle of the locally brewed Pilsener Beer, which comes in a big bottle.

Checklist – 28 new birds for the area and 17 life birds for me.

Tomorrow – owling at 5:00, breakfast at 6:30, and the rest of the morning on the 'easier' trail loop that Kathy and I did on Sunday while Dave had turista. Then more road birding in the afternoon, weather permitting.

A note on the weather: it has been surprisingly cool for a country that is ON the equator. Elevation has a lot to do with that in Quito (8,500'), at Yanacocha (11,000') and at Las Gralarias (6,000'). It's also been cloudy almost all the time and that keeps things cool. Rain has not been as expected, either. It rains every day, but mainly in the late afternoon and at night. The only hard shower while birding was yesterday as we mucked our way back from a very hard trail walk. ROBE falls rapidly with increasing rain and declining spirits. To deal with the clouds and rain forecast, you just tie your raincoat around your waist and go. Hats are in order, and Kathy carries a tiny umbrella that works fine.

Oh! A highlight of this morning's road walk was two Capuchin Monkeys. Charlie heard them call or hoot, and we finally found them high in a tree near Botrosa Road. Like the Howler Monkeys earlier, they were watching us watch them. Beautiful, big animals, dark brown or black, with cinnamon fur around face and chest. They leaned on their long arms while they watched our curious antics and whispered about living too close to the road.

To bed early, thinking about missing Lynda's birthday, and wishing her a happy day and many more from the Equator.

## Day 7 - Wednesday - January 14, 2009

Up at 4:30, owling by 5:00 on the Botrosa Road. We heard Poorwill very well, but it wouldn't come in where we could see it. We also heard Choco Screech Owl and Mottled Owl. The morning is always special for birding, and this one was no exception. It's nice being outside to watch the day begin.

Breakfast – fruit with yogurt, scrambled eggs and toast. I've pretty well got the coffee recipe worked out, with lots of sugar and milk. If I slurp quickly, I can get two cups down before Charlie's chair scrapes, announcing that breakfast is over. We birded "easy" trails from 7:00 to noon or so. No rain at all and excellent views of many birds including Indigo-crowned Quail Dove and Red-capped Manakin. Dave's claim: "The best forest birding day we've ever had!"

Lunch was a wonderful salad of tuna on lettuce with tomato and cucumber, and then Chinese fried rice with chicken (imagine that), peas and carrots blended in.

Porch birding after lunch, then a 30-minute nap. It was raining at 3 p.m., so we dawdled a bit, then drove toward the river to car-bird. We only had a short dry window, so we spent extra time in the van. Kathy talked a little about her teaching assignments in Eastern Europe and the recently liberated USSR in the early nineties. Dave told stories about Harris Corporation, including his responsibility for escorting the dependents of the employees out of Iran when the Shah was overthrown.

Cell phone service is excellent in most of Ecuador but doesn't measure up near Reserva Canande'. Juan Carlos has found several high spots where service is available if you stand up straight and position your feet just so. He said the ground around all these 'phone booths' is littered with prepaid cell phone calling cards. You can tell when the phone booth is in use by the small motorcycle parked at the base.

Back to camp around 5:00 for porch birding. I did a little prepacking for tomorrow's departure (already?) and did my last sink load of laundry before relishing what I hope is my last cold shower for this trip. Dinner was excellent – noodle vegetable soup, then a hamburger patty with 'freedom' fries (*papas fritas* – you may still call them French Fries), broccoli and green beans. The cold beer was perfect with dinner, and we enjoyed tea during checklist.

Checklist was quick tonight – a relatively short list, with just 11 new ones for my list.

This is our last night at Reserva Canande'. Five quick nights, four days of good to excellent birding. Breakfast will be early tomorrow, with an hour or two of road birding on foot, and a 9:00'ish departure for Las Gralarias. Canande' has been very good, with comfortable accommodations and excellent food.

**Day 8 - Thursday - January 15, 2009**

Up at 6:00, breakfast at 6:30 – we ate fruit and toast, although eggs were offered. We birded the road on foot until about 8:00, then packed and left for the ferry crossing. We took a picture of the *Bienvenidos* sign, which turned out to be another phone booth. We stopped again a little farther down the road, near some Cecropia trees with lots of fruit, which is a favorite of tanagers. Emerald Tanager and Scarlet & White Tanager visited the fruit while we watched, both excellent and sought-after birds that we had missed earlier.

Next stop was the Rio Canande' ferry crossing. We were concerned about high water after all the rain, but no problem and no waiting. The road from the river to lunch was long and rough and I had had too much coffee and juice this morning. No stops, so the last hour before lunch was quite long. I had noted that Kathy is very careful about fluid intake while birding and learned anew why her method was right.

We stopped in the middle of a heavy downpour at a little restaurant in Los Bancos, called Mirador Rio Blanco. It caters to birders, and we were able to enjoy our tea and coffee while admiring the birds that visited the hummer feeders and fruit feeders right outside the huge and clean windows. We had great looks at Palm and Blue-gray Tanagers, which had been only spots in the canopy earlier, and added a new beauty – Silver-throated Tanager. We also saw Pallid Dove at six feet; until now, this beauty had been nothing but a haunting call in the jungle!

The coffee at La Mirador was excellent (MUCH better than at Canande') and served with hot *leche'*. Do I mention food enough in the journal? And did I mention that it was raining like hell and had been for most of the afternoon? We watched a little TV news, in Spanish of course – US Airways Flight 1549, with 155 souls on board, had made an emergency landing in the Hudson River. and Tommy Muniz died. We learned later that all aboard the aircraft survived, thanks to Captain Chesley "Sully" Sullenberger, his skilled flight crew and quick rescue work on the river. Our best guess was that Tommy Muniz was a comic actor of some renown. We still don't know who won the BCS Football Championship.

Charlie struck up a conversation with a young Israeli man who had just begun a three-month birding adventure in Ecuador. Charlie is outgoing, with a ready smile, and gave him some helpful tips about where to go and who to contact. In return, he got some great info about birding in Israel and Jordan, places he will bird for the first time in March or April when he visits his new Swedish girlfriend, who works for the Red Cross in the Middle East.

A short drive brought us to Las Gralarias. Jane Lyons greeted us enthusiastically and began pumping us about our week's birding. As we talked, the lights flickered a few times and then the power went out completely. It was to stay out until 1:00 p.m. Friday, and as I write this by candlelight at 6:55 p.m. Friday, it went out again! Jane would tell us Friday that most of Ecuador was without power. Terrorism? Bad wiring? Landslides? Who cares? The real deal was that the much-anticipated hot shower was out, after five days of cold ones, and dinner was by candlelight. Fish, hot rolls, and lentils for dinner, with a fabulous dessert of passion fruit, oranges and cream. Checklist was also done by candlelight – 15 life birds.

## Day 9 - Friday - January 16, 2009

Well rested, and only slightly aromatic, we birders were up at 0400. Still no electricity, as the country-wide conspiracy continued. Kathy quoted Juan Carlos, as he emerged from his room in the dark: *"No hay luz, no hay agua, no hay nada!"* (There is no light, there is no water, there is nothing!). Kathy gifted me later with a T-shirt adorned with those words that I treasure.

Despite the gloom, we were off to the famous Angel Paz Reserve, home of the Andean Cock-of-the-Rock and hand-fed Antpittas. We arrived at 0515 and joined two other groups for the slippery walk down to the Cock-of-the-Rock lek in the dark. This lek is used daily throughout the year and is busiest during mating season in June when 15 to 20 bright red, gray and black Cocks–of-the-Rock really put on a show.

Dave and Kathy had been here in 2007 and told tales of slipping and sliding while trying to hang on to their flashlights. Two years later it was still wet and slick, but new steps and rope handrails had been installed, so the trip was much less hairy than last time - timing is everything. We arrived at a thatch-roofed blind, crowded in as comfortably as 14 strangers can, and immediately heard the birds. I mentioned their red, black and gray coloration – think of a GIANT Scarlet Tanager, with intense blood-red head, back, chest, belly and rump, and black wings and tail. Then add a big patch of inner flight feathers that cover the lower back with pearly gray. Top it off with a huge, red, laterally compressed hump of feathers that cover the bill. Oh, forget it – you had to be there. Put it on your bucket list.

During breeding season, the show involves many males and the females even show up on occasion to be impressed. According to Charlie, only one or two of the most dominant males mate with all the females. The rest of the boys are jockeying for position for next year. During the winter off-season, far fewer birds show up, but the status-determining or -confirming work is done anyway. We saw three males, enough to get the idea.

We moved on to watch Senor Angel Paz call and feed Giant and Yellow-breasted Antpittas. His patience and consistency with these funny little birds has built enough trust with "Maria" and "Willie" that they come out into the open when he calls, to eat bits of worms while a bunch of ecotourist birders watch. Angel is very clear with the birders, directing them where to stand and what not to do. He has turned a strange hobby into an ecotourism industry; he charges for the 'lek and worms' tour, serves you breakfast afterward, and then sells you a t-shirt, hat, photograph, wooden pot or binocular harness, all emblazoned with his name and logo. All this takes place in the middle of his raspberry farm, with a few cows scattered around for authenticity.

We tramped up the hill for tea, coffee and plantain balls, served by Angel and his family. Juan Carlos, who did not join us for the birds, played some kind of gambling game with coins with two of Angel's boys. I don't know who had more fun; Juan Carlos claimed to be the big winner.

Dave had chosen not to take the last and steepest stretch down the hill to see the Yellow-breasted Antpitta. He birded his way back up, pausing to watch the hummingbirds at the feeding station on the edge of the raspberry orchard, then getting his boots washed by Angel's daughter. He struck up a conversation with Rodrigo, Angel's brother, who told him about the problems of too much rain on raspberries (they rot) and eventually showed him a female Orange-breasted Fruiteater on her nest. Pretty good communication, given Dave's limited command of Spanish and Rodrigo's almost non-existent English. We all trooped up the road later to see the bird, whose green coloration was perfect camouflage. The bird literally materialized before my eyes after I'd looked right at her for 10 seconds or so.

Our companions at Senor Paz' Reserve included a delightful couple from Scotland who had recently spent a week in the Galapagos Islands. She sounded like a classic Scot, but he confessed to being from South Africa after I accused him of being a fake because of his more British accent. A group of four very serious guys turned out to include the number two birder in the world, John Hornbuckle. The ranking is based on the size of your World List – Hornbuckle's is in the 8,400 range. Charlie knew who he was and chatted him up a bit. Somehow, I converted Hornbuckle to Hornblower, which delighted Charlie. With a grin, Charlie asked to see Hornblower's hands; said he'd seen his hands so many times in learned birding journals, holding banded birds, that he was sure he'd recognize him from his hands alone. Anyway, Hornblower was miffed because he 'needed' Moustached Antpitta for his life list, and Senor Paz had not been able to coax one into view, despite a gallant effort. Charlie commented later that the young birding guide leading Hornblower's group was under a lot of pressure to produce.

We visited Milpe Reserve in the afternoon, a small wooded park just off the highway. It produced some good birds, including the Club-winged Manakin, which makes a sound with its wings that sounds exactly like a big truck's back-up alarm. Rain eventually drove us out, but we ate lunch under cover in their nice gazebo, watching a herd of hummers at the standard array of feeders. Lunch was a big bowl of cantaloupe and guava fruit, followed by two personal-size pizzas each. Charlie helped with the surplus.

We headed back to Las Gralarias in the rain. The road was steep and wet enough that Charlie moved from his shotgun seat in front to the back of the van for ballast. The power was on when we arrived – hot showers were once again in the offing, but only after Jane adjusted her on-demand hot water equipment. Then – heaven! Dave knuckled under and shaved and was immediately banished from BAS. Jane's cook and waitress, local sisters, came in and lit a fire in the fireplace. We warmed our buns and then hung socks on the screen to finally dry. Juan Carlos went home to Quito to see his family. He'll be back tomorrow, prepared for a three-week birding tour as Charlie's driver with two Brits that he'll pick up at the airport on his way back.

With dinner scheduled for 7:00, the power went out again at 6:45. The candlelit dinner was wonderful – chicken curry, tomato and cheese salad, *zanahorias* (carrots) and a bowl of something green. The lights came back in time for checklist – 28 life birds today, the higher number because we were at a different elevation which supported different birds. Moving a few hundred feet up or down in Ecuador can take you into or out of a microhabitat with different plants and critters.

Jane showed us her other guests as we left the dining room. When the lights are on, hundreds of moths of many species are attracted to the well-lit wall outside the dining room. There's also a friendly Tarantula that hangs out on the wall near the boot-washing faucet. It's recommended that you shake out your boots before putting them on in the morning. Don't want to squish a spider, do you?

I'm writing this by candlelight; the power went out yet again at 8:45. No matter – I've had a shower and bed is next. Breakfast is at 6:00 tomorrow, then fill-in birding with Charlie around Las Gralarias. We'll meet Jesus, our return-to-Quito driver, in the morning. Then lunch with Jane, Charlie, Juan Carlos, Jesus and the two Brits, who are brothers on their third trip to Ecuador. Charlie and Juan Carlos will take them straight back to Reserva Canande' for four days, and then head south for the rest of the trip. Tomorrow is our last birding day. After lunch we'll head for Quito and the Hotel Eugenia with Jesus. On Sunday morning, we fly home. A long week has somehow passed, yet a very short week in many ways.

**Day 10 - Saturday - January 17, 2009**

Breakfast at 6:00 was quick. Still raining and still no power. Kathy didn't feel well and declined both breakfast and birding. Jesus, our driver back to Quito, was here already. With Jesus at the wheel (quite an image, don't you think?) Dave, Charlie and I spent the morning at several rainy locations, but under cover, with good birds (15 lifers!) We met a couple from New Mexico, living in Ecuador for seven months, and building a house on land next to Jane's. No idea why they left the US or how they wound up in the restaurant where we met them. We shared a cup of coffee on the covered patio, watching the hummers on the nearly empty feeders. As we watched, the owner brought out a full feeder; the birds knew it was full and were on it before the owner's hand fully let go.

We drove through the town of Mindo, headquarters of the first dedicated Important Bird Area set up by Jane Lyons when she settled in Ecuador with a conservation agenda 15 or so years ago. It remains a birder's Mecca, full of hotels, hostels, and cafes with bird themes. Dave remembered being here two years ago with Edison Buenano, the guide for that trip. Hoping to see Torrent Duck, which favors rushing streams, we visited the bridge that produced a "Torrent Donkey" for Dave and Kathy on the earlier trip. As they were birding nearby, a donkey wandered from under the bridge, braving the fierce current, and headed for an island where it apparently spent some of its time. A member of their party dubbed it a Torrent Donkey to honor its bravery in wading the *Rio Nambillo*. Today, the river was truly a torrent, but with neither duck nor donkey in sight. We did see Ringed Kingfisher, Spotted Sandpiper and Black Phoebe, which also adorns fences in the American West.

Back to Las Gralarias for lunch. The power was back on and Kathy was feeling much better. We met Charlie's new clients from England, brothers named Keith and something else. Despite his British speech, Keith was very nice and easy to understand. His portly brother, whose name I didn't catch after he said it twice, was grumpy and spoke in a rumble not recognizable to me as English. *Buena suerte*, Charlie!

We did our last checklist, and I bought a couple of souvenirs from Jane. I gave Juan Carlos a new Vortex cap and a tip for his kindness and trouble. Dave and Kathy invited Charlie to visit Georgia – he seemed interested and might show up one day. It was a somewhat sad farewell; we enjoyed Charlie very much and we all "got on" quite well. Dave mentioned something his son Paul had spoken of, from his own life as a fishing guide: "You can't and don't allow yourself to get attached to your clients, even though they may welcome friendship. Clients go home, and you have to dedicate yourself to your next party."

We left for Quito at 3:00. We talked and laughed about the week, the ups and downs, the food and the people. And, of course, the birds. The hotel was ready for us and promised to bring breakfast to our rooms this evening. Wow!

I called Sonja at 5:15 – this call cost me ten bucks and was well worth it – it was a joy to hear her voice! I had thought yesterday that the only bad thing about the trip was being completely out of touch for so long. She said exactly that right away. It was a brief chat, with promises for more once I reached Miami. She is fine, the store is good, the kids are fine, but she promised two big issues for later. So – home tomorrow. We've been gone at least a month, or was it 15 minutes? A knock on the door about 9:00 this evening brought the promised breakfast. It turned out to be a single slice of ham on white bread and a glass of OJ. An echo ran through my mind, "a far cry from The Hotel Quito!" Jesus will pick us up at 6:30. We expect only a brief hassle at the airport, and our plane leaves at 9:20.

## Day 11 - Sunday - January 18, 2009 ...... And, so it ends.

Jesus picked us up at the hotel and took us to the airport in plenty of time. It was a glorious morning, the first real sunshine we've had all week. Quito sits in an inter-Andean Valley, with the city washing up the slopes on either side. In the sunshine, it is a beautiful sight, despite the peeling paint. The mountains are so green, and the sky a particular high-altitude shade of blue. The trip to the airport takes only a few minutes – it seemed like a long trip the evening we arrived.

The airport is not busy, and the uniformed staff is pleasant. American airports and airlines should take note. We quickly check in, hand off our luggage and head for the "vig" line, where we each pay our $40.80 USD "Exit Fee" – governments everywhere seem to know how to steal from the people.

We drift through the winding line of gift shops toward the airline gates. No one is looking for anything in particular, although Dave reveals after a while that he wants some Mello hard candies, which are more to his taste than anything he has found in the States. We enter a shop he remembers from last year, but it no longer carries this Ecuadorian candy. I find a magnet for Sonja's refrigerator, that Kathy will no doubt turn upside down on her next visit (she's shiftier than her innocent look might say), and Kathy splurges (her term) on a beautiful and authentic shoulder bag. Dave, sweet tooth unsatisfied, buys *nada*.

We find a coffee bar and get a cup of coffee at American prices. Kathy offers me her Hotel Eugenia sandwich, which she has been protecting in her carry-on; I refuse politely, then remember how scrumptious mine was and accept. Such is our departure day breakfast....

Off to the gate, where we are questioned and allowed in. But, security is onto us and in a few minutes, Kathy is whisked away to have her luggage searched. She returns in a while to tell me that I am the one being questioned. It seems that all of our bags were registered under Kathy's name, but the bag they wanted to search was mine.

Remember the leaf on which the ROBE formula was written? I have it in my bag, tucked into the handwritten version of this journal – could the drug dogs have sniffed it out?

The tiny female security person leads me and three other hapless travelers to the baggage area, a covered shed that felt like it was too close to the airplanes on the runway. Under the watchful eyes of several young, lean soldier types in gray and black camo uniforms, my veteran suitcase is opened and searched.

You should know that this generously sized, wheeled, blue Samsonite bag had been to Italy and France during my Emory post-graduate international business trip, to New Zealand with my Dad, carrying his junk to a rendezvous with his WW II memories after his recovery from leukemia therapy, and back to Europe in 2001 to visit Sonja's homeland, where I bounced it down the escalator off the carefully engineered baggage cart I tried to take backwards down the moving stair. It had history and pride and integrity, and here it was, $3.00 lock mysteriously broken, being fondled by a corrupt official of the Ecuadorian Government. It contained no drugs, no booze, no contraband, and no souvenirs (Sonja's magnet was in my pocket), and somehow my dirty undies, damp socks, and rubber barn boots kept my illegal but valuable leaf safe from discovery.

Interestingly, the closest drug dog was a handsome but slightly pudgy Yellow Labrador, who checked our status later as we walked through the passageway from waiting area to plane. He was a good judge of character and sock odor both times and ignored me and my bag.

I was escorted back to the waiting area; all of us, including our airport security escort, were frisked and electro-wanded as we re-entered the main terminal. Dave and Kathy breathed a huge sigh of relief at my apparent innocence, and we soon were cleared for boarding.

The plane was full, but boarding was smooth. Dave and I were together, thanks to a gracious fellow passenger who traded seats with one of us, but Kathy was in the middle seat of the middle row, four or five aisles away. She waved gaily and settled into her isolation. You may remember her rule about minimal liquids during travel; once again it served her well. A breakfast of omelet, yogurt and fresh pineapple was served; both Dave and Kathy lamented later that this was the last truly fresh pineapple they would see until the next birding trip. We all somehow passed up the opportunity to buy duty-free Scotch, fancy watches and French perfume, and dutifully filled out our immigration paperwork.

An easy flight to Miami. Dave dozed a bit, but woke up when I pointed out a long, narrow sandbar in the middle of the Caribbean, which I have since been unable to relocate with MapQuest and Google Earth. It was Robinson Crusoe's island, with nothing within a thousand miles and certainly an idyllic retreat except during hurricane season. We took a peek at Cuba as we passed over it, with neat fields and roads, and arrived in Miami on time.

Customs got one more shot at my Cecropia leaf in Miami, but we cleared with flying colors. The lines were fairly long but moved along well. Once we got to the desk, we were cleared immediately. I was amazed at the number of Latino folks who were in the American Citizen line. Ahead of us in line was a young woman who had been Kathy's seatmate. She was a mountain-climbing guide who had applied to several colleges in the mountainous parts of the US ("I have to be near mountains," she told Kathy,) and had come to the States to speed up the dual-citizen visa process that would allow her to qualify for financial aid from these schools. We picked up our bags, checked them through to Atlanta, and walked the parts of the airport Kathy hadn't seen on our way through last week to our gate.

I called Sonja, and after a warm reunion, caught up on the two 'big' issues she had kept from me last night. She had processed most of a home refinance and I was to meet the appraiser tomorrow, and there was a couple interested in buying our bird store. A relatively short wait in Miami, and we were on our plane, bound for Atlanta. Another easy flight – how can one ask for easier travel conditions? We picked up our bags, shuttled to the Park N Ticket lot and found Kathy's car undamaged. I re-enacted my role of Atlanta Driver and got us back to Epworth before 9:00 p.m. A quick hug and I was headed up Lickskillet Road for home. No way to say an adequate thanks to Dave and Kathy for a fabulous journey but delighted to be back in Georgia. In short, an unbelievable adventure, loaded with birds and memories, never to be forgotten. Would I go back? Emphatically YES, but only when the time is right, and I'd like Sonja to somehow share in the adventure and the wonder. For now, as Dorothy said: "There's no place like home."

## Post-trip Thoughts and Comments

*Note: These things cropped up while I was jotting down journal notes each day. They didn't fit the daily nature of a journal, but I didn't want to miss the thought when it came up.*

The local people are very pleasant – they wave, smile and toot their horns when they pass. Their homes are small, made of unpainted boards, with window holes but no glass. Many are on poles so there's room underneath for tools, chickens, the occasional cow or donkey, a motorcycle and laundry.

**A typical rural Ecuador home place. (Kathy Tickner)**

These people don't walk if they can ride. In the Canande' area, it's a long way to anywhere, so hitching a ride makes sense. There are very few cars, but lots of little motorcycles, often with two or more aboard. Many have three riders and four is not unusual. The front rider is usually a youngster, held in place by an older sibling behind. Everyone seems matter-of-fact about the crowding and the baby in front is sometimes sound asleep. Other transport includes small horses and donkeys. One horse had three kids on top. No open truck goes by empty – 4 to 15 *campesinos* is the usual load. We saw one road grader with four or five on the 'hood', three in the cab and three more on the back.

If you look up *Guia de los Aves* (Birding Guide) in your Spanish dictionary, you should find a picture of Charlie Hesse, our guide. His Spanish is excellent, allowing him to flirt with the kitchen girls and tell Juan Carlos, our driver, where we're going. He's extremely knowledgeable, focused, tireless, patient, great with his clients, tolerant of dumb questions and poor memories, has a great sense of humor, superior vision and even better hearing. I'd have seen about 11 species of birds on my own. And - Charlie can eat! He inhales his food while the rest of us are adjusting our napkins and choosing a fork. Then he waits patiently for Kathy to offer her extra. To balance, Charlie eats no sugar and quit drinking years ago.

Recreation is big! We drove by a soccer tournament on Sunday in Ocha, with several teams playing on a concrete pad and lots of fans watching. A little rain doesn't stop the action. Pool is popular with the young men. We saw several pool tables outdoors, but always under cover in a carport-like covered area attached to a house or store. A couple of places had two tables, possibly for tournaments.

According to Charlie, Sunday's goal is to get ripping drunk – many young guys were drinking beer and playing pool when we drove thru Ocha village. We passed a rustic roadhouse on the way out from Canande' with the typical architecture – an unpainted shed with beer posters in the windows and an attached lean-to covering the requisite pool table. A picture of Jesus was pasted to the door between the main building and the pool area. My comment, "Jesus is my bartender" drew a chuckle from Kathy.

Rubber boots are clumsy but worth it. They hurt like hell to start, 'cuz your toes jam against the front on the downhills but fit and comfort improve over time. Easy on and off, wash the mud off with a hose. Just be sure to shake them out each morning! Charlie had a frog in his one day, which did not survive the ride. Scorpions and tarantulas can add excitement to the daily boot-shaking!

Other conclusions:

I'd be a better birder if I could see.

I'd be a better birder if I could hear.

I'd be a better birder if I really worked at it.

I'll never get tired of Swallow-tailed Kites.

**THE 2009 ECUADOR BIRDING CREW**
From left: Dave Tickner, Kathy Tickner, Tom Striker, Charlie Hesse, Juan Carlos Cruz

# PART FOUR:
## LESSONS FROM THE BIRD STORE

*Bird feeding is second only to gardening as a hobby in the United States. It's pretty simple, right? Buy a plastic feeder at the big box store and a bag of bird food with lots of colorful seeds at the grocery store. Add a hummingbird feeder when you're ready and nail a pretty bird house to a tree for the bluebirds. Sometimes it all works - for a while. More often, the feeder gets chewed up by squirrels, a lot of the seed gets thrown overboard and rots or sprouts under the feeder. The hummer feeder becomes a sugar buffet for ants and picks up some mold in the corners. And the cute bird house is shunned by your blue-birds and stays vacant or is colonized by paper wasps who build a big and dangerous nest.*

*My experience as the owner of a bird feeding supply store con-vinced me of two things: you can have a lot more success attracting birds if you have a little guidance; and you don't have to spend any more money to do it right. Choosing the right seed is your most im-portant decision. You have lots of quality feeder choices, and there are ways to deal with squirrels and other critters. You can have humming-birds without ants or yellow jackets, and bluebirds will happily use a well-designed house in the right location. Finally, you can be a Purple Martin landlord with a reasonable investment and serious attention to the details.*

*I've heard a lot of success stories from customers and talked to feeder manufacturers, seed suppliers and bird experts over the years, and have included some fun details about bluebirds, hummers and martins that you may not have seen before.*

**The Fixin's - The "Good Stuff" in Birdman's Blend**

**A truly Squirrel-proof Feeder**          **Where is YOUR cat today?**

# 14

# Feeding Birds, and A Word About Cats

*Choosing the right seed and avoiding the junk! Different seed attracts different birds, with a variety of feeders for maximum success. Notes on my triumphant battle to trademark Birdman's Blend™. A sermon on free-roaming cats and research highlights on their destructiveness and the trouble the cats get into when allowed to roam.*

Over 60 million people feed birds in the United States, a hobby second only to gardening. Its widespread popularity is fairly recent, but bird feeding had some early fans. The concept of a backyard bird sanctuary goes back several centuries in Europe, where it was considered good luck to have storks nesting on the chimney and swallows nesting under the eaves. Henry David Thoreau scattered corn and bread crumbs outside his cabin on Walden Pond in 1845. Modern, year-round bird feeding may have originated in Mrs. E. B. Davenport's yard in Brattleboro, Vermont, according to Florence Merriam in her book, *Birds of Village and Field*, published in 1898.

I've been feeding birds for about 50 years and have learned a little bit from personal experience. I learned a lot more once we opened our bird-feeding supply store in north Georgia in 2003. Buying and testing seed and feeders ourselves allowed us to make solid, fact-based recommendations to our customers, getting them off to a good start or solving the problems that had frustrated them for years.

A bewildering variety of seed and feeders is available, and many folks plunge right in and wind up wasting time and money before they have much success. Others quit feeding because of the mess on porches and in gardens, or because squirrels dominate their feeders.

People wonder if feeding birds is harmful to birds by interfering with their natural search for food or making them dependent. Watching bird activity at your feeders will tell you that most birds are not there most of the time, and in fact continue their restless and constant search for natural food. During late summer and fall, when natural food supplies are at their peak, the question I heard most often in my shop was "Where are the birds?" The birds were out living their normal lives, ignoring fully stocked feeders!

My conclusion after 50 years of feeding birds in all seasons and in nine states is that feeding is not harmful if feeders and bird baths are kept clean and feeding is consistent. Starting a sizable feeding program and then not continuing it during times when natural food is scarce almost certainly puts birds at risk. Mid-to-late winter and early spring are critical times, when natural food is exhausted and extreme cold, snow or freezing rain can put birds in jeopardy.

Widespread bird feeding has undoubtedly changed the behavior of some birds, teaching them that feeders could be reliable sources in their unending search for food. Watching Northern Cardinals feeding their youngsters on a deck rail or branch near your feeder is compelling testimony. Increases in suitable habitat and consistent feeding have contributed to the northward expansion of historically 'southern' species like Northern Cardinal, Tufted Titmouse and Red-bellied Woodpecker. Recent studies have shown that nesting success is slightly better where winter feeding occurs.

Although the benefits to birds are pretty clear, most people feed birds for their own enjoyment, so they can see them better, see more variety, and enjoy the beauty of their plumage and their songs. As a customer once told me, feeding birds is relaxing and can be an affordable and effective substitute for professional counseling or therapy, at a little over $1.00 a pound!

Keep this in mind as you start or expand your bird-feeding program: The advice and knowledge you get from an independent "bird store" or franchise like Wild Birds Unlimited far outweigh the false economy at big box stores. The big boxes stock their shelves with bird stuff but often carry low-end products and junk seed and there's no bird expert on staff to help you make good choices. Some progressive hardware stores, nurseries and garden centers have begun to recognize the year-round value of a well-stocked bird-feeding department. A smaller number employ a knowledgeable birder to help customers make smart choices of seed and feeders. You may pay a little more at a specialty shop, but you'll only pay it once!

**Seed – Your Most Important Decision**

*Choosing a high-quality seed is the single most important decision you will make.* Sunflower seed should be the heart of your backyard feeding program, and black oil sunflower seed is the most popular choice. Its thin shell and high oil content make it a nutritious choice that can be cracked and eaten by most birds. Striped sunflower seed is larger, with a bigger kernel, but the shell is too thick to be cracked by many smaller species.

Many quality mixes add other seeds to broaden the appeal for the greatest diversity of birds – safflower, sunflower meats or chips, shelled peanuts and white proso millet are all quality ingredients in the right proportions. Very fancy blends may add pecans, other tree nuts and dried fruit. All these additives drive costs up, sometimes without attracting any more variety than a much simpler blend.

---

**CHEAP SEED WARNING**: Many apparently inexpensive "wild bird blends" contain large quantities of milo, cracked corn, red millet or wheat. These *filler* seeds bulk up the weight and lower the price but are generally not eaten by wild songbirds that come to backyard feeders. Up to 75 percent of these blends are not eaten and wind up on the ground under your feeders where they sprout into weed patches, rot or attract rodents. Snakes sometimes follow the rodents.

---

Milo is the seed of the sorghum plant, a group of once-wild grasses native to Africa and Asia that have been domesticated and cultivated for thousands of years. It has been a critical staple food for poor rural people in the semi-arid tropics of Africa and Asia for centuries. More recently it has been grown as fodder for livestock. Milo, or grain sorghum, is the third most important cereal grain crop grown in the United States and the fifth most important world-wide.

While milo is used as a bulk filler in inexpensive seed blends and is not favored by most backyard birds, it can be a good addition to seed mixes for some birds, particularly in the West. According to Melissa Mayntz, a veteran birder who writes frequently for birding magazines, Wild Turkeys, Ring-necked Pheasants and Gambel's and California Quail will readily accept milo, as will Western Scrub Jays (now split into California Scrub-Jay and Woodhouse's Scrub Jay),

Steller's Jays, Eurasian-collared Doves, White-winged Doves and Rock Pigeons. It will be eaten by ground-feeding birds like Common Grackles, Brown-headed Cowbirds and European Starlings, which are not necessarily welcome additions to your backyard because of their tendency to crowd out more desirable species.

In the Eastern US, milo is pretty much a filler in seed blends, and most of it winds up on your patio or on the ground, where it rots or sprouts if not cleaned up. The spilled milo can attract possums and bears, even if you're taking your feeders indoors at night. It will also attract rodents and rodents attract snakes. Read the label and avoid any mix that contains milo!

As a long-time owner of a bird-feeding supply store, I looked at a lot of promotional materials from quality manufacturers hawking their feeders. I was amazed at how many of these ads contained pictures of beautiful feeders filled with what I consider to be junk seed, light on sunflower and heavy on millet, cracked corn and milo. Whoever was responsible for working with the ad agency wasn't involved enough with personal backyard feeding to understand what a negative impression these pictures made on knowledgeable buyers like me.

By law, the components of all bird seed mixes must be listed in order of content on the label. Read the label and avoid blends with milo, red millet and wheat. "Cheap" seed is actually more expensive than high-quality seed in terms of cost per pound of edible seed or cost per bird fed. The mess and the risk of attracting unwanted critters are included at no extra charge.

I created a cheap seed display in my shop to show people how much junk seed was in a typical wild bird blend. I sorted a five-pound bag from the grocery store and put the components in plastic containers, as shown in the photo. Sorting those little seeds was challenging and I made a mess in my wife's kitchen that I'm still hearing about.

## Here's what I found in a 5-pound bag:

| | | |
|---|---|---|
| **Black Oil Sunflower** | 5 ounces | Give Sunflower an "A" grade |
| **White Proso Millet** | 18 ounces | Give Millet a "C+" or "B-"grade |
| **Milo** | 57 ounces | Give Milo an "F" in the East, a "D"in the West |

**From Left: Milo (4 Cups) Millet (1 ½ Cups) Sunflower (Less Than ½ Cup)**

## Other seeds that can be offered separately or in blends:

Sunflower Meats (shelled sunflower): The kernels of sunflower, sunflower meats are like peeled shrimp for birds. They are very nutritious, with no waste at all. Because there is no protective shell, sunflower meats are vulnerable to mold and deterioration. Sunflower meats are also expensive, so offer no more than can be eaten within a day or two.

Safflower: This medium-sized white seed is not quite as well liked as sunflower by most birds, but is very attractive to Cardinals, House Finches, Mourning Doves and others. It's a great additive to a quality mix. Interestingly, Common Grackles don't like it at all. Better yet, a feeder filled with safflower seed can be hung unprotected from squirrels since most squirrels will not eat it. Make it a part of your feeding program. It may take several days for your birds to become accustomed to safflower seed, so be patient if you haven't offered it before.

White Proso Millet: This tiny, buff-colored seed is inexpensive and a nice addition to sunflower seed in mixes for ground feeders like sparrows, towhees and doves. It's the preferred seed for Painted Buntings.

Niger/Nyjer: This tiny black seed is the preferred food for goldfinches. Redpolls, Pine Siskins, House and Purple Finches love it as well, as do Cassin's Finch and Rosy-finches in the West. Once mistakenly called thistle, Nyjer seed is the fruit of a species of aster plant (*Guizotia abyssinica*) native to Ethiopia in Africa, and now also grown in India. The Wild Bird Feeding Industry (WBFI) recently trademarked the name Nyjer to help with pronunciation and reduce confusion with the less desirable thistle seed.

Nyjer has a short shelf life as a result of the heat treatment required by the U. S. Department of Agriculture (USDA) when it is brought into the United States. Heat treatment is required to prevent germination of weed seeds that may be part of the mix.

Finches will reject feeders containing stale Nyjer seed; this is the primary cause of complaints about failure to attract finches. A newly purchased bag of Nyjer doesn't ensure freshness, since many big box retailers warehouse it for a long time before sale. Inquire about the freshness of Nyjer when you buy it or buy it exclusively from a birding specialty shop or other reputable supplier. Damp or wet Nyjer will be rejected as well, so check your feeder after wet weather and remove any wet clumps.

Nyjer & Chopped Sunflower: This mix of Nyjer and finely chopped sunflower meats is a recent addition to the seed shelf. It is more attractive to finches than straight Nyjer and can be offered in a standard finch tube or sock.

Shelled Peanuts: Tufted Titmice love peanuts and they're eaten readily by jays, chickadees, titmice, nuthatches, wrens and woodpeckers. Pine Warblers and bluebirds will take a few. Offer them in your regular mix or separately in a mesh peanut feeder or open tray. Like sunflower meats, shelled peanuts are no longer protected by a shell, so they are susceptible to mold. Reduce the risk by blending peanuts 50/50 with sunflower seed in a peanut feeder; chickadees, titmice, and nuthatches will help the wrens and woodpeckers eat the blend quickly.

Whole Peanuts: How birds know they like peanuts is a mystery to me. After all, goobers are a root crop, right? Doesn't matter; once they're out of the ground and in the feeder, birds love 'em! I can understand that the aroma of shelled peanuts is attractive to birds, and they see what they're going to get. Whole peanuts, in the shell, require a different level of understanding! Titmice and Blue Jays love whole peanuts and will pick them out of a tray or fly-thru feeder or off a deck rail. Put a few out and watch the fun!

**Other Foods to Consider**

Suet:  In raw form, suet is the fat that forms around the kidneys of beef cattle.  It is very high energy and serves as an excellent substitute for insects in the winter. Older birders may remember asking the local butcher for suet from the butcher shop. This was the real thing – big white chunks of beef fat, fresh from the cutting table. Can't do this anymore, since most meat is pre-trimmed before it gets to your local mega-grocery. That's probably lucky, because those same older bird-ers tried to melt the suet on Mom's stove and wound up stinking up the kitchen and piling up huge numbers of demerits. I used to just put mine in a mesh potato or onion bag and hang it up. This was fine for the cold winter months, but that natural suet got pretty gamey after things warmed up in the spring.

Today there's a wide variety of commercial suet available, in ev-ery flavor imaginable. It comes in 12-ounce cakes, 3-ounce plugs, big 3-pound bricks and bigger 4-pound slabs. Properly formulated suet dough can be used in temperatures up to 100° F for year-round use.

Newer additions to the suet department include fruit-flavored and peanut nuggets, nuggets for bluebirds and even pepper-treated nug-gets to discourage squirrels. Nuggets can be offered in a tray feeder, a special nugget feeder or mixed into your regular seed blend.

I recommend starting with peanut or peanut butter suet; the strong aroma helps attract your first customers. After that, the sky's the limit, with suet ranging from cherry, berry, apple and orange flavors through fruit 'n nut, woodpecker blend, insect blend and even mealworm cakes. I have a hunch that flavored suet and fruity seed mixes are blended as much for the discerning birder as they are for the bird.

Seed Cakes, Blocks & Logs: Seed logs are a relative newcomer to the bird feeding marketplace. Commercial blocks are made up of a variety of seeds, nuts, fruit and insects that are compressed into a flat or rectangular block or round cylinder ranging from 12 ounces to 20 pounds. Some versions are bell-shaped or formed into balls, and hol-iday versions are shaped into wreaths, snowmen, Santa Claus, even Christmas ornaments! Gelatin or another edible binder is used to hold the whole thing together. Do-it-yourselfers use gelatin, flour and corn syrup to make their edible glue.

The small flat cakes fit nicely into a standard suet cage. Large blocks can be offered in commercially available large wire cages. The cylindrical seed logs have a hole drilled through the middle and are threaded onto an open spindle-type feeder, often equipped with a roof and a round perch. The really huge blocks are created for game birds or intended to attract and distract squirrels away from your regular feeders. They are set out on a stump or feeding table and should be sheltered to protect them from the rain.

Seed blocks and logs attract a lot of birds, especially those that are comfortable clinging to something. Woodpeckers, wrens, chickadees, titmice, nuthatches and Pine Warblers come to mine. Like any other seed offering, these blocks attract lots of the usual bandits: squirrels, chipmunks, possums and raccoons, so a baffle may be necessary. Crows can peck them apart in no time if they're not protected.

Fruit: Many birds love fruit and natural fruit is a staple in summer and fall – dogwood, blackberries, poke berries, crabapples, and holly berries. Offering fruit to tanagers and orioles is a common summer feeding strategy. Apple slices, orange and grapefruit halves, grapes and grape jelly are welcomed. Raisins can be chopped and soaked in warm water to soften them. Dried fruit is an expensive ingredient in premium seed mixes. Birding friends in Atlanta have had success attracting migrating warblers and tanagers with melon slices and grapes skewered on sturdy twigs in fall!

Mealworms: This is the traditional live food for bluebirds during the nesting season, although most feeder birds will eat them if they're offered. Not actually a worm, mealworms are the larval stage of a beetle (*Tenebrio molitor*) and are available from birding specialty stores, bait shops and internet merchants.

A mealworm feeder can be as simple as a clean plastic suet tray thumbtacked to a stick or as elaborate as a Plexiglas and wood box with bluebird sized holes in the ends that keep big birds out.

Bill Thompson III, the editor of *Birdwatcher's Digest*, a popular birding magazine, warns against feeding mealworms during the insect-rich summer months. Too much protein can stimulate more energy-demanding breeding cycles than are healthy for bluebirds; two broods are normal, three are unusual. Thompson's experience with summer-long mealworm feeding once resulted in four broods in a season, possibly weakening the adults as winter approached.

## BIRDMAN'S BLEND - A STORY IN ITSELF!

When we owned Blue Ridge Bird Seed Company, our most popular seed mix was Birdman's Blend™, a mixture of black oil sunflower seed, safflower, sunflower meats and shelled peanuts. We called the non-sunflower additives "The Fixin's" and added just enough that the diversity of ingredients attracted a wider variety of birds than straight sunflower, but at a much lower cost than other branded "quality" blends. Birdman's Blend™ was mixed to my own recipe and became the main reason for the store's success.

I developed the recipe for Birdman's Blend™ when I was still an amateur. I got tired of the milo mess that came for free in the wild bird blends I was buying. I started experimenting by adding black oil sunflower to my cheap blend, which attracted more birds but didn't reduce the mess. I eventually dumped the cheap blend and started with sunflower seed as the base ingredient, then added a variety of quality seeds and even dried fruit. I played with additives and quantities in search of the combination that attracted a lot of birds at a reasonable cost.

Once I had the recipe, I used it at home in the Atlanta area for years, mixing in bulk in a big trash can. This worked so well that I moved the trash can into my new bird store in 2003 and kept mixing. I created labels and sold Birdman's Blend in 5, 10 and 20-pound bags, then added refillable two-gallon plastic jugs and five-gallon buckets with high-quality twist-off lids. Our customers loved the convenience and economy of our buckets, and there were more than 2,000 refillable buckets in customer hands by 2017.

"The Fixin's" became an interesting extension of Birdman's Blend. A lot of our customers were vacation-home owners or only occasional visitors to the mountains. Once acquainted with Birdman's Blend, they wanted to use it at home. Seed is heavy and bulky and mailing pre-mixed Birdman's Blend was impossibly expensive. We decided that sending a bag of "The Fixin's" to our distant customers might work if we could find an economical way to do it. It turned out that the U. S. Postal Service offers a variety of shipping boxes in the category of "if it fits, it ships!" We packaged "The Fixin's" in bags that fit the USPS medium box and sent them to our customers with instructions to mix them with sunflower seed bought close to home. Our customers loved it and remained loyal to Birdman's Blend – long distance!

A second brand extension happened when we offered "The Fixin's" as a no-mess patio blend to people who couldn't deal with the mess created by the shells of sunflower seed. Our "No-Mess" blend was more expensive but just right for apartment dwellers and those who wanted clean patios and sprout-free gardens.

Mixing small quantities of your own seed blend at home is a pretty reasonable activity. Mixing it in large enough quantities to supply a growing retail store is a bird of a different color entirely! While we were in the trash can stage, we ordered sunflower seed, sunflower meats and safflower in pallet-sized loads from our local agricultural cooperative. Shelled peanuts came from a well-known bird seed dealer in Kennesaw, Georgia. Their redskin peanuts made a "pretty" blend but were pretty expensive, and we eventually changed to another source.

Our limited backroom space was full of raw materials for Birdman's Blend, and the seed barrel seemed to empty in no time. We tried to increase mixing efficiency with stirring sticks, golf clubs, canoe paddles and even a shovel. Nothing worked very well, and we stuck to rolling our sleeves up and mixing literally by hand, while thinking about buying a small cement mixer. In 2009, as monthly seed sales were exceeding three tons, I met a fellow store owner at a trade show who recommended calling his seed supplier to see if they would mix to my recipe. (The cheers you hear are from the back-room seed mixing crew...)

Business Manager Lisa Jones answered my call to Burkmann Feeds in Bowling Green, Kentucky in March of 2009. I told her about Birdman's Blend and the need to get away from trash can mixing. She asked for the recipe and an estimate of monthly volume and called back with prices and delivery details that changed our lives at Blue Ridge Bird Seed Company! Any small retailer will tell you how critical it is to find quality suppliers, especially for fast-moving consumable products like bird seed. Burkmann was a dream to work with, and their pricing structure actually improved our margins. Equally important, the periodic near-mutinies in the seed room simply went away when we stopped mixing our own seed.

At about the same time, I realized that Birdman's Blend was a valuable asset to the business because of its popularity, and that I should do something about protecting the brand name and the recipe. I researched trademarks and patents and concluded that trademarking the name was the most practical. I eventually contacted Legal Zoom for help, since dealing with the U.S. Patent and Trademark Office (PTO) directly looked a bit intimidating.

Legal Zoom helped me through the fairly simple application process, charged me about $650, and then quietly went away. To be fair, the fee included $275 to pay the reviewing PTO attorney to struggle through the complicated details of naming a bird seed blend.

I eventually received a nice letter from the PTO attorney in Washington denying my application because "Birdman's Blend" was *Merely Descriptive*. The file went into a drawer and I went away to sulk.

A month or two later, I stumbled across my Birdman's Blend file, felt the bile rise once again, and began working on a response to the PTO's refusal to register the name as a trademark. I ignored an offer of more help from Legal Zoom and wrote my own *Response to Office Action* to try to turn the tide.

Briefly, the PTO had two reasons for rejecting Birdman's Blend:

- "Birdman" simply describes *the intended user or group of users*.

- "Blend" is *something produced by mixing*.

My response argued instead that "Birdman" was not the user, but the man who invented the seed blend (me!) and suggested that my education, experience and credentials qualified me as an expert. Secondly, rather than something produced by mixing, Birdman's Blend was "a <u>specific</u> mix of quality seeds in the proper proportions that delivers significantly better value in attracting birds than any of the widely available inexpensive wild bird blends and many high-quality but more expensive seed blends." In summary, "Birdman's Blend is a specific product, formulated by an expert, to a particular formula."

I also cited two examples of previously registered trademarks for seed blends with names that fit the PTO's definition of *merely descriptive* – *Birder's Blend*™ (Kaytee Products) and *Birdwatcher's Blend*™ (SMG Brands, Inc.) and suggested that if the PTO registered these marks, they had to register mine:

*"These prior registrations create a precedent that precludes refusal of Birdman's Blend on the basis that the proposed mark is*

*merely descriptive."*

<u>The trademark was granted</u>, bringing my brief legal career to a close!

The popularity of Birdman's Blend with my customers was the major reason we were able to survive the recession caused by the housing and credit crisis from 2008 to 2012. It was our most valuable asset when it was time to sell Blue Ridge Bird Seed Company at retirement time. When we sold the store in May of 2017, monthly sales of Birdman's Blend were averaging about 10,000 pounds, and the new owners began making plans to expand sales to other independent bird stores and garden centers.

## Enough about Seed; let's talk About Feeders

When I started feeding birds in 1970, I made my own feeders – I had to! There were no bird stores, hardware stores sold nails and pipes, and commercially made feeders were rare and available only from a catalog, often sight-unseen. Today there are about as many different kinds of feeders available as there are seeds in a pound of sunflower, maybe five pounds! They range from cheap plastic junk to stylish (and expensive) garden decorations. Copper roofs and etched glass add both beauty and expense, while motors, weight-sensitive perches and protective cages promise to keep squirrels out.

The variety of feeder styles, materials and costs can be bewildering. It's wise to start slowly, know your budget and get some advice from the experts about quality and warranties. Bird feeding is beneficial to the birds, but keep in mind that being able to see them from your favorite rooms and porches is equally important. Take a little time to decide where you want feeders around your home and yard before you go shopping!

Seed feeders come in four basic styles: hopper, tube, platform, and globe. Suet feeders take many forms. A variety of feeder styles will attract a larger variety of backyard birds. Knowing what birds each feeder type attracts is helpful and matching each feeder style to the proper food is very helpful. Regardless of style, the feeder should be durable, comfortable to use for both birds and people and easy to fill and clean.

<u>Hopper Feeder</u>: Typically made of cedar, metal or recycled plastic materials, this house-shaped feeder is *non-exclusive*, meaning all birds can use it. It's perhaps the best all-around feeder design for attracting

a variety of large and small birds. Hoppers typically have solid ends and roofs, with plexiglass front and back panels in a "V" shape which funnel seed down as it is eaten and allow you to see how much seed is left. They offer large seed capacity and a hinged roof for filling and weather protection. They can be hung or post-mounted, and stocked with sunflower, safflower or a quality mix. Plastic lumber made from recycled pop bottles has become popular in recent years because it is durable and doesn't rot or fade. Removable metal screen bottoms provide excellent drainage and make cleaning a breeze.

Seed Tube Feeder: Simple plastic tubes with open feeding ports and metal or plastic perches, stocked with sunflower seed, safflower or a quality mix. Tubes are considered *exclusive*, since they *exclude* larger birds that don't like the small perches. However, when a seed tray is added, they become much more attractive to larger birds like Cardinals. Unhappily, the tray makes your tube more vulnerable to squirrels.

Finch Tube Feeder: Originally a plastic tube feeder designed to offer Nyjer seed through tiny feeding slits in a plastic tube. Newer designs include metal tubes made of fine screen or mesh that allow several birds to cling without perches and may be more durable. Nylon mesh socks are an inexpensive and less durable alternative. "Upside-down" finch feeders have the perches above the feeding slits, presenting no problems for acrobatic goldfinches while deterring the less nimble House Finches.

Elevated Platform or Tray Feeder: Another *non-exclusive* feeder, an elevated platform feeder is versatile, attractive to large and small birds and even some ground feeders. It can be hung or post-mounted, sometimes beneath a hopper feeder to create a very attractive feeding station. Some have a roof for weather protection and a screen or perforated bottom to improve drainage and to air dry seed after rains.

Globe Feeder: These come in several forms. The original globe is a clear plastic hanging ball with feeding ports accessible only to small, acrobatic birds like chickadees. A recent addition is a grapefruit-sized ball made of wire mesh instead of plastic. Chickadees, nuthatches and other "clingers" love to hang on them, often upside-down, and pull sunflower seeds through the mesh. The other type of globe feeder is really a plastic or wire mesh tube inside a round wire cage that allows small birds in but keeps big birds and squirrels out.

Ground Feeder: A modified tray, perfect for ground foraging species like Mourning Doves, sparrows, juncos and towhees. Seed is kept off the ground to reduce spoilage and screen or mesh bottoms allow drainage and air drying after rain or snow. A quality mix with sunflower seed can be used, along with White Proso Millet. Straight safflower will reduce squirrel and grackle activity.

Window Feeder: Window feeders can be small versions of hoppers or trays. Mounted with suction cups or hung from a bracket, a window feeder brings small birds close enough for easy viewing, certainly close enough to safely entertain an indoor cat. Installed on a quiet window and stocked with sunflower, safflower or a quality mix, a window feeder can be a delight.

Suet Feeder: Suet is a great energy source during the winter although birds will actually consume more animal protein (insects and suet) between March and August than they do all winter long. A variety of metal cages and drilled logs allow you to use commercial or home-made suet and seed cakes to attract birds of the tree trunk zone – woodpeckers, nuthatches, brown creeper (if you're lucky), chickadees and wrens. Kinglets and Pine Warblers will come to suet in the winter as well.

Suet feeders are available to fit every size and shape. The little one-cake metal cage is popular if a bit homely. Some come with plastic, wooden or copper roofs to dress them up a little. Upside-down suet feeders repel Starlings. A cage suet feeder inside a bigger cage repels bigger birds, squirrels and crows. Tail-prop suet feeders make it easier for larger woodpeckers to feed. My favorites are the cedar logs with three or four holes drilled through them to accommodate suet plugs. That cute downy woodpecker looks more natural and more comfortable on the log than he does on a wire cage.

## A Word About Cats

House cats, whether well-cared-for pets or ownerless in-the-wild feral cats, are tremendous predators of birds and small mammals. The hunting instinct is very strong despite many generations of careful breeding and domestication and the availability of an incredible variety of carefully formulated foods and treats. Fat cats may be a step slower, but they still hunt when allowed to be outside.

Historically, estimates of cat predation were based on counts of the prey brought back to the house. A recent study involving 60 cats equipped with 3-ounce mini cameras showed that most kills are not brought home, suggesting that earlier kill estimates were woefully low. The KittyCams Project, sponsored by the Warnell School of Forestry and Natural Resources at the University of Georgia tracked the activities of these cats for a combined 2,000 hours as they roamed in suburban Athens, Georgia in 2010 and 2011.

*The findings, reported at www.kittycams.uga.edu, are more than disturbing:*

*About 30 percent of the sampled cats were successful hunters and killed, on average, two animals a week. Almost half of their spoils were abandoned at the scene of the crime. Extrapolating from the data to include the millions of feral cats brutalizing native wildlife across the country, the American Bird Conservancy estimates that kitties are killing more than 4 billion animals annually. And that number is based on a conservative weekly kill rate, said Robert Johns, a spokesman for the Conservancy. "We could be looking at 10, 15, 20 billion wildlife killed (per year)," Johns said.*

Equally disturbing was the frequency of dangerous behaviors by these free-roaming cats:

- 45 percent of the project cats were witnessed crossing roads.
- 25 percent came in close contact with another cat.
- 25 percent were eating or drinking substances away from home.
- 20 percent explored the storm drain system.
- 20 percent entered crawlspaces.
- 18 percent climbed trees or walked on roofs.

Many cat lovers support the Trap, Neuter and Release (TNR) Program, which is purported to reduce the overpopulation of feral cats. The American Bird Conservancy has been an outspoken opponent of the practice, which releases neutered cats back into the outdoors where they continue to kill birds. It claims that feral cat population reductions are a myth, and that, as the risky behavior statistics from the KittyCams Project show, feral cats can lead short, harsh lives. There's a simple message here:

**If you care about birds, or you care about cats, keep them inside.**

---

"The sneaking, cruel cat hunts for the love of hunting. The most petted, pampered tabby is still a bird hunter." Joseph H. Dodson *Your Bird Friends and How to Win Them, 1928*

**Young Bear on a Sky Café – daytime! (Joan – Blue Ridge Bird Seed customer)**

**The classic unprotected feeder situation**

# 15

# Dealing with Critters

*You can't put a sign on your feeder that says "birds only." Sunflower seed delivers 1800 calories per pound and attracts squirrels, black bears and many other critters. This chapter tells how to deter squirrels with baffles and red pepper and offers advice on squirrel-resistant feeders. Bears are expanding their range in North America, love bird seed and will often destroy your feeder or take it with them! Our guidelines reduce damage and keep bears wild.*

Bird seed is nutritious; sunflower seed delivers about 1,800 calories per pound. Birds love a good seed blend and are not alone in their affection. Fox and Gray Squirrels, Red Squirrels, Flying Squirrels, Chipmunks and Raccoons will eat seed when they can get at it, and we often make it too easy. Possums are less nimble but can climb to feeders. I've caught both Red and Gray Foxes snacking on spilled seed at night. Black bears are becoming more common in many parts of the United States and present a special challenge.

Seed thieves are a fact of bird feeding life in most of the eastern United States. You can decide to love the critters and let them share your seed and suet, or you can put them on a diet by using a squirrel-proof feeder, installing one or more baffles, using pepper-treated seed they can't eat, and taking your feeders in at night.

## Baffles

A baffle is simply a physical barrier between hungry critters and your feeder. Properly installed, baffles prevent squirrels from getting to your feeder. You can install a baffle above a hanging feeder or mount one on your metal pole or 4x4 post below the feeder.

Hanging Baffle: A hanging baffle should be made of metal or heavy plastic and be wide enough that a squirrel can't slip around it. It should either tip under the squirrel's weight or have a steep slope that slides the squirrel off.

Post-mounted Baffle: A post-mounted baffle should be mounted 4.5 to 5 feet off the ground to prevent a squirrel from jumping over it. A variety of baffle designs is available: a flat disc, a slanted cone type and a cylindrical stove-pipe design. Disc and cone-shaped baffles should be 24 inches in diameter. Stove-pipe baffles should be at least 16 inches long for squirrels and 28 inches long for raccoons. In all cases, your baffled pole setup should be installed in the middle of an open area about 20 feet across. Squirrels will try to jump to your feeder above the baffle and the feeder must be 10 feet away from any launch point. Look up - squirrels will drop to your feeder from an overhead wire or tree branch if one is available!

**"Hot" Seed**

Pre-Treated Seed: Several varieties of hot seed are available, pre-treated with a sauce made from pepper. The pepper sauce irritates the mucus membranes of mammals, including the eyes, nose, mouth and throat of squirrels, chipmunks, raccoons, possums, bears and humans. Birds may take a few days to adjust to the hot seed, but the pepper does not harm the birds. In fact, pepper plants and parrots evolved together in South America to mutual benefit. The parrots feast on the pepper fruit and poop the seeds everywhere, spreading the pepper plants!

A couple of doses of burning eyes and stinging nostrils is usually enough to teach the squirrels to stay away. Hot seed is pretty expensive; we recommend mixing it about half and half with your quality seed mix to start. You can cut back to one-third hot seed and two-thirds regular seed after the squirrels have some experience.

Pepper Powder and Pepper Liquid: Squirrel-Away™ and Brown's Fire Mix are pepper powders you can mix with your seed in any quantity. It's a fine dust and seems to stick better if you pre-treat your seed with a spray-on edible oil product like PAM.

Cole's Flaming Squirrel™ Seed Sauce is a concentrated liquid pepper that can be mixed with or sprayed on bird seed, suet kibbles and flower bulbs to reduce squirrel problems. A customer recommended that the hot pepper liquid just be wiped onto the feeding ports of a tube feeder; when a squirrel sticks its nose into the feeding port, it gets a real snootful and is discouraged right away. This is an economical approach but may expose you to the hot sauce when you touch the feeder.

*Caution: Hot seed and pepper-based products can be very irritating to people, too. Eye protection and gloves are recommended when using either pepper powder or liquid pepper.*

## Other Solutions

Slinky – a couple of expandable springs are on the market, resembling the metal Slinky you used to play with on the stairs as a kid. They fasten to the feeder pole below the feeder and gently let the squirrel down when it tries to climb the pole.

Greased Pole – many people have experimented with applying a slick substance to the feeder pole, including axle grease and petroleum jelly. These may work but are toxic and will harm the squirrel when it licks its paws after sliding down. Squirrel Slip™ is a safe product made of coconut oil and soy that works well without hurting the squirrels. It must be reapplied after rain or heavy squirrel use.

Baffles, liquid and powdered pepper products, slinkys, and Squirrel Slip are available at most birding specialty stores. Pre-treated hot seed may be available as well. Trained staff will be delighted to help you choose the solution to your situation.

## Squirrel-Proof Feeders That Really Are

Skeptical people claim frequently that "there's no such thing as a *squirrel-proof feeder!*" I heard this most frequently from the husband or know-it-all friend that came into my bird store with an otherwise motivated customer. While this may be technically accurate, a good *squirrel-resistant feeder*, <u>properly installed</u>, will reduce seed theft by 90 to 95 percent. Smart as they are, squirrels will sometimes just jump on an otherwise squirrel-proof feeder to set it swinging enough to spill some seed. The result of using a well-designed and properly installed squirrel-resistant feeder is a much more enjoyable and affordable bird watching experience. Make the investment: Good squirrel-proof feeders pay for themselves!

Realistically, your goal is to keep the squirrels off the feeder, so the birds can get on it, and there are a number of very well-designed feeders that really do keep squirrels under control and dramatically improve your bird-feeding success and bird-watching pleasure. We have tried virtually every squirrel-resistant feeder on the market over the years and have found several that we can recommend without hesitation. At first glance, these feeders appear to be expensive, but they pay for themselves many times over in seed savings and in the joy of watching birds instead of squirrels. Our favorites are made in the USA or Canada and offer excellent warranties and readily available replacement parts.

**The Yankee Flipper ($150 - $175):** Introduced by Droll Yankees in 1999, this unique feeder is battery-operated and rechargeable, with a weight-sensitive, circular perch under the feeding ports that is activated by the weight of a squirrel. The perch rotates briskly until the squirrel is slung off or leaves on its own.

Like the airplane, the Yankee Flipper was invented by a bike shop owner. Paul Artigues, who lived in Atlanta, was known for his creative solutions to problems. According to Betsy Puckett, former owner of Droll Yankees, Paul was having squirrel troubles like everyone else and was searching for a method to deter them. He was lying on his couch in his home, looking up at his rotating ceiling fan when the idea of a feeder with a motorized, rotating or spinning perch came to him. Paul and a partner developed prototypes, filed for patent protection and created a video of the revolutionary Yankee Flipper in action, which they sent to several bird feeder manufacturers. Betsy and the Droll Yankees team had just returned from the annual Birdwatch America trade show in Atlanta and found the video in the mail stack on her desk. They went back to Atlanta right away.

Droll Yankees offers three other squirrel-resistant feeders of similar design (The Tipper, The Whipper and The Dipper) that use a collapsing perch concept to drop the squirrel off ($90 to $130). All of these feeders must be installed far enough away from post or shepherd's hook that the squirrel can't hang on to the post and pull the feeder toward itself without engaging the squirrel-resistant mechanism. Don't simply take my word for it; log into You-Tube on the internet and search for Yankee Flipper. There are lots of funny and instructive videos that feature some frustrated squirrels.

**The Arundale Sky Café ($80):** Developed by a family-owned company in St. Louis in 1975, the Sky Café was our top selling squirrel-proof feeder in our mountain town because it is perfectly designed for vacation cabins with big decks. It's a large capacity hopper feeder with a huge dome top and big tray. Originally made from recycled Plexiglas, it's now made of Lexan, which is less brittle. Replacement parts are readily available and inexpensive.

The Sky Café can be hung from a tree limb, five feet out from the trunk and five feet or higher above the ground, or it can be hung from the Erva Swing Arm from a deck post. The Swing Arm is four feet long and available with both screw-on and clamp-on bases. Tree-hung or deck-mounted, the large dome top keeps the squirrels from reaching it from above and they will not jump to it from your deck rail, even though it's less than four feet away. A really determined squirrel will crawl out on the limb or Swing Arm and down the hanging chain, hang on with its back feet and stretch down toward the rim of the dome top. It can't reach the rim and will slide off out of sight if it lets go of the chain. Oh no! Poor squirrel.....

**Brome Squirrel Busters (a family of six feeders - $30 to $100)**: Squirrel Busters have won the Best New Product award each time a new one has come out. The first four models (Squirrel-Buster Plus, Classic, Mini and Standard) are sunflower seed feeders, suitable for all birds. Squirrel-Buster Finch and Squirrel-Buster Peanut are recent additions. All are high quality designs of powder-coated metal and plastic, with internal spring mechanisms that make them work smoothly without exposure to the weather. Perches are wide enough for Cardinals to use comfortably. The tops are designed to keep squirrels out. All can be hung virtually anywhere, since the weight of the squirrel closes off the feeding ports and the squirrel quickly leaves in frustration. Squirrel Busters come with an excellent warranty and most bird stores stock replacement parts.

Note that most squirrel-proof feeders are designed to frustrate and repel Gray Squirrels and Fox Squirrels, the big guys that weigh at least a pound and often as much as two pounds. The cute Red Squirrel or Pine Squirrel of the northern US and western mountains is much smaller and may not be heavy enough to depress the weight-sensitive springs that close the feeding ports on the smaller feeders or trigger the motorized perch of the Yankee Flipper. Chipmunks present a similar weight problem. The Squirrel Buster Plus and Squirrel Buster Standard offer adjustable springs that allow you to dial Red Squirrels and chipmunks out of the buffet. Flying Squirrels are much smaller than gray and fox squirrels, weighing just 2.5 to 4 ounces and may present a problem even for adjustable feeders. They are nocturnal, and problems can be eliminated by bringing vulnerable feeders inside at night.

**Things To Watch Out For**

A lot of supposedly squirrel-proof feeders have flaws that you can't see in the bird store. Those little metal houses with a lift-up top for filling and one or two spring-loaded perches work fine for a while.

Sooner or later, a smart squirrel will figure out that it can lie on the roof and reach over enough to get its mouth on the seed without activating the perch. The design also puts the steel springs (not stainless steel, which doesn't rust) on the outside so they will eventually either be popped off or corrode.

Feeders with designs similar to the Squirrel Busters often have skimpy outer cages that allow the squirrel's teeth to get at the plastic inner tube and have external springs that will corrode and cause the feeder to stick open or closed. Well-designed feeders last a long time, like decent binoculars. Do your homework to help you choose a quality feeder, then invest in the best one that fits your budget.

## Dealing with Black Bears

Talking about black bears in a birding book? Yep – many thousands of people live in bear country or own a vacation home or cabin in bear country. If you're one of them and you feed birds, you're going to get acquainted with black bears.

**Black Bear Distribution in North America (National Geographic)**

Many areas in the USA and Canada support a healthy population of black bears. In fact, populations are growing even in populated areas.

These shy adaptable creatures do amazingly well despite the growing numbers of people with whom they share vacationland. There may be 900,000 black bears in North America, with the largest populations in Alaska (100,000), Washington (25,000), Oregon (25,000), California (23,000), Maine (21,500), Minnesota (20,000), Idaho (20,000), Colorado (12,000) and Pennsylvania (10,000). My home state of Georgia is home to about 4,000 black bears. Many other states have populations ranging from a few to several thousands. Reforestation and the demise of the family farm have created suitable habitat, and professional management has eliminated illegal trapping and shooting, although most states allow managed hunts under controlled conditions.

Male black bears can reach 500 pounds, while females weigh 90 – 300 pounds. The record is an 880-pound male from Craven County, NC. Black bears mate in May through July and 2-3 cubs are born in January, weighing less than a pound each. The sex ratio is 50:50 at birth, but males are killed at a higher rate, so the sex ratio among mature bears is often one male per 2.5 females. Cubs stay with their mother for about 17 months; the cubs are forced into independence in their second summer, just before their mother is ready to mate again.

### Hello 9-1-1? There's a bear in my yard!

Imagine that you're a second-year black bear cub, it's July and Mom suddenly tells you she has a date and you have to leave. You've been kept safe and well fed, and suddenly you're on your own. It's a shock, but she has showed you where to find food and you adjust. As you wander around, you bump into other bears; if you're a female, you get along without problems. But – if you're a young male and bump into another, larger male, he makes you feel very unwelcome and runs you off. You learn to avoid male bears, follow the forested river valleys, and suddenly find yourself in a densely populated suburban neighborhood, with cars, dogs and people. In a day or so, the word gets around, somebody calls 9-1-1 or the DNR to report that you're in a tree in their backyard, and suddenly you're on TV, with Traffic Copter 2 in the air, flashing police cars on the street, and a crowd of kids and dogs under the tree. If you're lucky, you don't get hurt when the tranquilizer dart hits you and you fall out of the tree. If your luck holds, you wake up tomorrow, safely back in the woods, but missing a tooth and wearing a radio collar.

Bears are very intelligent, can see in color and hear at least twice as well as we do. They swim well enough to reach island campsites and a lean bear can run at 30 mph. They are usually silent (except in movies) but use a variety of grunts to communicate with cubs and other bears. They may make loud blowing noises or clack their teeth when frightened. Hibernation periods, when a bear's metabolic rate is cut in half and body temperature may drop to 88° F., vary from seven months in the far north to a few weeks or months in southern states where food is more available year-round.

While black bear populations have increased in recent years, the potential for conflict with people has increased as well. Vacation home construction in remote areas puts people in contact with black bears and the outcome is dependent on how people respond when bear habitat overlaps with backyards.

Dr. Lynn Rogers is the world's expert on black bears. Now retired, he has spent more time with bears than any other biologist. When I say, "with bears," I mean right next to them for periods of 24 hours or more. Visit his website at www.bears.org to read his words about bears and check out the slide shows of his interactions with black bears in the wild including bathing with bears and sitting on a stump watching a sow and three cubs from 10 feet away.

Much of his work was done in Northern Minnesota, where I started my career as a forester. In the winter of 1973-74, I had the privilege of helping Dr. Rogers locate a female in her winter den, weigh and measure her and her twin cubs, and return them to their den without harm. An awesome experience.

Rogers believes that bears are timid by nature and will avoid conflict if they can. He claims the greatest misconception about black bears is that they will attack in defense of cubs. Bears will hear or smell you first and slip away without incident. In any event, if you encounter a bear, use caution, talk softly while backing away, avoid eye contact and don't run. In the unlikely event of an attack, you should make noise, act aggressively and fight back. Pepper spray is an effective deterrent.

One of my most memorable moments in the woods as a forester happened while I was doing trail reconnaissance work a mile or so from a road on the Huron National Forest in lower Michigan. I walked right up on a female black bear and three cubs; she may have been as surprised as I was when we saw each other from 50 feet. I stopped and yelled, "Hey bear!" as loud as I could. Mama coughed a warning to her cubs, who scampered off immediately, then she followed them into the woods. No aggression or threatening behavior from either of us – she just took her kids out of my vicinity. I waited a minute or two and continued down the trail.

If you live in bear country, you should expect to see a bear sooner or later. We are the intruders here, we have an obligation to honor their presence and existence, and should be prepared to change our behavior to minimize the damage from the encounter. Don't let your garbage become an attractant, keep your dog food and bird seed inside, reduce or stop feeding birds until the bears move on, and encourage your neighbors to do the same. Whatever you do, don't feed them!

Bears can live 20-30 years when left alone. The average life span is 3-5 years where humans and bears conflict. The bears' future depends on how well we understand and tolerate them. I live in the North Georgia Mountains, where black bear habitat is increasingly invaded by second homes and vacation developments. *So what, you ask? You live in the woods, in the middle of a National Forest with thousands of acres of wild country, perfect habitat for bears.* The fact is, you don't have to live in the mountains to encounter a bear. Georgia has 159 counties, and black bears have been reported from every one of them! Sometimes they're just passing through, but often they're moving into the county, settling down and raising cubs. Despite the growing population, many people live in bear country for years and <u>never</u> see one.

As a bird store owner, I hosted an annual Saturday Seminar on black bears each spring for 14 years, with the enthusiastic support of biologists and wildlife technicians from the Georgia Department of Natural Resources. These are the folks who answer the phone when an irate cabin owner calls to complain about a damaged bird feeder, a yard full of trash, or even a bear in his kitchen! The DNR folks are delighted to get an opportunity to talk with 40 or 50 homeowners about how to deal with bears. Educating my customers allowed me to sell seed year-round instead of enduring seasonal restrictions imposed by the DNR because people do stupid things.

A fun video shows black bears in places they shouldn't be, followed by war stories told by the biologist. The story about a female bear spending the winter under someone's deck gets everyone's attention, especially the part where mama brings her cubs out in April. We look at bear skins and a skull, see pictures of big barrel traps, and check out the tranquilizer gun. I bring out some damaged feeders, bent hardware and chewed-up seed buckets to prove we're not kidding. Then the biologists tell us about the things <u>we</u> do that get bears in trouble.

Black bears are attracted to garbage, pet food, bird seed and BBQ grills that we leave outside, easily accessible to bears. After giving our seminar guests a moment to nod knowingly and look guiltily at each other, we start talking about human behavioral change. In the old days, the biologists trapped trouble bears and took them to a more remote location. Two problems with that: 1) Somebody else built a new cabin in the remote location, or 2) The bear traveled back to its home territory, crossing roads and becoming road kill. The DNR doesn't do that anymore.

---

On the topic of moving nuisance bears, Ed Quinn, who owned a used book and wine store (the wine was new) in Blue Ridge, Georgia, told me about calling the DNR to report a bear that was hanging around his cabin in the boonies.

*"It's eating the cat food and getting on the porch. It's a little too tame" said Ed.*

The DNR biologist promised to come out with a big barrel trap and capture it.

*"We take bears like this to a really remote place in the National Forest."*

*Where's that?" asked Ed.*

*"Oliver's Trail, off the end of Cashes Valley Road."*

*"Oh," said Ed, "that's where I live."*

---

## Safety Rules for Bears

Over the years, we've developed some safety rules that are very effective in reducing damage and keeping the bears where they belong: in the woods, eating natural foods. Luckily, black bears are much more active at night than during the day; most of their raids on homes and cabins happen at night, which makes it easy to keep them out of trouble.

1. **Never, ever, feed bears.** One person feeding bears can create a problem that affects the entire neighborhood. Fed bears get used to humans, lose their fear, and become dangerous.
2. **Don't leave trash or garbage outside.** Keep it in a bear-proof container or in a container in a secure basement, garage or shed. If you have garbage pickup, put your container out

the day of disposal, <u>not the night before</u>.

3. **Keep pet food inside if you can – <u>Always bring it inside at night</u>**. Bears are omnivores, which means they're not picky eaters. Cat and dog food are tasty treats.

4. **Keep your BBQ grill clean and covered.**

5. **Avoid bird seed that contains milo.** Milo is generally not eaten by our birds but is often a filler in inexpensive wild bird mix. It usually winds up on the ground under your feeders and will attract bears and raccoons at night, even if you take your feeders inside.

6. **Bring bird feeders inside every night.** Limit the number of feeders you use during the warm months when bears are awake and active and bring them inside every night. If you are part-time in bear country, leave your feeders inside while you are away.

**Follow these rules whenever the bears are not hibernating.**

April 1st to November 15th is the bears-active season in the southern Appalachian foothills. Our north Georgia bears semi-hibernate during the winter but may emerge briefly during warmer periods. The winter of 2012-13 was an exception – bears were active all winter and we followed these rules every night! Birders in other locations should adjust the rules to fit local winter patterns. Deep South and Florida bears don't hibernate. Bears in the Appalachians and Rockies will den earlier and stay asleep longer, as will those in the northern states.

**Bonus**: Raccoons, opossums and flying squirrels are equally attracted to pet food and bird seed and are active year-round. If you follow the rules for dealing with bears, you will eliminate night raids by these animals, too. *Caution: Raccoons seen during the day may be rabid and should be reported.*

A little humor about the difference between Black Bears and the more dangerous Grizzly Bear:

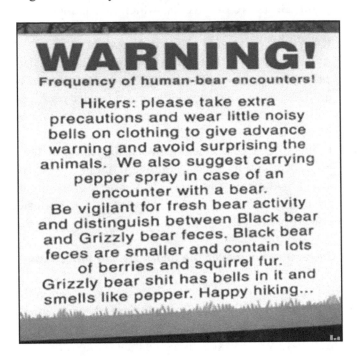

**Determined Bear**

**Midnight Cub**

**Eastern Bluebird Pair (orange throats) on A Simple House (Brian Lupa)**

# 16

# Attracting Bluebirds

*Habitat requirements and breeding biology of our three native bluebird species. History of the unfortunate introduction of European Starlings and House Sparrows, foreign species that disrupt and kill nesting bluebirds. Details on nest box design, installation and maintenance, with advice on dealing with insect pests.*

Bluebirds are among the most beautiful of birds and are favorites among backyard birders because of their willingness to move into a nest box and raise their families in our yards. Their song is cheerful, and they are among the first birds to return in the spring.

North America is host to three species of bluebirds: Eastern, Western and Mountain. They are members of the Thrush family of birds, closely related to robins. The range of the Eastern Bluebird extends south to Nicaragua, while the Mountain Bluebird nests beyond the Arctic Circle. Together, they are distributed continent-wide. Eastern and Western Bluebirds are generally found at lower elevations, while Mountain Bluebirds range from lowland prairies and sagebrush flats to high mountain meadows and alpine zones above timberline.

The Eastern Bluebird is the most widespread of the three bluebirds. Its back, wings, and head are blue, and the throat, chest and flanks are orange; males are much brighter than females. The orange throat makes it easily distinguishable from the Western Bluebird, whose throat is blue. The male Mountain Bluebird is brilliant blue from head to tail, with lighter blue on breast and belly. Females are grayer overall, with pale blue feathers on wings and tail.

Eastern and Western Bluebirds prefer open habitat with scattered trees, including open backyards, farmlands and orchards. They like elevated perches to hunt insects from and are often seen perched on fences and overhead wires. Mountain Bluebirds may use treeless terrain, including lowland prairies, sagebrush flats and alpine zones above timberline. Wide open prairie without perches is not ideal blue-

bird habitat although Mountain Bluebirds may winter in open grass-
land, desert and plowed fields.

**Western Bluebird (blue throat) (Barb Hauer)**

The diet of all three species is a mix of insects and berries. Beetles, grasshoppers, crickets, caterpillars, ants and bees are favored
when available, along with spiders, earthworms, small snails and the
occasional small lizard or tree frog. Dogwood, hawthorn, elderberry
and holly berries are eaten by Eastern Bluebirds, while Western and
Mountain Bluebirds consume mistletoe, juniper, elderberry and hack-
berry fruit.

All three species of bluebirds are migratory over much of their
ranges, retreating from regions with heavy snow and extreme cold
in the winter. Eastern Bluebirds have the largest range and can be
found year-round over much of it, wintering as far north as Illinois,
Ohio and New York during milder winters. Sustained cold and deep
snow can put bluebirds in danger, and both severe winters and spring
snowstorms have probably contributed to the decline of bluebird populations in the past. Once winter retreats, bluebirds return quickly to
breeding areas and their cheerful song is a welcome sign of spring.

## Population Decline and Recovery

Once abundant in rural and agricultural areas of North America, Eastern and Western Bluebirds experienced serious population declines that began after World War I. A series of severe winters, changes in farming and orchard practices, urbanization of once favorable areas, and competition with House Sparrows and European Starlings for nesting sites led to this decline. Mountain Bluebirds were not affected as much since they nest in more remote situations that were less prone to human disturbance, and away from the disturbed habitats frequented by House Sparrows and Starlings.

Habitat loss was a major cause of the decline of bluebirds. Imagine the bluebird's world in 1920 – much of the US population was still living in rural and agricultural areas and there were no sprawling suburban neighborhoods or shopping malls. Many farms were essentially non-mechanized, with small fields broken up by woodlots and brushy waterways. Pesticide and herbicide use were very limited. Wooden fence posts had not yet been replaced by metal and older posts offered holes for nesting. Apple orchards were made up of what we now call heritage varieties, tall trees with large limbs that were often left unpruned. Broken limbs and knotholes provided many more nesting cavities than the smaller, more compact trees of modern orchards.

Between the 1920s and the 1970s, Americans moved to town. Suburbs spread outward from growing cities, swallowing farmland. Modern mechanized agriculture required larger fields, fewer woodlots and greater use of chemicals. Old fences came down or were replaced by new fences with metal posts. Old orchards were bulldozed or abandoned; many were overtaken by brush and larger trees or smothered in Kudzu, particularly in the South.

Kudzu is a rapidly growing, climbing vine introduced from Japan at the 1876 Centennial Exposition in Philadelphia. A member of the pea family, Kudzu was heralded by claims of its value for erosion control and as a livestock forage. During the 1930s and the 1940s over a million acres of Kudzu were planted. Its use in erosion control was somewhat effective, but the benefits were overshadowed by its habit of climbing over trees and shrubs and killing them by heavy shading. In practice, Kudzu makes poor hay, and never came close to meeting expectations as livestock feed. Kudzu is a perfect example of the unintended consequences of meddling with the natural order by introducing a species from another continent.

Years ago, my brother bought a fixer-upper just outside Atlanta, with three acres of Kudzu in the backyard. My Dad and I helped John spray his Kudzu patch with herbicide; as we pulled the dying vines into piles for burning, we uncovered a small shed and three apple trees!

**Could there be any potential bluebird nest holes under there somewhere?**

Many people recognized the plight of bluebirds, including Dr. Lawrence Zeleny, a bluebird enthusiast and author of books and articles about bluebirds. His book, *The Bluebird: How You Can Help Its Fight for Survival,* published in 1976 by Indiana University Press, raised awareness with national conservation organizations. Dr. Zeleny asked the National Audubon Society and National Wildlife Federation to sponsor programs for education and bluebird recovery but was turned down.

In frustration, Dr. Zeleny and others formed a new organization dedicated to bluebird conservation called The North American Bluebird Society (NABS). Founded in 1978, NABS gathered recognition and support after an article was published in Parade Magazine, the Sunday newspaper supplement distributed to 15 million households every week. The November 25, 1979 article by Joan Rattner Heilman, *You Can Hear the Bluebird's Song Again,* brought 80,000 responses, asking for the new NABS brochure and seeking membership in the new society. NABS offered workshops and distributed nest box plans and bluebird recovery was underway.

Ironically, the Eastern Bluebird may be flirting with trouble once again. Breeding Bird Surveys across their range showed steady population increases from 1966 until 2000. Since then, the rate of population growth has slowed dramatically. Bernie Daniel, retired environmental research scientist and current president of the North American Bluebird Society, has suggested a number of possible reasons for the slowdown including weather conditions and localized House Sparrow competition. Two surprising factors may be involved as well – (1) dramatic decreases in insect populations worldwide and (2) decreasing numbers of *bluebirders* putting up and maintaining fewer nest boxes! NABS membership includes few young people, who are increasingly urban and less connected to the land. Disturbing trends, worth watching.

## Bluebird Biology

Bluebirds are cavity nesters, using old woodpecker holes, rotted-out knotholes and other natural cavities in trees and fence posts, and artificial nest boxes that are properly constructed and located in suitable habitat. Mountain Bluebirds use the usual woodpecker holes and bird houses when available, but can be quite flexible, sometimes nesting in holes in dirt banks and cliffs, and holes in buildings, and may use old nests of Cliff Swallows, which build a jug-like nest under bridges or building eaves.

Bluebirds begin nesting in late February in the southern US and late March to late April in northern states. In the west, bluebirds follow the melting snows northward and move to higher elevations as winter retreats. Like other migratory birds, they seem to sense that nesting should wait until warmer temperatures, blooming plants and trees and emerging insects signal that conditions are right to incubate eggs and feed hungry nestlings.

Bluebirds build tall, cup-shaped nests of fine grasses or pine needles. Nests are almost always neat, never littered with twigs, feathers or trash. They're also sanitary because the adults remove droppings produced by the nestlings. A typical clutch is 4 to 6 light blue eggs, rarely white. My experience in north Georgia is that the first clutch is five eggs, with smaller clutches in second and third nestings. The female does not begin incubation until all eggs are laid, ensuring that they will hatch at the same time. Incubation takes 13 to 16 days for Eastern Bluebirds, a day or two longer for the larger Western and Mountain Bluebirds. The young birds leave the nest about 18 to 20 days after hatching. They are physically ready to fly but need a little practice. The adults will tend the young birds for several weeks after fledging, although the female may begin building a nest for the next brood almost immediately.

## Competition for Nesting Cavities

A number of birds compete with bluebirds for nest holes, including some native species: Chickadees, titmice, nuthatches, House Wrens, Tree Swallows (east) and Violet-green Swallows (west). Chickadees, titmice and nuthatches are woodland birds and are more likely to nest in a bluebird box that is located close to the forest edge or on a tree. Proper location of your bluebird box on a post in an open area reduces competition problems with these cute birds. Putting up a second box may allow you to enjoy nesting bluebirds along with other welcome cavity nesters.

My experience with Carolina Chickadees and Brown-headed Nut-hatches in north Georgia is that these hard-working birds start nesting before the bluebirds do and will do their best to defend a nest box once they're in it. In this case, the early bird gets the box!

Tree Swallows and Violet-green Swallows are beautiful birds and should be welcomed in your bluebird box if they happen to get there first. Their nests are similar to those of bluebirds but are often lined with feathers. Fortunately, they get along well with bluebirds and a second house located nearby or even on the back of the same post will allow both species to raise their young in your yard without conflict.

House Wrens are tough competitors, building nests of twigs, coarse grass and feathers that can almost fill a nest box. Their nesting range rivals that of any bird in the New World, ranging from Canada through Central America and to the southern tip of South America. Bright and cheerful like other wrens, they can be aggressive nesters and fierce competitors of bluebirds. They are capable of breaking bluebird eggs and killing small nestlings, often removing eggs and dead bluebirds from the nest box. Like other songbirds in the United States, they are protected by the Migratory Bird Treaty Act and it is illegal to harm them. Again, locating your nest box on a post in the open, away from thickets and brushy edges, will even the odds and give your bluebirds a chance.

A couple of non-native species have put a lot of pressure on blue-birds in the last century, European Starlings and House Sparrows. Both were brought to North America through the efforts of "acclimatization societies," groups organized with the purpose of exchanging plants and animals from one part of the world to another. Members of these groups shared romantic notions of bringing to America all the birds mentioned in Shakespeare's plays. Clearly no one yet understood the ramifications of such introductions.

Sixty European Starlings (*Sturnus vulgaris*) were released in 1890 in New York's Central Park by a New York druggist named Eugene Schieffelin, with the help of the American Acclimatization Society. Another 40 birds were released in 1891. For several years, the birds rarely strayed from Manhattan. The first successful nest was discovered in the eaves of the American Museum of Natural History, across the street from Central Park, and the news of its finding was met with great joy. Little did they know....

Once starlings got some reproductive momentum, they moved fast. By 1928, they had reached the Mississippi River and were in California by 1942. The impact of huge flocks of these birds was well-known by then, especially their damage to grain fields, feed lots and fruit orchards. The droppings from a single starling roost, holding a million or more birds, created a disease and cleanup nightmare. Droppings have been linked to numerous diseases, including histoplasmosis, a fungal lung ailment that afflicts agricultural workers; toxoplasmosis, particularly dangerous to pregnant women, and Newcastle disease, which kills poultry. In 1960, a flock of starlings brought down an airliner taking off from Logan Airport in Boston, killing 62 people.

**European Starling**

**House Sparrow Pair**

Despite numerous and creative attempts, starlings have proven themselves ineradicable. Balloons, artificial hawks and owls and itching powder were tried without success. An Interior Department consultant suggested placing grease around feeding sites, hoping starlings would carry the glop back to their nests to interfere with incubation. Live electrical wires were strung on the columns of the U.S. Capitol to discourage roosting. Loudspeakers broadcasting starling alarm calls were used to discourage birds around the White House. Poisoned pellets were used in Nevada and California to reduce feed lot damage, killing an estimated 9 million starlings between 1964 and 1967. Other attempts were made to interfere with reproduction using radioactive Cobalt-60. Roman candles set off near starling roosts were ineffective. More recently, Starlicide, a focused pesticide developed by Ralston-Purina to combat starlings, has been used effectively to kill starlings in concentrated feeding situations like grain elevators and feedlots. Starlicide is toxic to starlings and gulls and will kill seed-eating birds like pheasants and Northern Bobwhite if used irresponsibly. Despite all efforts, European Starlings number perhaps two hundred million birds in North America.

---

**Four & Twenty Starlings, Baked in a Pie** – Perhaps the most creative solution was advanced by the U.S. Department of Agriculture in 1931. ''When the breasts of these birds have been soaked in a soda-salt solution for 12 hours and then parboiled in water, which is afterwards discarded, they may be used in a meat pie that compares fairly well with one made of blackbirds or English sparrows.'' The author cautioned that the gamy taste was not for everyone.

---

Starlings do most of their damage to bluebirds by taking over natural nesting cavities. They are too big to get into man-made nesting boxes with the recommended 1 ½ inch entrance holes.

The other alien nest competitor is the House Sparrow (*Passer domesticus*), formerly known as English Sparrow. House Sparrows have been closely associated with people for at least 10,000 years. They are most successful in urban and suburban environments where seed, grain and insects are plentiful and bird feeding is popular, and in grain-producing regions of the United States where food is abundant. They are rarely found in natural woodlands away from homes and other human development.

Eight pairs were released in Central Park in 1851 by Nicholas Pike, the well-intentioned but misguided director of The Brooklyn Institute, possibly to control canker worms that were infesting the park's trees. According to reports, they did not thrive, so another 25 pairs were released a year later. During the next 20 years, they were released in eight other cities and by 1870 were established as far south as Columbia SC and Galveston TX, with thriving populations in San Francisco, Cincinnati and Salt Lake City.

By 1890, their true nature as agricultural pests and destroyers of native birds was known, and eradication efforts began. Shooting and poisoning were encouraged, and bounties were established in several states. Joseph H. Dobson patented the Dobson Sparrow Trap in 1906 and made it available at the bargain price of $8.00 (f.o.b. Kankakee, Illinois). The clever wire trap featured a one-way funnel entrance and a removable inner cage. Despite this and other efforts, the House Sparrow population was estimated to be 150 million birds in 1943.

Formerly common in rural and farming areas, they have declined as farms have become more mechanized. A story which is probably true suggests that House Sparrows flourished after introduction in cities where horses were central to local transportation. Partly digested oats in "horse apples" were plentiful and available.

House Sparrow nests are variable, but cavities are preferred. Tree hollows, crevices in buildings and signs, and abandoned swallow burrows in banks and cliffs are all suitable. Loose gutters, grocery store letter signs and loose overhead panels in older gas stations and fast-food restaurants are often used. Of course, birdhouses offer perfect nesting cavities, and the aggressive sparrows will drive away meeker species like swallows and bluebirds. They will break eggs, kill baby birds and can injure adult bluebirds.

## House Sparrow Control

House Sparrows are a non-native species considered a serious pest, and thus House Sparrow nests, eggs and young and adults are not protected by U.S. federal law (e.g., the Migratory Bird Treaty Act). However, you need to check on any state or local laws that may apply to trapping and dispatching House Sparrows before taking any action.

Active House Sparrow control is critical in areas where they are abundant. Weekly monitoring of nest boxes and removal of House Sparrow nests, eggs and nestlings will eliminate fledging from those boxes. However, the male House Sparrow will continue to defend the box, rebuild the nest and drive off other birds.

The tenacious male House Sparrow can be captured by holding a plastic grocery bag over the entrance hole after dark and rapping on the box. The male, which commonly overnights in the box, will fly into the bag. Relocating the bird just moves the problem elsewhere, so the bird should be humanely euthanized. Detailed advice on how to do this is available on the Sialis website:

http://sialis.org/hospdispatch.htm

House Sparrow populations have declined in North America since 1900. Mechanized transportation literally put horses out to pasture and removed the oat-laden horse apples from city streets. Modern urban areas and suburbs are better-groomed, offering fewer nesting sites. Replacement of aging gas stations and restaurants reduced the number of crevices in drooping roof panels. Installation of motion-activated entry doors in grocery stores and other 'big-box' retail stores made it harder for the birds to sneak inside to roost or nest, although some House Sparrows have learned how to activate the doors!

The dramatic success of the House Finch in the East may have had a significant impact on House Sparrow populations, particularly in the South. If you look up House Finch in a field guide published before 1970, you'll see that the House Finch was widespread in the American West but had only a toehold in the Eastern United States, typically shown as a spot on the map near New York City. Pet shops sold the birds as Hollywood Finches in the 1940s and 50s but eventually ran afoul of the Migratory Bird Treaty Act of 1918 and released their birds in Central Park to avoid prosecution. The released finches settled right in and became fully naturalized throughout the Eastern United States by the 1990s. They are aggressive birds and compete successfully for the same locations preferred by House Sparrows – openings in buildings, hanging plants and those floppy roofs on gas stations.

Interestingly, when visiting friends and relatives in older urban neighborhoods in Chicago and Boston, I have found House Sparrows to be holding their own. Bird feeders stocked with wild bird mixes containing Milo attract House Sparrows may be part of the problem. In locations and seasons when insects and loose grain are less available, House Sparrows are often found in grocery store parking lots and around restaurant dumpsters, eating spilled Cheetos®, French fries and other crumbs.

**Gotta Know the Habitat** – House Sparrows have become much less common in Blue Ridge, Georgia, the north Georgia mountain town I call home, and are very hard to find in December, when we schedule our local Christmas Bird Count. In fact, our typical tally was zero for House Sparrows most years prior to the 2016 Count. In 2016 and again in 2017, my regular Christmas Count birding partner Barb Owens and I sneaked quietly into the local Home Depot to find our House Sparrows. 2016 yielded eight birds in the outdoor, but covered, part of the Garden Department, and 2017 produced about 20 sparrows in the tropical plant room above the bird seed display!

**Christmas Bird Count "Patch": Home Depot for House Sparrows!**
**(Barb Owens)**

**Nest Boxes**

Bluebirds prefer to nest in open areas with scattered trees and low ground cover like farmland, meadows, golf courses, parks, school and business campuses and cemeteries, where they find the insects they need, along with wild fruits like dogwood, hawthorn, serviceberry, elderberry and pokeberry in the brushy edges of these habitats. Bluebirds do not nest in heavily forested areas. Completely open spaces are also less desirable, but the presence of fence wires, fence posts, telephone lines, and other hunting perches improve the chances of nesting. Suburban neighborhoods with well-developed landscaping also offer prime habitat for bluebirds. The mix of open lawn, shade trees, smaller trees like dogwood, redbud and holly and shrubbery for cover make ideal habitat. What is missing from most of these habitats is suitable cavities for nesting.

A LOT of widely different nest box designs have proven successful over the years – vertical, horizontal, wedge-shaped, cylindrical, with round or oblong entrance holes and even horizontal slot entrances. Nest box plans are available on the internet on the NABS website:

www.nabluebirdsociety.org/nestbox-plans/

**And at Nest Box Builder:**

http://nestboxbuilder.com/nestbox-plans-for-bluebirds.html

A suitable nest box should be made of ¾ inch to 1 inch thick cedar, redwood, cypress or pine. Exterior plywood is okay, but treated lumber is not. Redwood sometimes cracks or splits under dry conditions, and pine is less durable and may warp, although White Pine is quite stable. Five or six-inch diameter PVC pipe works well, as does cement fiber siding material, although it is heavy and only light colors should be used. An important advantage to using thick wood materials is the insulation value they provide, in both hot and cold weather.

Most commercially available boxes are cedar, which is stable and durable but will eventually discolor. If you must paint your nest box to meet personal or neighborhood association décor standards, paint only the outside in a very light color to avoid overheating. Pine boxes can be treated with Linseed oil or a water-based paint or stain. The inside should not be painted. Galvanized, zinc-coated or stainless-steel screws should be used for assembly.

**Ultimate Bluebird House (Songbird Essentials)**

Lumber made from recycled plastic bottles is becoming more popular as a nest box material because it is very durable and will not rot, fade or discolor. If plastic lumber is used, it must be light-colored to avoid overheating. The slick surface will not provide toeholds to help fledglings climb out of the box. Horizontal saw cuts on the inside surface below the entrance hole will help. Hardware cloth is not recommended for an inside climbing ladder because the bluebirds can get their feet caught in it.

The box should have interior dimensions at least four inches x four inches. Five inches x five inches is ideal for Eastern and Western Bluebirds, and the larger Mountain Bluebird does better in a box that is 5 ½ x 5 ½ inches inside dimensions. Five nearly grown bluebirds take up a lot of space! A larger space allows the female to build her nest toward the back of the box, which helps deter some predators.

The round entrance hole should be 1 ½ inches in diameter for Eastern Bluebirds, or 1 9/16 inches for Western and Mountain Bluebirds, and located 4 ½ to six inches above the floor. An oblong entrance hole should be 1 ⅜ inches wide and 2 ¼ inches tall. Slot entrances should be 1 3/8 inches tall.

All entrances should have smooth edges to avoid injuring the bluebirds. The well-equipped do-it-yourselfer will use a Forstner bit, which produces a smoother and more precise hole than a spade bit or hole saw. Round and oblong metal hole guards are available at birding specialty stores; these "portal protectors" prevent squirrels and woodpeckers from widening the entrance hole.

No perch is necessary for the agile bluebirds, and a perch actually makes the nest box more accessible to House Sparrows. A couple of shallow, horizontal saw cuts beneath the entrance hole will give the adults some traction. Similar saw cuts below the hole on the inside will help the nestlings climb out when they're ready.

An overhanging slanted roof offers shade and some protection from hawks and raccoons. A shallow saw kerf cut into the roof at a slight angle just back from the edge will divert rainwater and keep the entrance area drier. A four- or five-inch overhang is recommended where Cooper's and Sharp-shinned Hawks are common. These hawks have learned that young bluebirds get excited by the slight vibration caused by an adult bluebird landing on the top of the box when bringing food. Older nestlings are big and agile enough to poke their heads outside as they anticipate being fed. A hawk landing on the box creates the same vibration, and a short overhang allows the hawk to easily snatch a young bluebird as it pokes its head out. The long overhang makes it harder for feral cats and raccoons to reach the nestlings inside as well.

The nest box should have ventilation holes to allow air flow and prevent overheating. Small triangles can be cut out of the upper corners of the sides and corners of the bottom, or small holes can be drilled through the sides of the box, angled up slightly to prevent rainwater from running into the nest box.

Opening the nest box is critical for monitoring and cleaning, so the front, the top or the side of the box should be hinged to allow access. The best commercial box opens from both sides, with a Plexiglas panel on one side allowing viewing without danger of baby birds falling out. A hinged top or side-opening door is preferable to front-opening because either allows the female to escape through the entrance hole if she is disturbed. Otherwise, she may feel trapped or burst out into your face as you peer in. The door should be held closed to prevent predators from entering. A double-headed nail inserted through a hole in the side or front and into the door edge works well. Galvanized or brass fasteners with screw threads and an L-shaped top are used on many commercial nest boxes and are readily available at hardware stores and home centers.

## Predator Control

Bluebird landlords owe it to their tenants to keep nest, eggs and babies safe from predators. Raccoons, cats and snakes are the most likely varmints to prey on your bluebirds.

Proper box placement can reduce raccoon problems. Boxes in pastures or grasslands are less likely to attract raccoons than those in more wooded areas. Once the box is properly located, the best strategy is to keep the raccoon from getting to it. Several preventive methods work equally well with snakes and cats.

Two things to work on – access from a nearby tree, and access from the ground. Cats and squirrels are good jumpers, so locate your box at least 10 feet from any trees. Stopping access from the ground requires an effective baffle. Baffles are much easier to install on a smooth metal pole or a metal T-post normally used for fencing.

Three proven baffles are recommended by the North American Bluebird Society:
1. The Zeleny Cone Baffle, a 3-foot diameter cone made of galvanized sheet metal or aluminum.
2. The Kingston Stove Pipe Guard, an 8-inch diameter stove pipe or vent pipe, at least 24 inches long.
3. PVC Pipe Baffle, a length of 4-inch or 6-inch diameter PVC pipe with end cap, at least 24 inches long.

Note that Rat Snakes and Black Snakes can practically stand on their tails to a height of three feet, so a 36 inch to 48 inch long pipe is recommended where these snakes are prevalent.

Detailed materials lists and installation instructions for these baffles are available on the NABS website.

## Nest Box Location

Mount your nest box on a post or pole in an open location. Boxes mounted on trees are likely to attract other cavity nesters like wrens, chickadees, titmice, and nuthatches. Galvanized pipe, metal fence posts, and treated landscape timbers all make suitable posts. Well-designed bluebird poles are available from birding supply stores, including two- piece units that step-into the ground and are easily moved.

The nest box should be mounted so it's about five feet off the ground. Height doesn't matter to the birds, but the five-foot level makes monitoring and cleanout convenient for people. I've seen natural bluebird nest holes 40 feet up in trees and as low as two feet above the water in a flooded tree in a local park. Face the box away from prevailing winds and toward a nearby tree or shrub that fledging birds can fly to on their first flights from the box. Avoid facing the box west because the afternoon sun shining into the entrance hole can make the box dangerously hot.

Bluebirds are territorial. A strong male will defend his territory against other bluebirds that try to nest near his nest box, so bluebird boxes should be located 75 to 100 yards apart. A house, barn or other visual barrier between nest boxes will shorten the required spacing, so a one-in-front, one-in-back placement may be workable on a large lot in suitable open habitat.

Tree Swallows in the east and Violet-green Swallows in the west will compete with bluebirds for nest boxes. Swallows and bluebirds get along pretty well, so placing a second box 5 to 15 feet away from the first will allow the two species to nest close together. Some bluebird landlords have had success with swallows by mounting boxes back to back on the same post! The highly territorial swallows will chase other swallows away but will not fight with a nearby bluebird.

**Troublesome Insects**

Blowflies can be a problem for bluebirds. Similar to the common house fly, and sometimes called bluebottle flies, they belong to the Calliphoridae family of insects. They lay their eggs in nest material and sometimes on or near the bodies of nestling bluebirds. Infestations are worse in poorly drained nest boxes and those with old nests that have not been cleaned out. The blowfly larvae suck the blood of nestlings, weakening them and causing anemia. If larvae concentrations are low and if the young bluebirds are well fed, bluebird mortality is unlikely.

Preventing blowfly infestations is difficult. However, problems can be reduced by removing old nests immediately after each brood is fledged, since damp nest material is attractive to blowflies. Very high-quality commercial nest boxes are equipped with a platform made of vinyl-covered wire mesh that effectively raises the floor of the nest box about one inch. The mesh platform helps keep the nest dry, and blowfly eggs are more likely to sift through the nest material and fall to the bottom of the nest box where they fail to hatch.

Paper Wasps are another troublesome pest that builds umbrella shaped nests that hang from the ceiling of bluebird boxes. If wasps invade a box, the adult bluebirds will often abandon the nest, even if there are eggs or hatchlings. Wasp nests can be prevented by coating the ceiling and upper sides of the nest box with a very thin layer of Vaseline (wipe off the excess), rubbing the ceiling and upper walls with unscented Ivory soap, or rubbing the same areas with candle wax, crayon wax or household paraffin. If a bluebird nest is already in place, cover it with a paper towel to prevent soap or wax flakes from falling in when you treat the box.

Coating the interior with inert soap or wax is probably the safest way to deter wasps. Chemical insecticides meant for garden use should never be used. Spraying with a pyrethrum-based insecticide made for use with caged birds is safe and can be very effective. The active chemical in these sprays is Pyrethrum, which is naturally found in Chrysanthemum flowers, and has been used safely for many years.

## Monitoring and Cleaning

One of the joys of hosting bluebirds is following the progress of nesting by peeking into the nest box to monitor nest building, count eggs as they are laid and to watch the nestlings grow. Careful monitoring will not disturb the birds and early detection of blowfly infestations and wasp nests can be very beneficial.

Monitoring will tell you right away what species is using your nest box. If it's not bluebirds, don't be unhappy, welcome them and put up another box. Chickadees, wrens and nuthatches are more likely to use a box on a tree or placed too close to the edge of the woods. Swallows do well in perfect bluebird habitat and will tolerate bluebirds in a nearby second box.

## Identification of Nests and Eggs by Species

| BIRD SPECIES | NEST MATERIALS | EGGS |
|---|---|---|
| Bluebird | Very clean; grass or pine needles | 4 – 6, light blue, rarely white |
| Swallow | Coarser grasses; usually feathers | 5 – 7, white, smaller than bluebird |
| Chickadee | Moss & plant down, lined with hair | 5 – 8, tiny, white w/ brown speckles |
| Titmouse (rarely) | Moss, grass, lined w/ fur, feathers, sometimes scraps of snakeskin | 5 – 7, small, cream-colored with brown speckles |
| Brown-headed Nuthatch | Bark fibers, grass, twigs & hair. | 5 – 9, white, spotted with reddish-brown |
| House Wren | Twigs; bulky and lined with feathers and coarse grass | 5 – 6, buff-colored with dark brown speckles |
| House Sparrow | Grass; bulky, dome-shaped, lined with feathers, plastic, paper, etc. | 3 – 6, white to greenish-white, with brown or gray dots at larger end |

Egg laying will begin as soon as the nest is finished, with one egg laid each day, typically in the morning. To avoid disturbing the female bluebird during this sensitive stage, do your monitoring in the afternoon. Once the eggs hatch, watch for the adult to leave the nest box after a feeding and keep your monitoring peeks brief. Your monitoring should be limited to watching from a distance when the chicks are 12 days old. At this age, they are mobile enough to leave the box early if they're disturbed.

Make a note of the date that incubation starts so you can plan to be nearby on fledge day. Watching young bluebirds take their first flights is an unforgettable experience. As fledge day approaches, the adults will stop feeding and will call to the young birds from outside the box, encouraging them to fledge.

Since bluebirds will build a new nest on top of an old one left in the nest box, the nest box should be cleaned out after every nesting. If the old nest is not removed, the new nest built on top will be too high in the box, making the eggs and nestlings vulnerable to raccoons and other predators. I learned a neat trick to make cleaning quick and efficient from a man who took care of the bluebird and swallow boxes at the John C. Campbell Folk School near Brasstown, North Carolina, a total of about 50 boxes. He put a two-inch tall cut-off bottom of a thoroughly cleaned plastic or cardboard half-gallon milk carton in each box. After nesting, he just slid the container and nest out into his trash bag and put in a new carton bottom. Simple and sanitary!

If the milk carton method is not used, scrape the old nest out with a spatula or ice scraper. If you find parasites or if the box seems dirty, spray the interior with a dilute bleach solution (one-part bleach to 10 parts water.) I like to leave the door open for a day or two for thorough drying and sun sanitizing.

Bluebirds will use nesting boxes for winter shelter, with six or more birds in one box. It's a good idea to do another cleaning right before nesting begins in the spring to remove accumulated droppings. Mice sometimes build nests in empty boxes in winter, and a late winter cleaning will remove them.

> How readily the bluebirds become our friends and neighbors when we offer them suitable nesting retreats!
>
> John Burroughs

**Male Ruby-throated Hummingbird (Brian Lupa)**

**A yard full of hummers in Michigan (Bob Anderson)**

# 17

# Attracting Hummingbirds

*Hummers are the jewels of the garden. We explore their close relationship with the flowers they pollinate, along with diet details, their overnight mini-hibernation, and their amazing flying skills. Nesting is covered in detail. Guidelines for gardening to attract hummers blend with advice on feeders, nectar preparation and fending off ants and wasps.*

Hummingbirds are the almost magical acrobats of your garden. Their bright colors and amazing flying ability make them favorites for many, and their arrival after a long winter away is another promise that spring has returned. Many people who don't feed any other birds put out hummer feeders to bring these avian jewels into their yards and gardens.

Hummingbirds are found only in the Americas, with the greatest abundance by far in the tropical jungles of South America. North America is poor in hummingbirds compared to Central and South America. Of the 342 known species, only sixteen nest regularly in North America, and just one, the Ruby-throated Hummingbird, nests in the eastern half of the United States. In dramatic contrast, Columbia has 180 species and Ecuador, the size of Colorado, has 132 species.

**What's in A Name?**

All hummingbirds are not called "hummingbird" – in fact, they carry a lot of other names that add a touch of glamour and style: *Topaz, Coquette, Emerald, Hermit, Mango, Brilliant, Mountain-Gem,* and *Bee* are just a few. How would you like to be a *Barbthroat, Sapphire, Woodstar* or *Plumeleteer*? Does *Goldentail, Racquet-tail, Lancebill* or *Puffleg* suit you better? How about *Sabrewing, Sicklewing, Inca, Sunangel,* or *Blossomcrown*?

You get the idea. My favorite may be the *Green-tailed Trainbearer*.

Why are there so many species in South America and so few in North America? The answer lies in the role of hummingbirds as pollinators, combined with the vegetative and climate zone diversity in South America, particularly in the Andes mountain range. From sea level to over 15,000 feet in elevation, the Andes exhibit virtually all the climatic zones known on earth. Within each climatic zone, the diversity of plant communities is incredible, with many highly evolved flowering plants within each community.

Hummingbirds are highly evolved pollinators and nectarivores (nectar eaters) that scientists have organized into nine distinct "clades" or groups. The word *clade* comes from an ancient Greek word meaning *branch* and refers to a group of organisms that consists of a common ancestor and all its lineal descendants. Each hummingbird clade is closely associated with a particular clade of nectar-bearing flowering plants, and their role as pollinator is critical.

Abundant moisture and the frost-free climate in much of the Andes support year-round plant flowering and reliable hummingbird feeding opportunities without the need for migration, so plants and their pollinating hummingbirds are together year-round. Flower shape and bill shape are closely matched between specific plants and the hummingbirds that feed on them and pollinate them. This specificity allows as many as 140 species of hummingbirds to co-exist in the same geographic region. Plant groups and the hummingbird groups they were so dependent upon remained close together through long periods of time. As the Andes Mountains rose during mountain uplift over the past 10 million years, its plant communities evolved, and hummingbirds co-evolved with them.

While North America also has climate zones, the diversity of plant life within each zone is far less, and hummingbird / plant relationships are far more general. The seasonality of North America brings at least brief periods of winter-like weather that limit the availability of food for hummingbirds. Even limited migration takes them away from their favored plant communities.

Even in the "sky island" environments of southeastern Arizona, where isolated mountain ranges have climate zones ranging from hot desert to cold boreal forest, limited moisture reduces plant diversity. The dozen or so nesting hummingbird species in these sky islands are rich by North American standards, but pale in contrast with Columbia or Ecuador.

## Flight

A large part of our fascination with hummingbirds comes from their amazing flying skills. Hummers can fly forward, backward, sideways and straight up. They can even turn a backward somersault in flight and wind up flying upside down. Their ability to hover in one place is perfectly suited to hanging in the air in front of a flower for long enough to gather insects and suck nectar from the flower.

Many birds have adaptations that give them specific flying abilities – broad wings for soaring; slender, pointed wings for rapid flight, short wings and long tails for maneuverability - but hummingbirds win the prize for physical adaptations. They have hollow bones; fused vertebrae and fused pelvic bones that reduce weight; proportionally large chest muscles for power; tiny feet to reduce drag; longer, stronger bones in the "hand" portion of the wing for flexibility and control; and a large heart that efficiently pumps oxygen-filled blood to the flight muscles.

Hummingbird wing structure is unique, with a specialized ball-and-socket joint where the wing attaches to the sternum, allowing maximum rotation. The "arm" bones are much shorter than in other birds and most of the wing is really a combination of "wrist" and "hand." This structure allows the hummingbird wing to stroke forward and backward instead of up and down as most birds do. The wings move in a horizontal figure-eight pattern, generating lift on both forward and backward strokes. Hummingbirds wings beat from 8 to 200 times per second, depending on the size of the bird. Larger hummers have much slower wingbeats.

## Metabolism

Hummingbird metabolism is incredible, the fastest of any animal species. Only insect metabolisms are faster. Daytime body temperature is about 109°F, suggesting that internal fires burn hot! When feeding, up to 90 percent of flying time is spent hovering, which burns calories at a tremendous rate. To keep up, hummingbirds feed frequently during the day, consuming one and one-half times their body weight each day in flower nectar, insects and spiders. An equivalent diet for humans would include 150 Big Macs® a day! Interestingly, hummers spend most of their time sitting or perching, to conserve energy. Studies have shown that hummingbirds spend only about 15 percent of their time feeding and 75-80 percent resting and digesting. They eat many small meals each day, returning to favorite perches to rest.

## Torpor

Hummingbirds survive the night by slowing their metabolism to conserve energy. This overnight mini-hibernation is called "torpor." Heart rate drops to about 50 beats per minute from 500, body temperature drops from 109° to 48°F, and respiration slows dramatically. Upon waking, the hummingbird heats up by shivering. It can fly only when its body temperature reaches 86°F. Despite this efficient adaptation, a hummingbird may lose 10 percent of its body weight overnight.

## Colors

The brilliant iridescent colors in hummingbird plumage are structural rather than pigment, produced by the refraction of light through tiny air bubbles on the surface of the feathers. When light strikes the surface of the feather, some light is reflected back, while other light passes through the air bubbles and is reflected back from the inner surface. When the thickness of the air bubble matches up with the wave length of the light, particular colors are produced. In poor light, otherwise bright parts of the bird can look dark or black. I'm pretty sure I don't understand the physics of hummingbird colors, but I thoroughly enjoy their beauty.

## Migration

North American hummingbirds generally migrate north to nesting areas in spring and south to frost-free feeding areas in the fall. Many hummingbirds winter in Mexico and Central America, but some, like Anna's, do not migrate and are permanent residents within their range along the Pacific Coast. Similarly, Ruby-throated Hummingbirds can be found wintering along the Atlantic and Gulf Coasts of the southeastern US and in Florida.

While the Ruby-throat is the only nesting hummingbird in the Eastern United States, a number of western species winter in the Southeast each winter, and an increasing number of hummingbird enthusiasts leave feeders filled until Thanksgiving in hopes of attracting a winter hummer. While the winter visitors are typically immature birds, some birds return to the same yards to winter as adults. Julia Elliott, co-owner of the Bird Watcher Supply stores in Georgia and a licensed hummingbird bander, has recaptured the same Rufous Hummingbird in a backyard near Macon, Georgia for five successive winters.

Male hummingbirds migrate before females in both spring and fall; male Ruby-throats reach Florida and warmer parts of the Southeast in February. Females may be 10 days behind. They challenge the advance of spring by reaching feeders in north Georgia in late March despite the scarcity of flowers and active insects.

Ruby-throats migrate across the Gulf of Mexico, flying up to 500 miles nonstop for twenty hours or more. Fishermen and workers on oil-drilling platforms in the Gulf have reported them zipping by their locations 200 miles from land, flying low over the water, or stopping to rest on their boats and drilling platforms. Strong headwinds and spring storms can interfere with migration and certainly cause mortality at times. There is evidence that fewer Ruby-throats cross the Gulf in fall than in spring, most instead following the Texas coast back into Mexico. Perhaps the hurricane season is a factor, and the genes of many birds with a tendency to fly over water in fall have been lost at sea during storms.

Migration is in daylight to allow stops to feed, except cross-Gulf migration, which typically starts at dusk. Flight is low altitude, barely above the water or treetops. Average speed may be 20 to 25 miles per hour. Hummingbirds are solitary birds and migrate alone. They do not attach themselves to geese or other birds as legends claim. They take advantage of tailwinds to speed them along and reduce demands on precious stored energy. Young birds have no experience and must navigate without parental guidance, which may explain why those young western hummingbirds wind up in the Southeast each winter. Hummingbirds migrate at a time determined by genetic programming; changes in daylength are a factor. They migrate when they are ready and will not linger just because your feeders are still out.

## Nesting

After mating, nesting is a single parent activity with the female doing all the work. Even if a male was interested in helping he would be chased away by the female! A typical nest location is a small forked twig protected by leaves overhead. She builds the tiny nest, little bigger than half a golf ball, using leaf bits, plant down, and lichens; spider webs hold the nest together, give it flexibility and allow the nest to expand as the nestlings grow.

Two eggs are laid, usually two days apart, and incubated for 12 to 15 days. The female feeds the nestlings a slurry of nectar and regurgitated insects until they are ready to fledge after about three weeks. Mom will continue to feed the young birds for another week or so until they become independent. One brood is typical, but a second nesting is possible where the nesting season is long enough.

Occasionally a nest is built on something manmade like a chime or metal wall ornament, even a clothesline! Don and Noriko Carroll bought a house in Las Vegas and were delighted to discover a hummingbird nest built on a clothesline on the covered back porch. Using cameras and a combination of blinds and mirrors, they were able to observe and record nesting over three seasons. Their amazing experience with the Black-chinned Hummingbird they named "Honey" is captured in a stunning DVD entitled "First Flight – A Mother Hummingbird's Story."

---

**A Lesson in Nest Engineering**

The Arizona-Sonora Desert Museum outside Tucson is a blend of zoo, natural history museum, art gallery, botanical garden and aquarium. One of its most popular exhibits is the Hummingbird Aviary where visitors can watch as many as eight species of hummers carry out the business of nesting inside the building. When the Aviary was first opened in 1998, early nesting efforts failed because the nests fell apart. There were no spiders in the new facility to provide spider silk, the hummingbird equivalent of duct tape! Once spiders were brought in, hummingbird nesting was successful.

---

**Attracting with Flowers**

Hummingbirds can be successfully attracted to your yard and garden by flowers, feeders or a combination. A mix of annuals, perennials and shrubs can provide nectar and color from spring until fall. While red is the most frequently recommended color for both garden plants and artificial feeders, hummingbirds will happily feed from any color flower that produces nectar or harbors insects.

**Some of the most popular plants that attract hummingbirds:**

| Common Name | Scientific Name | Annual Perennial | Color(s) | Season |
|---|---|---|---|---|
| Bee Balm | Monarda didyma | Perennial | Red | Summer |
| Cardinal Flower | Lobelia cardinalis | Perennial | Red | Summer |
| Butterfly Bush | Buddleja sp. | Perennial Shrub | Purple, pink or, white | Summer |
| Trumpet Vine | Campsis radicans | Perennial | Orange-red | Summer |
| Snapdragon | Antirrhinum | Annual | Varies with variety | Until frost |
| Salvia | Salvia splendens | Annual | Red & purple | Until frost |
| Fuchsia | Fuchsia sp. | Annual except in deep south | Red, pink, purple & white | Until frost |
| Columbine | Aquilegia sp. | Perennial | Red, pink, blue & purple | Spring to early summer |
| Phlox | Phlox sp. | Perennial | Pink, red, blue & purple | Spring to fall |
| Butterfly Weed | Asclepias tuberosa | Perennial | Orange | Summer to fall |

Many flowers that attract hummingbirds have no fragrance. Like many birds, hummingbirds seem to have no sense of smell, and rely on sight to find food. If it's true that red draws hummingbirds to gardens and feeders, then one of my customers was on the right track when she told me that she stakes out a big red plastic tablecloth in her yard when the hummingbirds are due to arrive.

## Attracting with Feeders

Hummingbird feeders come in all shapes and sizes and range from purely functional to fancy and whimsical. They can be categorized as 'bottle' feeders or 'basin' feeders. Bottle feeders hold nectar in a vertical bottle or column and deliver it to a wider base with feeding ports. Basin feeders are shaped like flying saucers, with nectar stored in the base itself with feeding ports above the nectar in the basin cover. Most have at least a little bit of red coloring and many have white or yellow flower-like structures around the feeding ports. Your senses of beauty and budget should guide your selection, but there are some other things to consider.

A good feeder is easy to clean, with top and base that come apart easily. A wide neck makes it easy to slip in a cleaning brush; narrow necked feeders are likely to accumulate mold spots in those hard to reach places. The base should come completely apart, allowing access to the inside corners and feeding ports. Some, like the Dr. JB Feeder, can be safely washed in the top rack of a dishwasher.

Decorative features sometimes create other problems. Yellow "blossoms" around feeding ports attract wasps and yellow jackets – something about the color. Similarly, the plastic mesh bee guards on some feeders have tiny holes that accumulate gunk quickly and require frequent cleaning with a small brush.

Hummingbird nectar is sweet and a natural attractant for ants. Any feeder that leaks or spills makes the problem worse. I eventually banned from my store all feeders that delivered nectar through a little downspout at the bottom – the little cork with a tube running through it, similar to the water bottle attached to your hamster cage when you were a kid. A couple of environmental factors contribute to spillage with these feeders: wind and heating by the sun. Wind sloshes the nectar and it can spill; sun heating causes the nectar to expand and it will drip from a poorly designed feeder. The little downspout makes it easy to convert a pretty bottle into a feeder, and beautiful examples are sold at art and craft shows. They're pretty, but they leak!

**Nectar Protector Jr. – Red**

**Nectar Protector – Clear**
**(Larger Capacity)**

*(Product photos in this chapter courtesy of*
*Gold Crest Distributing)*

Even a well-designed feeder will attract ants. Somehow, they know that if they climb the right post, run across the bracket and climb down the hanging wire or chain they'll reach the feeder. A straightforward but ingenious gadget solves the problem quickly and inexpensively – the 'ant moat' – which is a small watertight cup filled with water and attached above the feeder. The ants follow their map up the post and across the bracket but will not cross the water-filled moat.

Several commercial models are available, and home-made versions are easy to make from spray-paint can tops, tuna cans, even obsolete film canisters. Ant moats come in a variety of colors including red, green and clear. A clear moat makes it easy to see when it's empty. Perky Pet® makes a chemical version that uses the insecticide Permethrin, which is safe for use around birds and household pets. A number of feeders offer built-in ant moats, either as a cup-shaped hollow at the top of a bottle feeder or a central cup in the center of a basin feeder where the hanging rod screws in. Keeping the ant moat full of water can be a challenge with small moats and especially so in low-humidity climates. The ant moat should be rinsed when nectar is changed and thoroughly cleaned frequently. A bonus feature of a clean and filled ant moat is that chickadees and titmice will use it as a water source and tiny bird bath!

### My favorite feeders?

- All the *HummZinger* models by Aspects, which are shallow spaceship-shaped dishes with feeding ports on top and a built-in ant moat in the center. They range from very plain (The *Mini*) to quite attractive (The *Fancy*). The HummZinger *Ultra* also has Nectar-Guard® tips on the feeding ports that prevent bees and wasps from contaminating the nectar.

- Dr. JB's Feeders, with their wide-mouthed flat-topped glass bottles, two-piece easy clean base and replaceable flower inserts. They're dishwasher-safe, and larger capacity bottles are available for locations and seasons with lots of hummers.

HummZinger Ultra – 12 ounce Model        Dr. JB's Clean Feeder – All Red Model

- Best-1 Hummingbird Feeders, in 8 ounce and 32 ounce models. They're inexpensive, the two-piece base is easy to clean, and replacement bottles and bases are available. The glass bottles have narrow necks, requiring a bent brush to clean, but the 32-ounce models are decorative, and the low cost balances out the cleaning issue.

**Best-1 8 oz**　　　　**32 oz Hummingbird**　　　　**32 oz Black-chinned**

- Classic Brand Hummingbird Feeders – Ruby (10 ounce), Garnet (20 ounce), Diamond (30 ounce) and Big Gulp (40 ounce) models, all with built-in ant moats. They're attractive, inexpensive, and easy to clean, with wide-mouth bottles and a range of capacities. The only negative feature is that the ant moats are small, requiring frequent attention.

**Ruby 10 oz**　　　**Garnet 20 oz**　　　**Diamond 30 oz**　　　**Big Gulp 40 oz**

## Feeder Location

Obviously, we want to put our feeders where they are visible and easy to watch. With that in mind, try to place your feeders out of the reach of cats, at least four feet off the ground and in a shady spot. Shade will keep the feeder cooler with less fermentation and lower risk of leakage from expansion. Make sure the feeder is easy to hang and take down, so it'll be easy for you to keep it clean and full. Remember that spider webs are needed for nest construction, so placing a feeder in or near a shrub or small tree where spiders are active may benefit female hummingbirds as they seek spider silk for their nests.

I was surprised to learn that praying mantises and even dragonflies will catch and eat a hummingbird, so be careful about placing a feeder too close to dense vegetation where a mantis might lurk. Don't put your feeder near a hummingbird nest (if you're lucky enough to find one) to minimize the risk of predation.

## Nectar

Hummingbird nectar is very simple – it's just sugar water, with a sugar concentration about equal to the concentration of natural nectar from flowers. The do-it-yourself formula is one part fully-refined white table sugar to four parts water. Hot tap water is generally adequate for mixing, although heating the water will dissolve the sugar faster. If your tap water contains iron or other heavy chemicals, or has strong tastes or odors, consider using bottled or purified water for safer nectar. There is no need to boil the water if your local water supply is safe. In fact, the nectar in your feeder will be contaminated the first time a hummingbird feeds from it. You can mix nectar in quantity and keep it in your refrigerator for two to three weeks.

Never use artificial sweeteners, which have no nutritional value. Honey is a wonderful natural sweetener but fosters bacterial and fungal growth when mixed with water. Despite its healthful benefits for humans, it is dangerous for hummingbirds, so don't ever use it. Food coloring may be harmful to hummingbirds and should never be added to your nectar.

Nectar in your feeder will only stay fresh for three to four days, especially in hot weather. The sugar begins to naturally ferment after a few days, and pollen and bacteria are introduced by the hummingbirds themselves as they feed. Rinse your feeder with hot water when you change nectar and watch for the development of mold. Thoroughly clean your feeder frequently, with warm soapy water and a brush. At least once a month, soak the feeder in a dilute bleach solution (one tablespoon of bleach per cup of water) to sterilize the feeder, and rinse thoroughly.

A new issue has come up with the popularity of less refined and raw sugars for human consumption - turbinado, brown sugar, raw sugar, sucanot, organic sugar - which are beige or brown in color. These 'health-food' products may have a place in human lifestyles, but they're not safe for hummingbirds. These sugars are refined by the same process as white sugar but without removing all the molasses and other non-sugar components. The result is a less-pure sucrose which contains about five times as much iron as white sugar. Iron is essential to hummingbirds, and they naturally get what they need from the insects they eat. Their bodies are programmed to store it when consumed and too much iron is harmful.

Sheri Williamson, author of the *Peterson Field Guide to Hummingbirds* and co-director of the Southeastern Arizona Bird Observatory, addressed this in an e-mail to Steve Holzman of the Georgia Ornithological Society in response to his question about less-refined sugars:

"What little iron these birds need comes from the invertebrates in their diet. Chronic iron uptake above this level will cause Iron Storage Disease, which kills the birds slowly and painfully by building up in their organs. This problem is well known in the zoo community, but the Arizona-Sonora Desert Museum still lost almost all of its captive hummingbirds to ISD several years ago."

Commercial nectar is available in granulated and liquid forms. Clear nectar is basically just table sugar and the red version is colored with natural dyes from flowers. The real value is convenience. Commercial mixtures with added vitamins and minerals are formulated for captive hummingbirds that are being rehabilitated but are unnecessary for wild hummingbirds eating a natural diet of nectar and insects and are a needless expense for the rest of us.

## Is Red Coloring Dangerous?

Much of the concern about red dye in hummingbird nectar can be traced to 1971 and Red Dye No.2, an artificial dye developed in 1878 and used in everything from sausage casings to ice cream, even women's makeup. After nearly a century of use, concerns about Red Dye No.2, also known as amaranth, were first raised by Soviet scientists in

1971, with claims that it caused cancer. The public outcry in the US was huge, to the point that the Mars candy company stopped making red M&Ms, *even though they had never contained Red Dye No.2!* Studies by the Food and Drug Administration (FDA) concluded that Red Dye No. 2, in high doses, could cause cancer in female rats and the dye was banned in 1976. Red M&Ms did not return until 1986.

The red color in modern commercial nectars is derived from flower parts. No definitive studies have been done that prove either harm or safety in these flower-based colorings. If you are concerned about it, don't use red nectar. Your feeder probably has more than enough red to be attractive without using red nectar.

## Honeybees, Wasps, Raccoons and Bears

Hummingbird nectar is attractive to lots of critters besides hummingbirds. Since it's about the same sweetness as natural flower nectar, it's a no-brainer for honeybees to load up! One of my customers sent me this picture of honeybees on her feeder, wondering what to do. She didn't want to harm the bees, but they had taken over the feeder, keeping the hummers away.

**Honeybees Love Nectar!   (Karol Weech)**

Our solution was to take the feeder inside and wipe it clean to remove any sticky nectar. While the feeder was inside, she filled a shallow saucer with nectar and set it on her deck rail 10 feet away from the feeder location. The honeybees quickly found the saucer and began gathering nectar. A few bees returned to the feeder when it was hung up, but most stayed with the saucer of nectar. The saucer was brought in after a day or so and the bees moved on.

Wasps, hornets and yellow jackets are much more likely to be a problem than honeybees. They are aggressive and can drive hummingbirds away. They can be dangerous for people as well, especially those with sensitivity to the venom, which can cause anaphylactic shock, a serious allergic reaction that can be fatal. Since they do not lose their stingers as honeybees do, they can sting repeatedly.

Reducing problems with wasps, hornets and yellow jackets starts with general sanitation. Be sure garbage cans are clean and covered tightly, and be sure there is no trash, empty soda cans or standing water nearby. Take pet food, water dishes and other sources of refined proteins inside. Fresh nectar is less attractive than old nectar that has begun to ferment.

The next step is to eliminate leaking hummer feeders. Basin-type feeders like the HummZinger are least likely to leak. Basin-type feeders hold the nectar well below the feeding ports, making it harder for wasps to reach it. Regardless of the type of feeder, keeping it squeaky-clean will reduce its attractiveness to attract these insects.

Wasps, hornets and yellow jackets are very attracted to the color yellow. Using feeders with no yellow parts may be helpful but the insects can smell nectar and will eventually find it. These pesky and dangerous insects can be trapped, using any of several commercially made traps or home-made traps. The least expensive commercial traps provide a variety of plastic funnels and other parts that can be combined with an empty soda bottle to make the trap. Some type of bait is placed in the trap to attract the insects. A protein-based bait is most effective early in the season – tuna fish, moist pet food or over-ripe meat. In mid-summer or later, a sugary bait like hummingbird nectar or non-diet soda works best. Yellow color increases effectiveness.

---

**Simple Wasp Trap**
(World of Hummingbirds http://www.worldofhummingbirds.com)
You can also make a wasp trap out of an old soda or water bottle. Cut the bottle in two (2) about one-third (1/3) of the way down the bottle. Turn the top of the bottle over and put it inside the bottle bottom like a funnel. Staple the two halves together. Use a hole-punch to put two holes on either side of the top of the bottle. Run a string through the holes to create a hanger. Put some bait inside the trap and hang it up. The insects will go in and cannot find their way out. Toss the trap when it is full.

---

Many of the inexpensive commercial traps and virtually all the home-made versions are functional but not attractive. Pretty glass hive-shaped traps are available that work well and cost less than $20.00. These traps have a raised bottom with a hole in the center; sugar water or non-diet soda is added to fill the depressed outer ring of the trap, and the exterior is left a little sticky to attract the insects. Eventually they find and enter the hole in the bottom of the feeder and cannot escape.

**Wasp Trap Kit (Gadjit)**

**Small Wasp Traps (Toland Home & Garden)**

Raccoons love nectar. I once had a lanky raccoon that visited my hummingbird feeder nearly every night. It took me a while to figure out why my HummZinger feeder was empty but undamaged each morning and my deck rail was sticky with nectar. I finally snuck out with my flashlight one evening and caught the ring-tailed bandit standing on the deck rail and tipping the feeder into his mouth. His aim wasn't very good to start, and he spilled a lot of nectar on his chest, his feet and my deck rail. I spied on him a few nights and his table manners improved. Eventually I took the feeder in at night and he moved on.

Sometimes even a big nectar lover can be gentle with the feeder. I found this photo floating around on the internet but have no idea of the source. The spruce trees in the background suggest that it's from the western United States or Alaska. Whoever took the photograph was pretty close to the action!

**Adult Male Purple Martin (Brian Lupa)**

**Mrs. Abernathy's Gourd Colony – Epworth, GA (Tom Striker)**

# 18

# Attracting Purple Martins

*A complete guide to attracting martins and maintaining a successful colony, including habitat requirements, properly designed housing, location and monitoring. New information on migration details the dangers, timing and speed of migration. Only one in ten martin landlords is successful; this chapter reveals the reasons for failure and the keys to success.*

You can never know too much about Purple Martins. I've had a successful colony since 2006, but don't know enough about them. They're wonderful birds, great big swallows that return to North America from their winter quarters in Brazil in early spring, readily accept properly located martin houses and gourds, and make cheerful sounds all summer long. Martins soar and glide much more than other swallows and can change direction instantly to catch an elusive insect in the air. Watching a flock of feeding martins in an early summer sky is entrancing and addictive!

I opened my bird store in the spring of 2003 and put up a 12-compartment martin house right away, with two big gourds attached. I had met a martin expert from the Purple Martin Conservation Association at the annual bird store trade show that January and was confident I could attract martins to the open lawn in front of my shop in downtown Blue Ridge, Georgia. It took three years.

The first subadult (one year old) male showed up in April of 2006, followed quickly by a female. They moved into one of the gourds and set up housekeeping. That was it, one pair, but they nested successfully and fledged five youngsters in early July. They were gone by the end of July, probably joining other martins in a pre-migration gathering where they loafed and fed heavily in preparation for a 4,000-mile trip to the Amazon Basin.

New martin housing like mine is first colonized by young birds from last year's hatch, typically from a nearby colony that is full.

Adult martins have extremely high site affinity or fidelity, meaning that they will return to where they nested last year. Many adults return to the colony where they were hatched year after year for their whole lives. Eventually, a mature colony may be full or nearly so, with no vacant compartments for last years' young to move into. Site fidelity is not as strong in young birds which haven't nested yet, and they will abandon their home colony if it is full when they return from migration, seeking nesting space in a new colony.

---

**Martin Site Fidelity:  There's No Place Like Home, Even After It's Gone.**

I used to drive to my store through a little housing development surrounded by open fields. For several seasons I watched Purple Martins around an old gourd colony that was active but falling apart; three whole natural gourds hung from crossbars with half a dozen broken ones, and the posts listed badly. The property changed hands one winter and the new owners 'cleaned up' by removing what was left of the posts and gourds. As I drove by in mid-March, I watched several adult martins hovering in the air exactly where their gourds had been. Sadly, the new property owners had no idea what they had lost; a wannabe martin landlord would have given his or her eyeteeth to take over that woebegone but still vibrant colony.

---

Martins require a suitable hole or cavity for nesting. They are secondary cavity nesters; that is, they do not excavate or create their own nesting holes but use natural cavities or those created by other birds, such as woodpeckers. Early records indicate that martins used woodpecker holes near water for nesting in pre-settlement days, although Native Americans were observed to provide hollow gourds on poles in their villages for martins and may have done so for hundreds of years.

Purple Martins are one of only three North American bird species that are known to have made a "tradition shift" in their selection of nesting locations. Chimney Swifts have shifted from hollow trees to chimneys and other manmade structures while Barn Swallows have shifted from cave mouths and other rocky niches to nest locations in barns and garages or under bridges and wharves. The shift for martins probably began with gourds provided by Native Americans and accelerated as settlers installed gourds and later houses for martins. In the eastern United States, martins have abandoned the use of natural cavities and nearly all martins nest in multi-compartmented houses or gourds. In the west, some Purple Martins continue to use natural cavities but have begun to accept loose arrangements of single-pair houses grouped on poles or pilings near water. Martins in the desert southwest continue to nest primarily in holes in trees or giant cacti.

Purple Martins are widespread in North America. They are most common in the eastern US and southern Canada, with smaller populations in the Pacific Northwest, the desert Southwest and northern Mexico. Purple Martins have suffered a serious population decline in the west. West Texas populations are stable, but trends are mixed in most of the eastern US, with notable declines in the north. Competition with European Starlings and House Sparrows for nest sites may be involved, despite the efforts of over a million caring "martin landlords" who have installed and maintained housing for them. Climate change, including earlier than normal warmth in the spring, may be a factor as well.

## Purple Martin Migration

Martins winter in South America, returning to the US as spring returns. Northward migration in spring may be erratic, the birds following weather warm enough for insect flight, and retreating with cold waves. Florida landlords welcome their birds in January, while it may be Mother's Day before martins reach Canada. Because martins eat insects they catch in flight, they are susceptible to starvation during periods of cool and/or rainy weather when flying insects are scarce. My birds have returned to north Georgia each spring in early to mid-March, only to leave for days at a time when the weather turned cold or wet.

The Purple Martin Conservation Association (www.purplemartin. org) was founded in 1987 by James Hill, III, and remains the world leader in research, education and conservation of Purple Martins, providing guidance and quality products in support of martin landlords.

Research done by PMCA suggests that when martins are ready to migrate, they can move very quickly. During the summer of 2007, twenty adult male and female Purple Martins nesting in a PMCA colony near Erie, Pennsylvania, were fitted with tiny geolocators weighing less than a dime. This was groundbreaking stuff – large birds like eagles and falcons had carried satellite transmitters that tracked migration, but they were far too heavy for songbirds. The much lighter geolocator used for martins contains a light sensor, a clock, a battery and a microprocessor. It collects data but must be retrieved to be read.

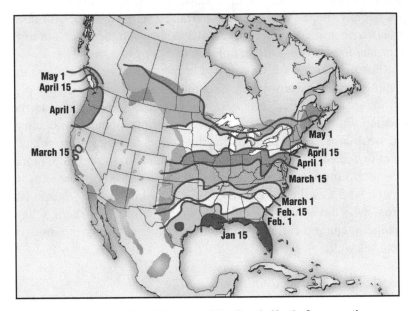

**Martin Migration Map (Courtesy of the Purple Martin Conservation Association PMCA)**

Worn like a backpack and secured with tiny loops around the legs, the geolocators record light levels every minute of the day and night. These recordings can be analyzed to approximate the location of migrating martins; timing of sunrise and sunset provides information about longitude - location east to west; dawn in New Orleans is much later than dawn in Pensacola, Florida. Day length helps with latitude – location north to south. Day length shortens as birds move south until they reach the equator, then lengthens as they move further south into Brazil. The combination of sunrise time and day length allowed researchers to pinpoint a martin's location within 40 miles east to west and 110 miles north to south.

To make things more interesting, martin migration occurs right around the spring (March 21) and fall (September 21) equinoxes, when day length is the same everywhere on the planet. As a result, there's a two-week fuzzy period around each equinox when latitude cannot be estimated.

Researchers had to recapture the geolocator martins to analyze the data when they returned to Erie after the 8,000-mile round trip to Brazil. After an agonizing wait of almost 10 months, two adult females were recaptured. The first, known as Yellow 2551, was recaptured on April 30, 2008, her geolocator loaded with astonishing information about her travels.

Before this amazing research, conventional wisdom held that Purple Martins migrated in a leisurely fashion, like other swallows. They are daytime migrants and feed along the way. There was little information about the speed or the route, and no answer to the question: "Do martins cross the Gulf of Mexico in migration?" *Birds of North America* is the most comprehensive reference for information about the life histories of birds that breed in North America. It is supported by the Cornell University Lab of Ornithology and the American Ornithology Society and updated frequently. Its species account for the Purple Martin stated: "Probably follows typical swallow pattern of leisurely movement, with migration in both directions spanning several months."

Apparently Yellow 2551 didn't get the memo, because her geolocator data revealed that she spent her last night in Brazil on April 12th and arrived at the Erie colony by the night of April 25th. She traveled 4,400 miles in 13 days, with nine flight days and four rest days. She flew from the Amazon Basin to the Yucatan Peninsula near Merida, Mexico, in five days. She rested two nights, then flew across the Gulf of Mexico non-stop, making landfall near the Texas–Louisiana border. Yellow 2551 rested two more nights near New Orleans, then headed for home with one more stopover in southern Illinois. She averaged nearly 500 miles per flight day. The second female took a more leisurely trip, arriving 27 days after leaving Brazil.

Similar geolocator research by PMCA and the Purple Martin Association of the Dakotas in 2011-12 traced the travels of another female which nested in Sioux Falls, South Dakota. Starting in early April 2011, she rocketed across the Gulf and reached her South Dakota colony in 15 days. Her return trip to Brazil again took her across the Gulf of Mexico but lasted 45 days. Interestingly, both migration legs in 2012 took her overland through Mexico, around the Gulf. Her spring trip took 31 days. Weather conditions were a likely cause, but no one knows.

What triggers martin migration, especially spring migration? The martins that nest in my colony in north Georgia probably leave Brazil in mid to late February in order to reach Blue Ridge in early to mid-March. Yellow 2551, the female from Erie, Pennsylvania, is apparently content to remain in Brazil until early April, a full month after my

Georgia birds have arrived at their home colony. She somehow knows that she must wait until temperatures and food supplies are adequate in Erie before starting migration. Perhaps further research will tell us more about this critical timing.

The first birds to arrive are adults, martins that are at least two years old. The male is a solid glossy blue-black. Adult females are much lighter, but with purple on their heads and backs. They're sometimes called "scouts," implying that they somehow send word back that the weather's fine and there are plenty of nesting sites available. They're really just aggressive adults ready to breed. They may stop at your colony during migration, but their homing instinct and strong affinity for their nesting colony will keep them moving. Note that adults that didn't breed successfully or whose housing is no longer habitable may attempt to colonize new housing or move into an existing colony.

Sub-adult birds may lag the adults by two to eight weeks. These are last year's young with no nesting experience, seeking available housing to colonize. They will continue to arrive for another four to six weeks; purple martins may arrive and begin nesting as late as the end of May in the South.

**Diet**

Martins are aerial insectivores, catching insects in flight. Martin diet is diverse and changes with insect abundance during the season. The menu includes dragonflies, damselflies, midges, flies, stinkbugs, leafhoppers, mayflies, flying beetles, butterflies, moths, grasshoppers, cicadas, bees and wasps. Contrary to myth and marketing claims, they don't eat many mosquitoes; stomach content analysis suggests that only two to five percent of their total diet is mosquitoes. Watching martins feed in flight will confirm this; they forage 100 to 500 feet up, sometimes higher, whereas mosquitoes are found within 20 feet of the ground, where you and I and other warm-blooded mammals hang out.

**Nesting**

Purple Martins begin nest building four to six weeks after arriving at their nesting colony. Once begun, nesting may span 70 days or more. My experience in north Georgia is that nest building doesn't begin until at least mid-April, despite spring arrival of adult birds between March 5th and 16th. Without fail, cold and windy weather drives my birds back south at least once in March and early April. The birds seem to know that insect food is not yet abundant enough to feed nestlings and wait for warmer weather and plenty of insects before nesting begins.

By mid-April in Georgia, though, the hormones must be raging, and nest building is underway. A variety of nesting materials may be used, including twigs, straw and pine needles. The landscape near my martin colony includes holly shrubs and a huge silver maple tree; prickly holly leaves, fresh maple leaves and even the winged samara fruits of the maple have wound up in nests. Male and female work on the nest together and construction may take a month to complete. A low mud dam at the front of the nest is often a finishing touch, perhaps built to ensure that eggs and baby birds don't fall out.

---

**No Dear – Let Me Do That.**

Martin households seem to have the same rules as human households. I installed a tiny camera in one of the big gourds in my martin colony, wired to a television inside the store. It allowed my fascinated customers and staff to watch everything: nest building, egg laying, turning the eggs, egg hatching, feeding, wing testing, and finally – fledging. During nest building, we watched both male and female bring in nest material and tuck it into place. We were amazed but not surprised to see Mama Martin look at the leaf Papa Martin had just placed so carefully, pull it out and tuck it in somewhere else. Sort of like moving the couch at my house. (For camera information: www. birdhousespycam.com )

---

The last stage in nest building is the addition of a layer of fresh green leaves, which may add moisture or act as an insecticide. Egg laying begins soon after the leaves are added, one egg per day and usually in the morning. Two to eight pure white eggs are laid, although a typical clutch is about five. Incubation begins when the second to the last egg is laid.

The female does nearly all the incubating since only she is equipped with a brood patch, a featherless area on her breast that is rich in blood vessels that deliver warmth to the eggs. The male may sit on the eggs briefly to maintain warmth while the female is away feeding. Incubation lasts 15 to 16 days, although cool weather may delay things. Hatching takes place over two to three days.

Newly hatched martins are tiny, featherless and pink and their eyes remain closed for a week to 10 days. Cold temperatures can be dangerous until the nestlings have enough feathering to maintain their body temperature without brooding by the female. Feathers begin to show after a week or so and the birds are fully feathered after about 25 days.

Both parents feed the nestlings for 26 to 32 days until they fledge. It's a full-time job! I was able to watch a lot of feeding over the years, thanks to our tiny camera. Small insects are offered during the first few days, but the size of the bites grows amazingly fast, and the nestlings are able to handle whole beetles and even dragonflies by the time they're about seven days old.

**My Bird Store Martin House**

The nestlings are ready to leave the nest about 28 to 32 days after hatching. For several days before that, they will move about the nest compartment or gourd, poke their heads out the opening and even come out onto the "porch" of a multi-unit house. Feeding slows dramatically three to four days before fledging; the young birds get hungry, lose a little weight and become anxious to leave the nest to be fed. The weight loss helps ensure that first flights are successful.

I've often wondered what that first flight feels like to the month-old martin that has been confined to a tiny box with four or five siblings with barely enough room to open its wings. Somehow, they know what to do and watching just-fledged martins is a treat! Takeoffs are easy enough, and they learn in-flight maneuvers quickly, but landings are a challenge for a while.

The adults will continue to feed the young birds for about two weeks, until they have learned to feed on their own. The young may return to the nest box for a night or two, but soon join the adults in small pre-migratory roosts. As migration time nears, small local flocks like mine will join other flocks in larger migratory roosts that may be used year after year. These roosts can be in marshes, on sandbar islands in large lakes or under bridges. The roost may be used for six to 12 weeks, although individual birds may stay for only a week or two.

---

**A Local One-time Roost Can Wreak Havoc**

I had never seen a large migratory roost until August of 2012, when Purple Martins began to gather each evening to roost on the roofs of several huge covered boat slips at the marina on Lake Blue Ridge near Blue Ridge, Georgia. The flock grew for several weeks until it reached an estimated 100,000 birds. As sunset neared each evening, the sky was full of small flocks coming in across the lake, and the light-colored metal roofs of the boat slips were blackened by the huge numbers of birds. Dramatic – but messy, since large numbers of birds produce large quantities of droppings. Thunderstorms washed the poop off the roofs and the accompanying winds blew the slurry on the boats moored below. Boat owner complaints brought representatives of the Georgia Department of Natural Resources and the Georgia Department of Health to the marina. As generally happens with events sponsored by Mother Nature, nothing important happened until the birds left. A few birds have gathered at migration time in recent years, but nothing like 2012.

---

## Starting Your Martin Colony

Attracting and hosting Purple Martins is both simple and complex, a substantial colony can be expensive, and a little luck is involved. Educating yourself about Purple Martins before getting started will save time, reduce frustration and help you avoid an expensive, wrong decision. Only an estimated 10 percent of installed martin housing is actually occupied by Purple Martins, for a variety of reasons. The keys to success are:

1) Suitable habitat;
2) Quality housing; and
3) Active colony management.

*Habitat is critical.* Your martin housing should be placed in the most open location available, at least 40 to 60 feet away from trees or buildings, yet within 120 feet of your home or other human activity. Remember that the interaction between martins and people goes back at least to pre-settlement times in North America, when Native Americans encouraged martins to live in suspended gourds in their villages. Claiming that the birds "learned" to live near people probably overstates what happened, but it is likely that natural selection played a role. Snakes, owls, crows, hawks and raccoons tend to shy away from homes and people, and martins nesting near humans should have a higher probability of raising their young. A watchful and alert martin landlord who monitors the colony will add to the likelihood of nesting success.

Trying to attract martins to an unsuitable location is frustrating and expensive. I have talked to many prospective martin landlords with vacation or permanent homes in the southern Appalachians. The very features that make their homes attractive often work against success with martins. Wooded hillside or ridgetop locations with spectacular views can be dangerously windy. Low maintenance landscaping usually means a too-small yard surrounded by trees. A heavily forested vacation home community is often a long way from the open habitats martins require for feeding. Weekend or part-time occupancy means the owners may not be present to open or close martin housing when needed and reduces their effectiveness as a deterrent to potential predators.

The other key element to habitat is where luck comes into play. Your colony must be where the year-old martins that will become your tenants can find it! Educating yourself before trying to attract martins should include scouting your local area for active colonies and martin feeding areas. Having an active colony within a mile or two of yours is a real positive; if the established colony is full, last year's young from that colony will seek other nesting options. They may have actually seen your colony last year while feeding prior to migration. Locating your colony within two miles of open feeding areas like farm fields, pastures and water increases your chances of success.

*Quality housing* can mean multi-unit houses, natural or plastic gourds, or both. Houses may be made of wood, aluminum or plastic, and should be white or a light color. White reflects heat, keeping the housing cooler in summer. Wooden houses provide insulation and can be works of carpenterial art but are heavy. Only untreated lumber should be used – cedar, cypress, pine or redwood, ¾ inch in thickness. Plastic housing should be thick enough to prevent a greenhouse effect caused by transparent material. A layer of insulation can be added to the attic of plastic or aluminum houses.

Whatever the material, the house or gourd cluster should raise and lower vertically on a telescoping pole, lanyard or winch system to allow frequent monitoring. The pole should be 12 to 18 feet tall; 15 feet is the most common height for commercially made systems. The likelihood of wind damage increases with height. Even lightweight aluminum and plastic houses will be heavy when filled with nests, nestlings and adult birds, so the pole should be anchored securely in concrete, with about 24 inches underground.

Expert recommendations on compartment size have changed based on research on nesting success. The old standard of six inch x six inch compartments is out of date, and deeper compartments are recommended to provide greater protection from reach-in predators like raccoons, hawks and owls. Larger compartments are more comfortable for two adults and four or five growing youngsters and reduce the chances of nestlings falling or jumping out prematurely. Newly designed commercial houses have 12 inch deep compartments or allow adjacent smaller compartments to be connected by removing panels or leaving interior connecting holes unplugged. Gourds should be at least eight inches in diameter, and 10-12 inch gourds are even better. My own experience is that large gourds were the first to be occupied as my colony grew.

Entrance holes should be STARLING RESISTANT! Entrance holes vary in size; traditional round holes are 2 1/8 inches in diameter, but a range between 1 ¾ inches and 2 ¼ inches is acceptable. The only problem with these round holes is that European Starlings can get into your housing and wreak havoc, killing adult martins and nestlings. If you're starting a colony or adding new housing, you should insist on Starling Resistant Entrance Holes (SREH) on any new house or gourds. A number of versions are available, but the standard crescent design is available on most commercially made houses and gourds and is very effective in keeping European Starlings out. Replacement entrances are available to retrofit existing housing and the investment is worthwhile if you are troubled by starlings.

Predator guards are recommended on all active colonies. Squirrels, raccoons and even snakes are capable of climbing your martin pole. Commercial predator guards are like cylindrical squirrel baffles for bird feeders, but larger in diameter and longer, typically 24-30 inches tall. They should be mounted so the top of the guard is at least four feet above the ground. Do-it-yourself plans are available on the PMCA website.

Owl and hawk guards are made of tubing or large-gap wire mesh, depending on house design. They are mounted on the face of the house in front of the entrance holes, preventing predatory birds from getting close enough to reach into the nesting compartments. As noted earlier, deeper compartments also reduce the risk of hawk and owl predation.

Where fire ants are a problem, Teflon tape or spray can be wrapped or sprayed on the pole, or a ring of grease or petroleum jelly can be applied to the pole.

*Active colony* management is the third key to becoming a successful martin landlord. Large compartments, predator guards and starling resistant entrance holes are a great start, but frequent monitoring is critical to success. As nesting gets underway, you can supply nesting materials - dry pine needles, twigs and straw - and create a wet area for mud. Crushed oyster shells and eggshells from your kitchen are a prime source of calcium to replace calcium used in egg production and to strengthen the bones of growing nestlings. Kitchen eggshells should be rinsed, dried in a 350° F oven and crushed.

Many landlords number the compartments and keep written records of nesting, clutch size, hatch date and fledge date. Daily walk-under inspections will reveal problems – feathers, eggshells, thrown-out nestlings, etc.

Housing should be lowered weekly to check for predator activity and insect infestations. Mites and blowflies are the most common nest parasites and can weaken or kill nestlings if not taken care of. The use of pesticides to control parasites was common in the past but is dangerous for adults and nestlings. Pesticides should not be used; nest replacement is the recommended solution today.

When re-raising the housing, ALWAYS return the colony to the same alignment and compass direction it was in before lowering. Martins are tuned to the exact location of their compartment via "natural GPS" in three dimensions and misaligning the housing may result in the martin pair finding the wrong compartment where theirs should be, with eggs instead of the nestlings they expected. They may become disoriented and abandon their nest.

When nesting season is over, and your martins have headed for Brazil, lower your housing, do final nest checks and update your records and clean the housing thoroughly. Remove old nests and mud dams, check removable floors for deterioration, scrub interiors and perches with a 10 percent bleach solution, and rinse with clean water. Allow the housing to dry for a day or two and replace the door stops. Many martin landlords store gourds and houses indoors to prevent winter damage or leave them in the lowered position to reduce wind damage.

**Supplemental Feeding**

Martins can starve during extended periods of cold or rainy weather, when their insect prey is unable to fly. Temperatures below 45 degrees, steady rain, heavy overcast and dense fog can limit insect availability. Very windy conditions can cause problems as well. Just because the martins are flying under these conditions doesn't ensure that they are finding enough food to nourish themselves or their nestlings. In fact, energy spent hunting unsuccessfully can hasten starvation. Drooping wings on perched birds are an indication that the martin is in trouble as its metabolism is beginning to break down and digest muscle tissue.

Supplemental feeding is a topic I didn't / don't know enough about! I have never tried supplemental feeding and really hadn't considered it until the spring of 2018 because my martins seemed to know when to return to warmer conditions during bad weather. I had never lost any birds to starvation that I knew of, but a March 2018 cold front brought a combination of sustained cold and frequent rain, and one morning I found a dead adult male on the ground under the colony.

Coincidentally, I had just received a newsletter from PMCA with a link to a video showing an emergency feeding project carried out by martin mentor and bander Tim Shaheen in May 2003 after 6 days of rain in central New Jersey. Shaheen's video is available on YouTube: https://www.youtube.com/watch?v=JNcZ6ip92h0. Several similar "training" videos are also available on YouTube. While other nearby martin landlords were losing half or more of their birds, Shaheen saved most of his by tossing crickets and mealworms into the air for the martins to catch, and feeding them scrambled eggs! He used a slingshot to launch the crickets higher but a flexible spoon works equally well.

Crickets were accepted readily, perhaps because they look like grasshoppers, a martin staple. They were kept frozen and thawed to room temperature before feeding. Once the martins recognized what all the arm waving was about, they leapt into the air to catch the offered food. Shaheen also offered all three foods, plus oyster shells, on an elevated four-tray divided platform designed for feeding.

Scrambled eggs are the least expensive of the supplemental foods, but completely unknown to Purple Martins, so both patience and training are required. Shaheen started his martins on scrambled eggs by offering them on a tray with crickets and mealworms. Eventually, one or two of the martins tried the eggs and the others quickly followed suit. Scrambled eggs can be tossed by hand or with spoon or slingshot once the martins have accepted them.

Supplemental feeding was a good wake-up call for me, after 12 years of being a successful martin landlord. The learning continues, and you should be alert to new techniques and products. It's not rocket science, once you know about it. Based on my recent education, it's smart to train your martins when the weather is good, so they're ready to benefit when feeding may save their lives. The delightful thing is that the martins, once trained, know where the food is coming from and will follow the landlord during feeding sessions.

**Reasons for Failure**

The experts at the Purple Martin Conservation Association have gathered a lot of information about success and failure regarding attracting martins. A relatively small percentage of the estimated 1 million Americans who maintain martin housing is successful. Clearly, educating yourself before spending the first dollar is the best thing you can do. If you don't have the right habitat and location or are unwilling or unable to actively manage your colony, you need to know that at the beginning and stick to squirrel-proof feeders and bluebird houses!

If you do have the right situation and have made the investment, you'll want to know what steps to take to improve your chances for success. Here, briefly, are the top ten reasons for failure, according to PMCA. Complete details are available for free in a downloadable PDF document from the PMCA website: https://www.purplemartin. org/uploads/media/top10-257.pdf

1.  Housing is too close to tall trees or in yards that are too enclosed.
    *Martins need clear flight paths to and from housing in at*

*least a couple of directions.*

2. Landlord allows other birds to claim the housing first.
   *Housing is left open to other cavity nesters before martins arrive, and these birds repel young martins which have not yet developed site fidelity.*

3. Housing is too far from human houses or activity.
   *Natural selection has taught martins, through better survival rates, that people provide protection from predators.*

4. Housing is not painted white.
   *White housing is cooler, and the dark entrance holes stand out better against white housing, making them more attractive to martins seeking nesting locations.*

5. Housing is opened up too early.
   *Related to #2. Early arriving scouts are not going to nest in a new colony. Keep housing closed until the subadult colonizers are due, four to six weeks after the adults.*

6. Failure to open martin housing at all.
   *Keeping other birds out is a balancing act! Open entrance holes attract potential martin occupants. Leave a few compartments open during late summer and fall migration.*

7. Vines and shrubs are allowed to grow up under the housing. Tall shrubs and vines say "predators!" to martins. Remove the bushes and vines!

8. Housing is not really "built to specifications."
   *Requirements are becoming better known and more precise and some published plans and commercially made houses don't meet specs. Large compartments and properly sized and placed entrance holes are critical.*

9. Housing is attached to wires or placed too close to wires.
   *Wires are squirrel pathways and martins know it.*

10. Landlords buy or build housing that can't be easily managed.
    *Houses mounted on stationary poles or poles that tilt down don't allow lowering for nest checks. Compartments must be easily opened for monitoring and cleaning.*

## Why Established Martin Colonies Are Lost

Even well-established martin colonies can be lost, all at once or over a period of years. Bad weather during migration and starvation conditions during adverse weather at any season can decimate a colony. Nest parasites like mites, fleas and blowflies can weaken adults and nestlings. Predation by raccoons or owls and nest site competition from starlings, sparrows, and otherwise beneficial birds like swallows and bluebirds can drive even loyal martins away. Quiet changes like tree encroachment and nearby pesticide use can have an impact.

Subtle things can make a difference. Part-time landlords who aren't in residence when housing should be opened will lose their martins. Better housing offered by a neighbor may tempt your birds to leave. Sloppy monitoring that doesn't consistently reorient housing to the proper compass direction and alignment can lead to individual nesting failures or reproductive failure for the entire house. Replacement of housing between seasons, especially if the new housing is of different design or in a different location, may disorient martins enough to cause them to leave. My example of the old but active gourd colony that vanished with new property ownership is an extreme example of this. Sadly, the death of the martin landlord will send a colony into decline if no one else takes over.

**Purple Martin Resources**

*The Complete Birdhouse Book* by Donald & Lillian Stokes, Little, Brown and Company, 1990.

*Stokes Purple Martin Book* by Donald & Lillian Stokes, Little, Brown, and Company, 1997.

*Enjoying Purple Martins More* by Richard A. Wolinski, Bird Watcher's Digest Press, 1994.

Websites

**https://www.purplemartin.org/**          **Purple Martin Conservation Association**

**PMCA is the world leader in Purple Martin research, education and supplies.**

**https://purplemartinplace.com/**          **Purple Martin Place**

**http://www.chuckspurplemartin-page.com/**          **Chuck's Purple Martin Page\***

*\*Chuck Abare is a terrific fan of Purple Martins. His website is newsy and conversational and very thorough. His section on Starlings and House Sparrows contains very graphic photographs and videos of the destructive habits of these two invasive species.*

**Early Morning Fight – Canada Geese (Brian Lupa)**

## Final Words of Encouragement

I hope you have enjoyed reading *Never Bird in the Road* and found some things that will make birding more enjoyable and successful. I had no idea what satisfaction and joy birds and birding could bring to me until I blundered into range of The Birding Bug. If you're new to birding, whatever your age, it's never too late to start. I've included the vital information that will save you time and money as you dive into birding for the first time or venture into new activities as you branch out as a birder. Birding is a marvelous hobby and you can devote as much or as little time as you want to it. Your skills and enjoyment will increase in proportion to your effort and commitment. Equip yourself with the right tools and equipment, choose the right seed, find a birding buddy, join a club or Audubon chapter, keep a monthly yard list, and you'll be amazed how quickly your knowledge, identification skills and enjoyment will grow.

**LET'S GO BIRDING!**

# Index